Trade Wars Are Class Wars

Trade Wars Are Class Wars

How Rising Inequality

Distorts the Global Economy and

Threatens International Peace

MATTHEW C. KLEIN

MICHAEL PETTIS

Yale UNIVERSITY PRESS/NEW HAVEN & LONDON

Published with assistance from the Kingsley Trust Association
Publication Fund established by the Scroll and Key Society of
Yale College.

Yale University Press books may be purchased in quantity for
educational, business, or promotional use. For information,
please e-mail sales.press@yale.edu (U.S. office) or sales@yaleup
.co.uk (U.K. office).

Set in Minion type by Integrated Publishing Solutions,
Grand Rapids, Michigan.
Printed in the United States of America.
Library of Congress Control Number:2019953857
ISBN 978-0-300-24417-5 (hardcover : alk. paper)

A catalogue record for this book is available from the
British Library.

This paper meets the requirements of ANSI/NISO Z39.48-1992
(Permanence of Paper).

10 9 8 7 6 5 4 3 2

Where the distribution of incomes is such as to enable all classes of the nation to convert their felt wants into an effective demand for commodities, there can be no over-production, no under-employment of capital and labour, and no necessity to fight for foreign markets. . . . The struggle for markets, the greater eagerness of producers to sell than of consumers to buy, is the crowning proof of a false economy of distribution. Imperialism is the fruit of this false economy. . . . The only safety of nations lies in removing the unearned increments of income from the possessing classes, and adding them to the wage-income of the working classes or to the public income, in order that they may be spent in raising the standard of consumption.

John A. Hobson, *Imperialism: A Study* (1902)

Contents

Acknowledgments

This book is a joint project between two authors who live six thousand miles apart—a genuinely transpacific partnership between San Francisco and Beijing. Although the finished product is ours, much of it was informed by the accumulated insights and talents of others. Like so much else in the modern global economy, our book would not have been possible without the contributions of people around the world.

Matt would like to begin by thanking the teachers who taught him how to write and think critically long before entering journalism, particularly Earl Bell, Ted Bromund, David Bromwich, and Donald Kagan. Their influence has been invaluable throughout his career. Matt would also like to thank his former Bridgewater colleagues for teaching him economics and finance, as well as for introducing him to Michael's writings on China and the balance of payments.

Michael would like to thank the brilliant Peking University students in his central bank seminar with whom he has discussed these and other issues many times and who force him to understand the basics.

Matt would like to thank the Marjorie Deane Financial Journalism Foundation for giving him his start as a writer with an internship at the *Economist*. He has been fortunate to have had many excellent mentors and editors over the years, including Ryan Avent, Clive Crook, Cardiff

Garcia, James Greiff, Brian Hershberg, Greg Ip, Izabella Kaminska, Zanny Minton-Beddoes, and Robert Sabat. Matt would particularly like to thank Sebastian Mallaby, who, almost a decade ago, hired Matt as a research assistant to work on a biography of Alan Greenspan. Sebastian encouraged Matt's ambitions at a time when becoming a writer seemed like the worst possible way to earn a living. He has always been a valuable source of advice on career decisions—especially the decision to write this book.

Preparing the proposal and finding the right publisher were not easy. In addition to Sebastian, we thank Tim Harford, Anna Pitoniak, Reihan Salam, Amir Sufi, and Martin Wolf, who were all incredibly generous with their suggestions and personal introductions.

Yale University Press has been a joy to work with. We would like to thank Seth Ditchik, Laura Jones Dooley, Dorothea Halliday, Kristy Leonard, Karen Olson, and Margaret Otzel for their support and guidance throughout the process. We also thank the anonymous reviewer, who provided useful suggestions for improving the manuscript. Bill Nelson transformed Matt's Excel spreadsheet into elegant illustrations.

Many ideas in this book are the product of conversations with others. Although many people contributed to our thinking, we especially thank Robert Aliber, Kenneth Austin, Ed Conway on Bretton Woods, Brad Delong, Niall Ferguson, Jacob Feygin, Marcel Fratzscher on Germany, Cardiff Garcia, Ambassador Jorge Guajardo, Stephanie Kelton, the formidable Wall Street veteran Robert Kowit, George Magnus, Sebastian Mallaby, Atif Mian, Julio Mota, Christian Odendahl, Zoltan Pozsar, Dani Rodrik, Reihan Salam, Martin Sandbu, Karthik Sankaran, Brad Setser, Hyun Song Shin, Amir Sufi, Srinivas Thiruvadanthai, Adam Tooze, Kellee Tsai on China's informal banks, Angel Ubide, Duncan Weldon, Martin Wolf, and Gabriel Zucman.

Brad Setser and Harry X. Wu also generously provided us with their data on China's manufacturing trade, global foreign reserve accumulation, and Chinese productivity. During our many meetings at the International Monetary Fund office in Beijing, our host, Alfred Shipke, along with Logan Wright, Rodney Jones, and Chen Long, spent hours agreeing or disagreeing about the evolution of the Chinese economy, from which Michael stole many of our best ideas.

Suggestions and critiques from Christian Odendahl and Adam Tooze improved the chapter on Germany and Europe immensely. Cardiff Garcia and Sebastian Mallaby provided valuable input on the introduction, the chapter on the role of the dollar in the global financial system, and the conclusion. Ed Eyerman and a Peking University professor who prefers not to be named read through the whole book and gave great advice, and Shenglong Tian was a great help through revision after revision. Matt's parents, Andrew and Lisa, and Matt's wife, Frances, each read the entire manuscript, including multiple versions of certain sections. Their questions and edits were essential.

One of the themes of this book is that choices made in one place can have unexpected effects elsewhere. Matt decided to work on a book without taking time off from his day job, and Frances felt the consequence of having a husband who was busy on countless nights, weekends, and early mornings. He is grateful to her for her understanding and support.

Trade Wars Are Class Wars

Introduction

Almost everyone in the world is connected by the global trade and financial systems. Whenever we buy something, go to work, or save, our actions affect billions of people thousands of miles away—just as people on the other side of the world unknowingly affect us every day with their mundane decisions.

Although these economic linkages have many benefits, they can also transmit problems from one society to another. People in one country are often responsible for unaffordable housing, debt crises, job losses, and pollution elsewhere. The Chinese government persecutes labor organizers and offers cheap bank loans to real estate developers, and American manufacturing workers lose their jobs. German companies slash wages as the German government cuts welfare spending, and Spaniards get a housing bubble.

The thesis of this book is that rising inequality within countries heightens trade conflicts between them. This is ultimately an optimistic argument: we do not believe that the world is destined to endure a zero-sum conflict between nations or economic blocs. Chinese and Germans are not evil, nor do we live in a world where countries can only prosper at others' expense. The problems of the past few decades do not have their roots in geopolitical conflict or incompatible national characters.

Rather, they have been caused by massive transfers of income to the rich and the companies they control.

Regular people everywhere are being deprived of purchasing power—and tricked by chauvinists and opportunists into believing that their interests are fundamentally at odds. A global conflict between economic classes *within* countries is being misinterpreted as a series of conflicts *between* countries with competing interests. The danger is a repetition of the 1930s, when a breakdown of the international economic and financial order undermined democracy and encouraged virulent nationalism. Back then, the consequences were war, revolution, and genocide. Fortunately, things are not yet nearly as dire now as they were then. But that is no excuse for complacency.

The escalating trade dispute between the governments of China and the United States is the most obvious demonstration of the risks. Between 2002 and 2010, voters in congressional districts where many businesses made goods that competed with imports from China elected increasingly extreme representatives—from both the left and the right. Donald Trump, who distinguished himself from other Republicans in part by his hostility to trade and to China in particular, won eighty-nine of the hundred counties most affected by Chinese import competition during the 2016 Republican primaries. Some estimates show that he would have lost the general election had it not been for the trade-induced radicalization of voters in Michigan, Pennsylvania, and Wisconsin.[1]

As president, Trump has followed through by levying punitive tariffs on most Chinese imports, by officially designating the country a "currency manipulator," and by blocking Chinese investments into U.S. companies. Unlike most of Trump's other policies, confronting China over trade has been popular across the American political spectrum. Charles Schumer, the lead Democrat in the Senate, praised the punitive tariffs in 2018 because "China is our real trade enemy" and "threatens millions of future American jobs."[2]

This political consensus is based on an important truth: Chinese government policies before 2008 destroyed millions of U.S. jobs and inflated the housing debt bubble. Things have improved somewhat since then, but the durability of this improvement is tenuous, at best, and the country remains a major drag on the global economy.[3]

Yet there is no economic conflict between America and China *as countries*. The Chinese people are not the enemy. Rather, there is a conflict between economic classes *within* China that has spilled over into the United States. Systematic transfers of wealth from Chinese workers to Chinese elites distort the Chinese economy by strangling purchasing power and subsidizing production at the expense of consumption. That, in turn, distorts the global economy by creating gluts of manufactured goods and by bidding up the prices of stocks, bonds, and real estate. Chinese underconsumption destroys jobs elsewhere, while inflated asset values lead to devastating cycles of booms, busts, and debt crises.

China's policies do not just hurt Americans—they also harm ordinary Chinese workers and retirees. Chinese workers are underpaid relative to the value of what they produce, and they are taxed too much. They are unable to access the goods and services they ought to be able to afford. They breathe dirty air and drink polluted water because many local government officials place the financial interests of politically connected business owners above the well-being of the public.

Some combination of falling employment and rising indebtedness outside of China was the inevitable consequence. Americans have borne much of these costs, thanks in part to the collusion of U.S. business interests with Chinese politicians and industrialists.

Tariffs and nationalist rhetoric will not resolve China's imbalances, but they will likely reinforce the mistaken belief—on both sides—that China and the United States have incompatible economic interests. Mishandling legitimate grievances could threaten international peace without even addressing the underlying problems. Class wars are already causing trade wars, as they have in the past. It would be a tragedy if they led to something worse.

At the same time, doing nothing is not an option. China is too large an economy for the rest of the world to passively accept the consequences of its internal distortions. It may seem strange to think of China's domestic economic policies as a legitimate subject for international diplomacy, but it is a necessary implication of the global connections that link humanity together. Convincing Chinese elites to allow Chinese workers to consume a greater share of what they produce is one of the great policy challenges of our time. Reversing the transfers from regular people to the rich over the past thirty years is in the interests of both the Chinese people and the American people.

The situation in Europe is far less likely to devolve into a military confrontation, but in some ways its intellectual confusion and domestic pathologies are even worse. Over the past few years, Europe, not China, has become the biggest threat to the world economy, and for similar reasons: governments, first in Germany and then across the continent, have raised taxes on consumption, slashed labor market protections, and pushed millions of people into low-paying part-time jobs. As in China, European workers are increasingly unable to afford what they produce. Since the start of 2010, household spending in the euro area has grown at barely half the rate of overall production.[4]

Although there are important differences between China and Europe—Europeans have cut spending on infrastructure investment to the point that bridges and roads are becoming unusable, for example— the similarities are more important for how they affect global economic prosperity. Today, the global impact of Europe's internal distortions is about as large as the impact of China's imbalances at their peak on the eve of the 2008 financial crisis.

Before 2012, Europe as a whole was not unbalanced relative to the rest of the world because domestic imbalances within certain countries, particularly Germany, were absorbed by other Europeans, particularly the crisis countries of Spain, Greece, Italy, Ireland, Portugal, and the Baltics. Germans consumed less than they produced, and they underinvested in their country, which produced large surpluses with the rest of the world. At the same time, Spaniards, Greeks, and the others experienced booms, spending far more than they earned and borrowing to cover the differences. In the years leading up to the global financial crisis, Spain had the second-biggest trade deficit in the world, behind only the United States, while Greece, a country of just eleven million people, had the fifth biggest. But Germany's pathologies—rising inequality, depressed consumption, and systematic underinvestment—were a preview of what was to come for the rest of the continent.[5]

Nationalists have responded by stoking ethnic prejudices while allowing elites to sidestep the fundamental economic issues. German politicians demanded that the Greek government repay its debts—many of which had been purchased by German banks during the boom—by selling islands. Tabloids went further and suggested liquidating national treasures such as the Acropolis of Athens. The Greek government responded by reviving long-standing demands for reparations for Nazi atrocities. As recently as 2017, Jeroen Dijsselbloem, then the Dutch finance minister and the president of the Eurogroup, blamed the entire crisis on people who "spend all the money on drinks and women and then ask for help."[6]

It is bad enough when tabloids make such foolish statements, but for policymakers to misunderstand the crisis so deeply and to apportion blame according to national characteristics is not just irresponsible but wrong. The European crisis was never about a conflict between fascistic Germans and dishonest Greeks—it was about income distribution. German policies developed in response to the twin shocks of reunification and the postcommunist liberation of Eastern Europe transferred purchasing power from workers and retirees to the ultrarich, which in turn forced Germany's neighbors to tolerate some combination of rising unemployment and soaring indebtedness. The sad result was that Germany's leaders undermined what should have been one of the most positive transformations of modern times: the creation of a healthy, unified Europe. The danger now is that Europe and the United States—the world's two largest economies—will enter a trade war of their own, undermining both global prosperity and an important alliance among the world's democracies.

Everything Old Is New Again

This is not the first time the global economy has been distorted by rising inequality. In many ways, the situation today resembles the world of the late nineteenth and early twentieth centuries. Back then, the extremely unequal income distribution in the rich European countries meant that workers could not afford to consume all the manufactures they produced. Meanwhile, the rich had lots of money to invest but lacked attractive opportunities at home. There was no point in building more factories when local consumers could not buy more goods. Had the distribution of income been less unequal, workers would have had more spending power and been able to afford to buy everything they produced, while the rich would have had an easier time generating their desired returns on investment.

The elites of the time rejected this option, but they also wanted to prevent unemployment from rising to the point that it could encourage revolutions. Their solution was to shift their excess output to captive markets abroad. Foreigners in imperial possessions and quasi-independent states would buy the goods locals could not afford, and they would pay for those goods by borrowing at relatively high interest rates guaranteed by occupying armies and gunboats. British, French, Dutch, and German investors financed projects in Australia, Latin America, Canada, Africa, India, China, and Southeast Asia. They also built railroads and exported everything from machinery to military hardware to luxury goods. Violent conquest was a logical consequence of the macroeconomic distortions created by extreme inequality.

This was recognized by astute observers at the time. According to the British economist and social critic John A. Hobson, the need to find outlets for "surplus capital which cannot find sound investments within the country" was the central explanation for American and European imperialism. The underlying problem was an economic and political system that "placed large surplus savings in the hands of a plutocracy." Income concentration gave the rich "an excess of consuming power which they cannot use" at the expense of everyone else. This was ultimately self-defeating, since "consumption alone vitalizes capital and makes it capable of yielding profits." Rich savers therefore had to search abroad to find "new areas for profitable investment and speculation." Eventually, this search encouraged powerful domestic interests to "place larger and larger portions of their economic resources outside the area of their present political domain, and then stimulate a policy of political expansion so as to take in the new areas."

The good news was that the toxic combination of inequality and imperialism could be peacefully resolved by changing the income distribution. "The home markets," Hobson wrote, "are capable of indefinite expansion" as long as "the 'income,' or power to demand commodities, is properly distributed" among the people. "There is no necessity to open up new foreign markets," Hobson wrote, because "whatever is produced in England can be consumed in England."[7]

Hobson made that argument in 1902. It went unheeded. Twelve years later, the world he described was destroyed by World War I, although the dynamics did not change. In the 1920s, rich Americans were the source of the glut and it was the Europeans who were forced to absorb it. More recently, Kenneth Austin, an economist at the U.S. Treasury Department, has noted that Hobson's insight applies just as well to modern China, Japan, and Germany, with the United States acting as a sink for foreign gluts. In the late nineteenth century, the 1920s, and today, the harm caused by extremely unequal income distributions was spread to other countries through the global trade and financial systems.[8]

Hobson recognized that everyone—or almost everyone—can become better off through transfers from the ultrarich to ordinary people, particularly in places where inequality is at its most extreme. He further appreciated that moderate redistribution within nations can peacefully resolve the economic conflicts between them. Unfortunately, his insights were ignored and forgotten. They also seemed unnecessary during the boom years of the mid-twentieth century. But the rapid increases in inequality and the deepening economic links across national borders since the end of the Cold War have made Hobson's wisdom more relevant than ever. The challenge is an intellectual one (getting people to appreciate this perspective) and a political one (defeating entrenched interests that benefit from the status quo).

To understand how all this works, it helps to have a historical perspective of how we got here.

From Adam Smith to Tim Cook

The Transformation of Global Trade

I nternational trade used to be simple. High transport costs and politically imposed constraints limited the flow of finished goods and
raw materials across borders. In the late eighteenth and early nineteenth centuries, British thinkers argued for removing tariffs and
other barriers to encourage specialization, while Americans and Germans proposed protecting infant industries to develop diversified domestic markets. The end of the Napoleonic Wars, the mass deployment
of steam engines, and the invention of the telegraph led to a boom in
trade until the early 1870s—which ended with what some have called
the world's first synchronized global financial crisis, the Panic of 1873.
From the late 1880s until World War I, high imperialism in the late nineteenth and early twentieth centuries led to increased trade within larger
blocs even as it limited trade between them.

World wars, the Great Depression, and revolutions upended the
political and economic order in the first half of the twentieth century.
Initially, the impact was to crush international trade to its lowest level
since the late eighteenth century, although these events also caused a
massive redistribution of wealth that left income more equally distributed within the rich countries than it had ever been. Eventually, these
forces created space for much deeper economic integration.

Even then, most trade at the time consisted of finished goods and commodities. The innovation of container shipping radically lowered transportation costs while advances in communications technology made it easier to oversee factories on the other side of the world. By the late 1990s, trade had been transformed. Companies spread complex manu-facturing supply chains across multiple countries to maximize efficiency and minimize taxes. Trade today looks nothing like it did before. Unfor-tunately, in spite of all these changes, the popular understanding of trade continues to be based on obsolete eighteenth-century models.

Pins, Cloth, and Wine

Adam Smith's *Inquiry into the Nature and Causes of the Wealth of Na-tions* opens with an account of a pin factory. Smith estimated that it took "eighteen distinct operations" to make a single pin. Just making the head required "two or three distinct operations." One worker would be hard-pressed to make more than a few dozen pins in a day if he were forced to perform all the steps himself. What the pin-makers—and Smith—realized was that each worker became thousands of times more produc-tive by focusing on specific parts of the process.[1]

Pin-making in Smith's day took place in a single building, but it can be understood as a series of trade relationships: the factory owner buys raw materials from suppliers, after which the first worker effec-tively buys some of the materials from the factory owner and makes the first set of improvements, preselling this unfinished good to the next worker, who makes more improvements before selling the modified good to yet another worker. The last worker in the chain ends up with finished pins ready to be sold to distributors. While businesses exist to simplify these implied transactions between employees and owners, Smith's insight—people accomplish more when they specialize—explains why pin-makers did not forge their own steel, much less mine their own iron and coal. All of these separate businesses trade with each other for what they need while focusing on how they can add the most value.[2]

International trade is simply an extension of this process across national borders: England is bereft of sunshine but rich in freshwater, while much of Spain is sunny and dry, so people in both Britain and Spain can benefit by trading food grown and raised in their respective climates. Forcing British farmers to plant olive groves and vineyards—rather than raise cows and sheep to trade for oil and wine—would be wasteful. As Smith put it back in 1776, "It is the maxim of every prudent master of a family never to attempt to make at home what it will cost him more to make than to buy. . . . If a foreign country can supply us with a commodity cheaper than we ourselves can make it, better buy it of them with some part of the produce of our own industry employed in a way in which we have some advantage" rather than pay extra for a locally made version.[3]

David Ricardo was born half a century after Smith. Whereas Smith was a Scottish academic moral philosopher, Ricardo was a Jewish financier who had become so wealthy after betting correctly on the outcome of the Battle of Waterloo that he was able to buy a seat in Parliament. After reading *Wealth of Nations,* Ricardo decided to spend his leisure time writing about economics and published *On the Principles of Political Economy and Taxation* in 1817. The book covered everything from Ricardo's explanation for why gold has a higher price than silver—"because fifteen times the quantity of labour is necessary to procure a given quantity of it"—to his theory that "the rate of profits can never be increased but by a fall in wages." Most significantly, Ricardo argued that trade between two countries could make both countries better off even when one country is more productive than the other in every way.[4]

In Ricardo's example, Portuguese workers could make both cloth and wine more efficiently than their English counterparts. At first glance, this might suggest there would be no reason for the two countries to trade. However, in his example, Portuguese capitalists earned relatively higher profits making wine compared to cloth, while English capitalists earned relatively higher profits making cloth rather than wine. Specialization would be good for both Portuguese and English investors, but only if the two countries could trade cloth for wine with each other. Without the ability to benefit from exchange, Portugal "would be obliged to devote a part of that capital to the manufacture of those commodities, which she would thus obtain probably inferior in quality as well as quantity."[5]

These arguments for specialization only went so far. Neither Smith nor Ricardo thought it would make sense to divide the stages of pin-making or textile manufacturing across national borders. Rather, they were thinking of the world as it was then—two hundred years ago. In those days, people happily traded raw materials and finished goods with each other across long distances but would not trade intermediate goods or services. The communications technologies available at the time— carrier pigeons and couriers on horseback or sailing ship—would not have been adequate for coordinating the various stages of production across disparate locations. Travel was dangerous, and wars were common. (One happy consequence of those difficulties was the invention of Port wine by British entrepreneurs to solve the twin problems of never-ending conflicts with France and the spoilage of conventional Portuguese wine during the long journey to England.)[6]

What many forget today is that Ricardo's argument made sense only under these primitive conditions. He realized that the superior productivity of Portuguese workers meant "it would undoubtedly be advantageous to the capitalists of England [that] the wine and the cloth should both be made in Portugal, and therefore that the capital and labour of England employed in making cloth, should be removed to Portugal for that purpose." He thought that this would be bad for England, but he was unconcerned because he assumed that "most men of property" would be "satisfied with a low rate of profits in their own country, rather than seek a more advantageous employment for their wealth in foreign nations." It was difficult to supervise investments in foreign countries before the invention of the telegraph and the steamship. Ricardo also thought that "the natural disinclination which every man has to quit the country of his birth" would limit capital outflows.[7]

Ricardo's subtle case for free trade depended on persistent differences in rates of return across countries, which in turn depended on investors' unwillingness to move money abroad. Those assumptions broke down as technology improved, communication costs collapsed, and global politics changed.

Hamilton, List, and the "American System"

On the other side of the Atlantic, a dozen years or so after Smith published *Wealth of Nations* and nearly thirty years before Ricardo published his *Principles,* George Washington and Alexander Hamilton presented a different vision of economic statecraft. For them, the development of domestic manufacturing capacity was a national security imperative. America was isolated diplomatically and geographically, vulnerable to naval embargoes, and far from any potential allies.

The United States, they decided, would have to become economically self-sufficient to guarantee its newfound political independence. As Washington put it in an address to Congress on January 8, 1790, "A free people ought not only to be armed, but disciplined. . . . Their safety and interest require that they should promote such manufactures as tend to render them independent of others for essential, particularly military supplies." To use the language of Ricardo, Americans would have to make both cloth and wine, regardless of what any economic theory might suggest.[8]

Washington established the need to industrialize. Alexander Hamilton, the first Treasury secretary of the United States and a leading advocate of a powerful federal government, was given the job of figuring out how to do it. His magisterial *Report on the Subject of Manufactures,* published at the end of 1791, would prove to be a founding document of the developmental state. Hamilton believed that manufacturing had value far beyond its contribution to national security: it would "diversify the industrious pursuits" of the citizenry, raise agricultural productivity, and encourage investment in machines. Moreover, he realized that America's status as an agrarian republic was a consequence of British imperial policy, not destiny. Under the right conditions, the new United States could transform itself into a manufacturing superpower—but those conditions needed to be created by a strong state to encourage the market to create the right sort of manufacturing capacity.

Hamilton's insight was that countries could only capture the productivity gains from the division of labor by rejecting the concept at the international level. The benefits of internal economic diversity were incompatible with national specialization. It was a rebuttal to Ricardo before the theory of comparative advantage had even been written.

Hamilton admitted that Americans might want to focus on farming in a world with perfect free trade and zero regulations. He was quick to point out, however, that in the real world, "the United States cannot exchange with Europe on equal terms." American exports were discriminated against even though the United States levied few tariffs on imports. The difference in treatment stemmed from the fact that Europeans did not depend on American farm output the way that Americans depended on European manufactures. The "want of reciprocity" would keep Americans in "a state of impoverishment." Activist government was therefore required.

According to Hamilton, Americans could not hope to compete with European producers unless the U.S. government was willing to match the "gratuities and remunerations which other governments bestow" on their manufacturing exporters. He therefore recommended raising taxes on foreign manufactures and using the money to pay "bounties" to American producers of high-priority goods. At the same time, he wanted to lower American manufacturers' costs by eliminating America's tariffs on raw material imports such as copper, sulfur, and silk. Government intervention would make American-made goods cheap relative to imports from Europe, encouraging Americans to buy locally.

The goal was to promote entrepreneurship and investment. Hamilton believed that the guaranteed domestic market would make it easier for Americans to start new businesses in what were then the high-tech industries of textiles, nails, glassmaking, and gun-making. Americans needed "the incitement and patronage of government," according to Hamilton, because they did not yet have the skills, the credibility, or the confidence to start self-sufficient businesses. The new and unfamiliar are always difficult—a situation made worse by the existing European tariffs and subsidies to encourage their own manufacturers and to prevent the development of manufacturing in the United States. Eventually, America's "infant" producers would grow and mature to the point that they would not need as much government support. Hamilton did not want to eliminate foreign competition, because that would be bad for American consumers, but he did want to tilt the playing field in favor of additional domestic production.

Hamilton's relative openness to imports can be explained by his expectation that the "parts of Europe, which have more Capital, than profitable domestic objects of employment" would help pay for his country's industrialization. Whereas Ricardo assumed that technological limitations and political barriers would prevent large-scale international financial flows, Hamilton believed that "a very material difference in profit" could "produce a transfer of foreign capital to the United States." The risks of investing in a country thousands of miles away would be offset by America's "advantages, which are with difficulty to be equaled elsewhere."[9]

Shortly after the report was submitted, Congress found itself debating how to raise revenue to provide security against attacks on the country's western border from America's indigenous inhabitants. The timing was propitious: Hamilton was able to overcome opposition to his moderate tariff plan by arguing that taxes on imported manufactures were necessary to raise revenue for national defense. The offsetting bounties, however, were not enacted mainly because of concerns about corruption, insufficient revenue, and objections that government subsidies for favored industries would violate the Constitution.

Ironically, America's position of neutrality in the decades-long wars between revolutionary France and counterrevolutionary Britain ended up imposing far higher barriers on U.S. imports than anything Hamilton had ever proposed. An indigenous manufacturing industry developed in response. By 1815, President James Madison was calling for more extreme versions of the policies Hamilton had suggested to preserve this new manufacturing base after peace had been restored in Europe. The so-called Dallas Tariff, named after the Treasury secretary at the time, was passed in 1816. It raised duties on many manufactured imports as high as 30 percent and imposed additional taxes on imports brought in on foreign ships.[10]

The United States was pioneering a new model. In parallel with the tariffs, the federal government was spending on internal improvements to facilitate the movement of people and goods across America's rapidly growing territory. Canals were being dug, roads and bridges were being built, rivers were being widened, railroad tracks were being laid down, and migrants were flooding into the Northwest Territory and the lands Thomas Jefferson had acquired in the 1803 Louisiana Purchase (funded, ironically, by the system of credit engineered by Alexander Hamilton that Jefferson had strongly opposed). American manufacturers were protected from foreigners but competed within the large—and expanding—domestic market.

This evolving American development model did not go unnoticed. Friedrich List was a German who had moved to Pennsylvania in 1825 after years of persecution by the duchy of Württemberg for "seditious activities." Before emigrating, he had tried to convince the German states to create a customs union to restore some of the manufacturing capacity that had been developed during the Napoleonic Wars. German industry would be protected against competition from Britain while free trade within Germany would create a vibrant domestic market.

After coming to America, List concluded that the United States was a model for German unification and economic development. In the 1820s he wrote a series of letters defending what he called "the American System" and criticizing the "erroneous" theories of Adam Smith for ignoring "the fracture of the human race into nations." List was concerned with how a country could "grow in power and wealth," with just as much emphasis on power as on wealth. Unlike what he derided as the "cosmopolitical economy" of Smith and other free traders, List wanted to put political institutions back into "political economy."

List believed that protective tariffs were necessary to make American manufacturing businesses competitive with British exports, which in turn would attract foreign capital and skilled workers from Europe. In a virtuous circle, greater production would, through higher wages, create additional demand for manufactured goods and American raw materials, boosting demand for labor and machines and ultimately growing the national economy and increasing national power. As he put it, "Consumption begets therefore production, as much as production begets consumption." Production could grow sustainably if it were transformed, via wages, into consumption demand, and consumption could grow sustainably if it were satisfied by additional production. Each should push the other forward. Even more than Hamilton, List believed that an activist government was required: he warned that "industry, left to itself, would soon fall to ruin, and a nation letting everything alone would commit suicide."

List did not think that his policy recommendation was universally applicable. For him, "every nation must follow its particular course in developing its productive powers." List thought that Latin America, India, China, Spain, and Russia would fail to benefit from his program because they lacked the "certain stock of freedom, of security, of instruction" necessary to develop productive industry. They were poor, in other words, because they lacked the institutions necessary for sustainable wealth creation. He criticized Spain in particular for the ways "the priesthood consumes the fat of the land and nourishes vicious indolence." America, however, like Germany, had the necessary "liberal institutions" to develop into a prosperous manufacturing nation.[11]

In 1841, List expanded his ideas into *The National System of Political Economy,* a mix of theory, history, and reporting meant to guide statesmen in what he hoped would become the new German nation. His thesis was that "free competition between two nations which are highly civilized can only be mutually beneficial in case both of them are in a nearly equal position of industrial development." A country such as Germany, which was less developed but "possesses the mental and material means" to become wealthy, should instead avoid free trade and "strengthen her own individual powers."

The United States, with its high external tariffs and a vast internal market, was "the best work on political economy one can read." Activist government policies promoting domestic trade and domestic production had combined with the native industriousness of the American people to transform an agricultural colony in "complete thralldom" to Britain into an independent and powerful nation-state.[12]

Although world trade expanded steadily after the end of the defeat of Napoleon in 1815 thanks to peace in Europe, tariff liberalization in Britain and France, and the technological innovations of steamships, railroads, and the telegraph, List nevertheless won the argument by the end of the nineteenth century. The United States levied tariffs on manufactured goods of about 45 percent from 1870 through 1913, and it aggressively expanded the size of its protected internal market in the nineteenth century with land purchases, negotiated annexations, and wars of conquest. The United States was not unique. Tariffs on manufactured goods rose across the world in the latter third of the nineteenth century. By the eve of World War I, most European countries were charging

20 percent tariffs on manufactures, with the notable exceptions of the United Kingdom and the Netherlands. The world's average effective tariff rate rose even further as the United States and Germany grew as a share of global economic output.[13]

High Imperialism and the Open Door

The spread of protectionism had a predictable effect: world trade began to shrink relative to economic output starting in the early 1870s. It would take a hundred years for international trade to become as important again as it was then. This presented a particular problem for the United Kingdom. Britain depended on export markets to absorb its excess manufacturing output, which generated the revenues needed to pay for food and industrial commodity imports. Unfortunately for Britain, the world's biggest and fastest-growing economies (the United States and Germany) were determined to limit British access as much as possible.

The United Kingdom had a solution, however: its extensive portfolio of overseas colonies. In addition to the so-called white dominions of Australia, Canada, and New Zealand, Britain had control over parts of southern Africa, all of the Indian subcontinent, Hong Kong, Malaya, and bits of the Western Hemisphere. In the last decades of the nineteenth century, the British Empire would dramatically expand to include much of Africa, the Middle East, and substantial spheres of influence in Asia. These territories would not be allowed to develop using List's "National System." Tariffs would be minimal, at least for British goods. The empire would serve as a sink for British exports and provide it with a secure supply of raw material imports.

Britain's apparent success with this strategy (scholars disagree whether the military costs justified any of the purported economic benefits) encouraged imitators. The French moved into North Africa and Southeast Asia. Japan seized the Ryukyu Islands. The Russians aggressively expanded their land borders south and west, which frightened the British into additional conquests—Afghanistan, Burma, much of East Africa, and most of southern Africa—ostensibly meant to secure the defense of India. Britain would also fight in Central Asia, Persia, and Tibet because of its fear of losing India. The scramble for Africa became

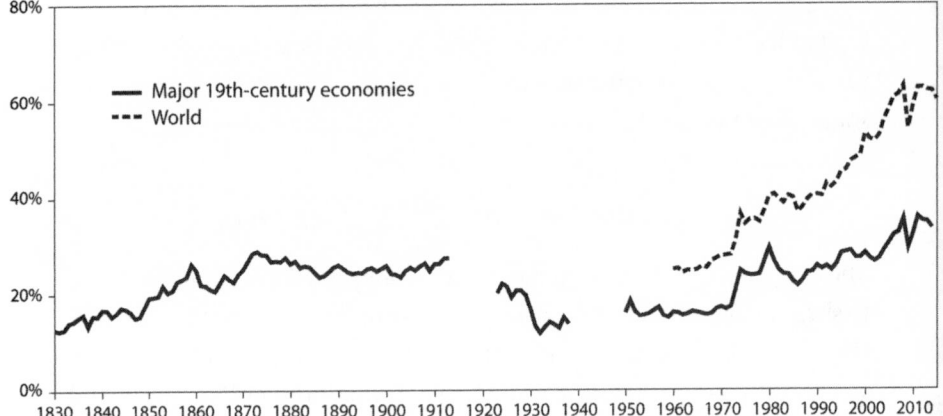

Fig. 1.1 World trade did not surpass its 1873 peak until the 1970s (total exports as a share of world output). *Source: Bank for International Settlements*

so intense that an international conference (known as the West Africa Conference) was held in Berlin in 1884–85 to prevent military clashes between the European powers.

By the eve of World War I, all of Africa except for Ethiopia and Liberia had been brought under European control. Japan fought China to take Taiwan and to establish dominance in Korea in the mid-1890s. Ten years later, Russia and Japan fought the world's first war between mechanized armies over control of Korea and Manchuria. While this period of high imperialism was not motivated solely by economic considerations, the desire to acquire export markets and investment opportunities was an important consideration. One consequence was increasing fragmentation of global trade within imperial blocs.

Although it annexed the kingdom of Hawaii and took Cuba, the Philippines, and Puerto Rico from the Spanish in 1898, the United States was less focused on acquiring colonial dependencies than the Europeans and more interested in encouraging internal migration to the West, often by violently displacing the indigenous population. America's imperialist tendencies were focused on expanding its own national borders—and its protected domestic market—through the project of Manifest Destiny. This created a distinct American approach to trade with other countries in the late nineteenth century: the Open Door Policy.

Confident of the prowess of its merchants and relatively uninterested in colonial conquests, Americans did not push for preferential access in any foreign market. American companies did not expect their government to directly control the foreign territories where they hoped to conduct business, nor did they expect protection from foreign competitors outside the American home market. The United States deployed military power to secure its investors' rights abroad, especially in Latin America, but it did not do so at the expense of other foreign investors. American investors did not need foreign investment opportunities until the end of the nineteenth century (the first foreign branch for a U.S. bank was not even established until just before World War I, in Buenos Aires), and even then diplomats simply wanted to prevent the Europeans, Russians, and Japanese from carving out exclusive economic zones in China. While the United States got the other powers to agree to refrain from partitioning China, it was less successful in ensuring that American traders could compete on equal terms in areas under foreign spheres of influence.

From World Wars to World Order

The U.S. principle of neutrality proved difficult to maintain during World War I. Substantial cultural and economic links to Germany were dwarfed by the far larger financial interests tying the United States to the United Kingdom. America's private-sector tilt to the British explains why German submarines targeted American merchant ships and why German diplomats tried to convince Mexico to attack the United States mainland—two decisions that persuaded Americans to enter the war against Germany. The United States had little military capacity compared to the European belligerents, but it more than made up for this deficiency with its abundant industrial base, its farms, and, belatedly, its fresh supply of young men. It took the American Expeditionary Force more than a year to arrive in meaningful numbers, and the doughboys had to fight using British armaments because Americans lacked the latest military technology. Once in France, however, the Americans helped bring a decisive end to the fighting on the Western Front.

Peace did not restore prosperity. Europe's economies were exhausted by the loss of manpower, the destruction of productive capacity, and the redirection of investment to serve the war effort. European reconstruction was impeded by high war debts and onerous reparations obligations. The Russian Empire had succumbed to the Bolsheviks, while China had entered what would become decades of civil war.

America, however, had profited as a supplier to the belligerents: the United States exported more than twice as much as it imported during the war, leading to "the largest favorable trade balance that has ever existed in any country," according to a report by the American economist John H. Williams in 1921. As the biggest undamaged power, it had tremendous leverage to make a new, better order. Unfortunately, it refused to do so. Reminiscent of China's suspicions today of global institutions, many Americans feared that the Europeans wanted to constrain U.S. power. As a result, the federal government focused myopically on getting Britain and France to repay their wartime loans even as it distorted the world trading system by hoarding gold. One consequence was a sharp drop in international trade, which fell from 27 percent of global output in 1913 to just 20 percent in 1923–28.[14]

The Great Depression a few years later caused international trade to collapse to just 11 percent of the world economy by 1932. Cross-border flows of goods and services remained below 15 percent of global production until the outbreak of World War II. Compounding the immediate impact of the collapse in business activity and cross-border finance was the wave of protectionism unleashed by the United States with the Smoot-Hawley Tariff Act in 1930. Punitive American taxes on imports from the rest of the world prompted global retaliation, breaking whatever had been left of an international economic system and unleashing competitive currency devaluations, rising tariffs, and deglobalization.

Fittingly, the United States, which had been reliant on foreign customers to absorb its excess production since the end of the nineteenth century and was at that time running one of the largest trade surpluses in world history, was among the biggest victims of the protectionism it had helped encourage as it lost access to many of its export markets. This is the great lesson of Smoot-Hawley: countries with large trade surpluses have them only because they cannot consume all they produce, which makes them extremely vulnerable to a decline in international trade.

Many countries, especially those that did not devalue their currencies, resorted to barter agreements to trade manufactures for commodities. (The most notorious of these was between Nazi Germany and the
Soviet Union.) Others retreated into trading with their imperial possessions. French exports to its colonies, protectorates, and League of Nations mandates jumped from 19 percent of the total in 1929 to 28 percent
by 1938. Over the same period, Italian exports to its African possessions
and to Ethiopia jumped from 2 percent of the total to 23 percent, while
Japanese exports to its imperial possessions in Korea, Taiwan, Manchuria, and China soared from 35 percent of the total to 63 percent.[15]

World War II led to a dramatic change in trade patterns compared
to peacetime. As it had in World War I, Germany resorted to seizing raw
materials from Eastern Europe. Britain became wholly dependent on resource imports from the empire and, to a lesser extent, the United States.
During this time the United States became the "Arsenal of Democracy,"
as President Franklin Roosevelt put it, thanks to its distance from the
conflict and ample spare capacity from the ongoing depression. Between
1938 and 1941, U.S. exports grew by 45 percent.

Japan, by contrast, lost access to imports from the United States in
protest of its depredations in China. That, in turn, helped persuade the
Japanese to invade Southeast Asia to gain access to oil, rubber, and other
industrial supplies. The Soviet Union, which had spent the 1930s as a pariah state trading mainly with the Nazis on a barter basis, became a major
importer of American supplies after it was invaded in 1941. America's
abundant productive capacity stood in contrast to the other belligerents,
all of whom struggled to satisfy their material needs with domestic—or
conquered—production.[16]

Shortly after the Allied landings at Normandy, representatives from
forty-four countries met in Bretton Woods, New Hampshire, to discuss
the postwar order. The goal was to prevent a return to the economic
anarchy of the 1920s and 1930s, which everyone agreed had been a principal cause of the war. While the conference focused on reforming the
monetary system and the regulations surrounding financial flows, delegates also supported a proposal for a new International Trade Organization (ITO) that would "reduce obstacles to international trade and in
other ways promote mutually advantageous international commercial

relations." As U.S. Treasury secretary Henry Morgenthau put it in his closing remarks at the conference, the "revival of international trade is indispensable if full employment is to be achieved in a peaceful world and with standards of living which will permit the realization of men's reasonable hopes."[17]

But this revival of international trade was to occur in a very different context than today. Transportation costs were still high enough then that it made little sense to spread manufacturing processes across wide geographic areas. Capital, too, was not mobile to anywhere near the extent that it is today. In fact, even though the two main architects of the final Bretton Woods agreement, Harry Dexter White and John Maynard Keynes, were as eager as Morgenthau to see international trade revive, neither had any interest in bringing back capital mobility, concerned, as they both were, by the way huge capital movements in the prewar period had distorted global trade and created massive imbalances, especially in the United Kingdom and the United States.

Creating new international institutions did not change the fact that Europe and Asia were in tatters when the war ended a little over a year later. Reviving trade required resources from the one country able to provide them. While the long occupation of Japan had already been planned, Americans only gradually came to realize the danger of leaving the Europeans to their own devices: persistent poverty would make them desperate and vulnerable to communist subversion, which in turn would cause them to withdraw from a global trading system that had become important to the U.S. economy.

Meanwhile, U.S. military demobilization was hitting domestic spending, which meant that American farmers and manufacturers were keen to find sources of external demand. This made for a powerful coalition of Americans determined to expand trade with Europe. One prong of this strategy was the Marshall Plan, which gave Europeans the resources to buy American exports and rebuild their own productive capacity. The other was a legal effort to open European markets for trade once they had recovered.

While the ITO originally proposed at the Bretton Woods conference died in 1950 after U.S. objections that it would have jurisdiction over domestic economic policy, the separate General Agreement on Tariffs and Trade (GATT) thrived under American leadership. The idea was to assemble a coalition of willing countries to reduce the most obvious barriers to international exchange—namely, tariffs and quotas. At the time, the United States dominated world trade and accounted for 35 percent of all manufacturing exports. That meant it could lead by example, lowering its own tariffs so that the Europeans and Japanese would lower theirs.

Americans continued to guide the world trade agenda toward further liberalization as GATT expanded and was eventually replaced, in 1995, with the World Trade Organization (WTO). All signatories agreed to basic minimum standards and to abide by the ruling of an impartial panel of judges in the event of disputes. Groups of countries could negotiate bespoke supplementary deals with each other if it meant furthering global trade.[18]

Despite these moves toward liberalization, the end of the war failed to restore trade to its pre-1929, much less pre-1913, importance. In fact, cross-border flows of goods and services relative to global output would not return to the zenith reached in the 1870s until the 1970s. While Western Europeans began integrating their economies to an unprecedented degree and Japan, bereft of its empire, embraced commercial relations with the West, these developments were outweighed by what was happening in the rest of the world. Half of Europe had been overrun by communists, as would China shortly thereafter. Decolonization led to new trade barriers across much of the world as the liberated countries attempted to industrialize, as the United States had, through import substitution. The international political environment would limit further growth in trade until the end of the Cold War.

Container Shipping

The postwar political constraints explain only part of the slow recovery in global trade, however. The other major stumbling block was high transportation costs, driven by the inefficiencies of the shipping industry. Although the 1950s were the era of the jet plane, the rocket ship, and the hydrogen bomb, moving goods from place to place was slower and more expensive in these years than it had been in the nineteenth century.

Relative to total economic output, international trade was about half as significant in the middle of the twentieth century as it had been less than a hundred years earlier. Moreover, the trade that did exist was dominated by basic commodities, rather than manufactures. By the 1980s, however, the world had been revolutionized by the commercialization of an elegant idea: the container. Once people figured out how to use them, plain metal boxes made transportation across long distances radically simpler and far cheaper. Trade volumes exploded to levels never before possible—and transformed the global economics of international commerce.

Cargo shipping in the mid-1950s would likely have been recognizable to Smith and Ricardo. Transporting bulk freight, such as oil, coal, and grain, was easy enough. Anything else, however, had to be carefully packed. Ships were not profitable to operate unless their holds were completely stuffed, which was a challenge when dealing with goods of different shapes, sizes, and weights. Cold-rolled steel, coffee beans, and clothes often traveled together to maximize the use of limited space. Loading and unloading this cargo took a lot of men—the big docks employed tens of thousands of workers to handle the traffic—and a lot of time.

Powerful unions were relentlessly creative at finding ways to reduce efficiency. Goods that arrived prepackaged into bundles, for example, would be scrupulously unpacked and then repacked by the longshoremen, who naturally charged by the hour, plus overtime. It could take a week to fully load a typical cargo ship, another week to unload it once it arrived at its destination, and yet another week to load the ship back up for the return trip. About two-thirds of the total cost of shipping goods across the Atlantic could be explained by the time spent in port rather than the voyage across the ocean.

While getting goods on and off the ships was the worst part, getting them to and from the docks was also expensive and slow. Much of America's maritime shipping went through Manhattan or Brooklyn, even though both were accessible only by trucks that had to fight through dense New York City traffic. London's riverside docks were surrounded by urban neighborhoods and narrow streets, which made it difficult to move goods from the rest of the country to the water. Some manufacturers had adapted to these constraints by building their factories as close to the ports as possible. Many others decided the cost of seaborne transportation was not worth the hassle and focused on selling to their local market.

The rest had to rely on trucks and trains—which were loaded in the same painstaking manner as the cargo ships—to bring their merchandise to the ports. After the cargo had been unloaded from a ship, it was kept in warehouses at the ports where it would be sorted (slowly) before being repacked onto trucks and trains bound for end users. These constraints meant that it could take several months to send a shipment of manufactured goods from the United States to Europe in the mid-1950s, even though the sailing time between Brooklyn and Bremerhaven, West Germany, for example, lasted only about ten days. There was no sense in producing goods for export unless the customer had already ordered it, and there was little reason to order goods from abroad unless local substitutes were literally unavailable.

Prepacking goods at the factory into standardized metal containers revolutionized this process. The same box could be used interchangeably across all modes of transportation. Trucks and trains could arrive at a port, drop off their cargo, get new containers, and roll off to their next destination in a matter of minutes. Even heavy containers could be moved quickly and safely by a handful of people using cranes. The hard work of packing and unpacking would only be done at the beginning and end of the entire trip, rather than at the beginning and end of each leg. That limited the risk of damage, which produced the added benefit of lower insurance premiums for customers.

Containerization also cut the opportunities for theft by longshoremen and teamsters, which explains why Scotch whisky exporters were among the earliest adopters. Moreover, container ships, unlike traditional cargo ships, could be loaded and unloaded simultaneously. When the first container ships were introduced, these innovations cut the time in port from days to hours. Ships now carry about ten times as many containers as they did in the 1960s, but the biggest ones still spend far less time in port than the typical freighter in the precontainer era.

American entrepreneurs began commercializing container transport in the late 1950s, but even after demonstrating the potential for cost savings and speed, the idea did not fully catch on until the 1980s. Longshoremen unions vociferously opposed changes that would eliminate most of their jobs. Many ports were slow to invest in the cranes, berths, and loading areas required for big ships carrying thousands of big boxes. The railroads feared that containers would compete with their traditional business of moving goods packed in boxcars. The cartels setting transoceanic rates wanted to protect the value of their existing fleets until their new container ships were ready. Regulators were used to a world where transportation and packing were linked and wanted prices based on the value of the good being shipped. Even the innovators in container shipping could not agree on common standards to make boxes interchangeable across transportation platforms.

The Vietnam War was the first catalyst for change. The port in Saigon was even worse than the docks in Brooklyn because standard cargo ships could not get close enough to unload directly. Supplies arriving from California had to be taken off the cargo ships waiting offshore and repacked onto shallow-bottomed barges, which then had to find space at one of the few available piers where Vietnamese longshoremen would do the same routine as their American and European counterparts. Corrupt Vietnamese generals often stole the most desirable items for themselves. Worse, most of the American soldiers who needed supplies were nowhere near Saigon. Getting them their gear from the docks required trucks driving on dirt roads for weeks, often in hostile territory.

Desperate for better results, the U.S. Army hired Malcom McLean, the original innovator of container shipping, to build and operate a container port at Cam Ranh Bay. He had two conditions: each box would be packed with a single type of item, and each box would be packed for a specific unit, which would be responsible for returning it. Within months, McLean had solved the army's logistics problem and shown the world what was possible with containerization. (He also profited handsomely by having his ships and empty boxes pick up Japanese goods for the return trip to California.)

In the 1970s, the world's shipping companies embraced the container, borrowing heavily to build new vessels able to carry far more boxes than the generation commissioned in the 1960s. The initial result was a glut of capacity that came online at the same time as the oil price quadrupled and the world economy had a severe recession. Many lines went out of business while the rest merged to survive. By the 1980s, however, the mortgages had been refinanced and the oil price had stabilized, which enabled the remaining lines to cut rates for increasingly demanding customers.

At the same time, governments were eliminating the cumbersome regulations limiting what truckers, railroads, and ship lines could do. Manufacturers and retailers could finally make long-term contracts coordinating the transportation of containers from inland locations in one country to inland destinations in another. Thanks to the low and dependable cost of moving goods, it increasingly made sense to spread complex production processes across the world. Adam Smith's insight into the power of specialization would be applied at a scale he would never have imagined.[19]

How Global Value Chains and
Ports Distort the Bilateral Trade Data

The drive south across the Detroit River from the U.S. city of the same name to the Canadian city of Windsor only takes about twenty minutes. For nearly a century, the big three American automakers have exploited this proximity by operating plants in both Michigan and the southern bit of Ontario. This Great Lakes motor vehicle manufacturing complex might be the first recognizably modern global value chain. Components, material inputs, and finished cars and trucks are constantly moving across the border. Trade between Canada and Michigan is more valuable than trade between Canada and China. Trade in motor vehicles and parts between the United States and Canada is worth more than a fifth of the total trade between the two countries.[20]

Thanks to the collapsing cost of transportation, especially by sea, cross-border manufacturing networks are now far more common and far more spread out than in the years when Chrysler, Ford, and General Motors first opened factories and offices in Canada. Most of the world's manufacturing takes place in one of three cross-border manufacturing networks centered on the United States, Germany, and China (previously Japan until about 2007). Trade of intermediate inputs within these networks explains more than half of all international trade, while cross-border trade of finished goods and services accounts for only one-third. (Energy and metals commodities make up the rest.) This is a far cry from the world of Smith and Ricardo or even the world of the 1960s. It is a consequence of containerization, liberalization, and the end of the Cold War.[21]

American exports of goods to Canada and Mexico are worth about as much as U.S. exports of goods to the European Union, China, Japan, and Korea combined. Much of the *value* of U.S. exports to its neighbors, however, comes from elsewhere. A seatbelt for an American-made car or light truck, for example, might have its fibers manufactured in Mexico, woven and dyed in Canada to take advantage of the abundance of water, sent back to Mexico to be sewn up, and then installed somewhere at a plant in the United States. At the same time, nearly half of the content of motor vehicles and parts imported from Mexico was originally made in the United States.[22]

Trade in goods and services among the twenty-eight members of the European Union (before Brexit) was worth about 50 percent more than trade between those same countries and the entire rest of the world. The German-led motor vehicle supply chain stretches east into Czechia, Hungary, Poland, Romania, and Slovakia, and southwest into Portugal and Spain. Nearly half of the value of exports sold by Germany's eastern neighbors comes from foreign components. More than half the motor vehicles produced by German car companies are made outside Germany, and about a third of the value of Germany's own automotive exports comes from its neighbors.[23]

Perhaps the most iconic transnational supply chain is the one developed to assemble electronics in China. In 2007, China ostensibly exported about $290 billion worth of "computer, electronic, and optical" products, but roughly $120 billion of the value of those exports (around 40 percent) came from elsewhere, particularly Korea, Japan, and Taiwan. Even though Chinese producers have since become far less reliant on imported components, global value chains still have an impact on the bilateral trade data. Even now, about a third of the value of China's imports from Korea and Taiwan originated elsewhere, reflecting those countries' positions in the middle of international supply chains. Taiwanese academics calculate that standard figures overstate the value of their country's trade relationship with China by a factor of three.[24]

The increasing importance of these global value chains means that conventional bilateral trade data no longer do a good job of measuring the actual value created by workers and machines in each country. Gadgets assembled in China (or, nowadays, Vietnam) and shipped to North America or Europe are filled with imported components, including components made in the United States, just as German cars are built with Eastern European parts and American trucks are filled with Mexican content. Yet the statistics produced by customs offices attribute all of the value of the imported inputs to whichever country happens to ship the finished product. Economists have recently begun producing alternative trade statistics that account for these transnational manufacturing networks. For the United States, imports are overstated by about 16 percent while exports are overstated by about 20 percent. Chinese imports and exports are both overstated by about 30 percent.[25]

The growth of transoceanic shipping among the three main manufacturing networks adds to the confusion. Although governments are reasonably good at tracking where goods came from and where they are initially shipped, it is much tougher for the customs offices to follow exports to their final destinations. American exports to the European continent often land in the major ports of Antwerp or Rotterdam before being moved to the major markets of France, Germany, and Italy. Similarly, many U.S. exports arrive in Hong Kong and Singapore before moving elsewhere in East Asia.

One strange result is that the United States consistently reports massive exports to Belgium, the Netherlands, Hong Kong, and Singapore. Official U.S. data imply that American businesses supposedly exported about $151 billion worth of goods to those four small countries in 2018. That would be more than American goods exports to China ($121 billion), or about as much as total U.S. goods exports to France, Germany, and the United Kingdom combined ($161 billion). Put another way, U.S. exports of goods to Belgium and the Netherlands ($80 billion, combined population of 29 million people) were ostensibly worth as much as exports sent to Germany and Italy together ($81 billion, combined population of 140 million). Meanwhile, the value of American goods shipped to Hong Kong and Singapore ($71 billion, combined population 13 million) was just below the value of U.S. exports of goods to Japan ($76 billion, population of 127 million). These numbers are artifacts of flawed international trade reporting rather than serious economic indicators.[26]

Combined, transnational manufacturing networks and oceanic ports mean that official figures on exports and imports are a poor guide to the countries that are capturing the profits and employment income from international trade. But another source of distortion in the data may be even larger.

How Corporate Tax Avoidance Distorts the Trade Data

International trade is conducted not by countries but by companies that have to pay taxes on their profits. Their efforts to pay as little as possible mean that official trade data often present a distorted picture of actual trade flows. The current account, which combines trade data with figures on cross-border investment income and remittances, is a better measure.

The reason is that corporate tax burdens vary widely depending on where those profits are officially earned. These variations have been exploited by creative problem-solvers at accountancy firms and within large corporations. People who in previous eras might have written symphonies or designed cathedrals have instead saved companies hundreds of billions of dollars in taxes by shifting trillions of dollars of intangible assets across the world over the past two decades. One consequence is that many companies avoid paying any tax on their foreign sales. Another is that many countries' trade figures are now unusable.

When the U.S. income tax was introduced in 1913, it assessed nothing on money earned abroad. Nobody seemed to mind until the 1950s, when American companies started aggressively relocating parts of their businesses to foreign countries to exploit lower tax rates. By the early 1960s this was starting to have a meaningful impact on the size of the tax base.

The Kennedy administration proposed that American companies

should pay U.S. taxes regardless of how they structured their operations internationally. Income would not be taxed twice, since businesses could credit any taxes paid to foreign governments against their U.S. tax bill. But there would no longer be any incentive to relocate jobs and factories purely for tax reasons. The principle underlying this worldwide system of profit taxation was called "capital export neutrality." The thinking was that the alternative territorial system effectively encouraged money to leave the United States for reasons other than underlying differences in productivity and costs. Defenders of territorial taxation said that they wanted every country's tax code to treat foreign and domestic companies alike. They called their position "capital import neutrality."

The Revenue Act of 1962 tried to split the difference by distinguishing between income from foreign subsidiaries that came from "active business" and income that was "passive." Profits earned from selling goods made in factories located abroad would not be taxed by the U.S. government as long as those profits were reinvested in the foreign operation. American companies would have to pay taxes only on profits sent home via dividends, debt buybacks, or mergers and acquisitions.

The resulting subpart F of the Internal Revenue Code penalized so-called passive income. Dividends and interest earned from investment portfolios would be taxed at U.S. rates by the federal government regardless of whether those profits were reinvested abroad or repatriated immediately to American investors. Crucially, income from royalties and licenses was considered passive. American companies would pay the full U.S. corporate tax rate on any income earned from their patents regardless of where they claimed those patents were located in their corporate structure.[27]

Everything changed in 1996 with Treasury Decision 8697. The new rule, which came to be known as "check-the-box" by practitioners, was supposed to make things simpler for tax filers and make life easier for Internal Revenue Service (IRS) examiners. Instead, it opened up massive loopholes in the corporate tax code. Among other things, income from royalties and licenses could now be treated the same as income from foreign factories. The IRS quickly recognized some of the implications and proposed a new rule to prevent arrangements "contrary to the policies and rules of subpart F," but political interference blocked any fix.

Once subpart F had been neutered, the creatives in law and accounting departments all across America began to exploit the new potential of "intangibility." Unlike factories or office buildings filled with workers, patents and other intellectual property occupy no physical space. They can be moved anywhere in the world by filling out a few forms.

The simple version of the scheme is to set up a subsidiary in a corporate tax haven and then sell the subsidiary the right to license the patents to the rest of the company. The parent company gets a regular payment from the subsidiary holding the patents, often quoted as a share of total research and development (R&D) costs, and the subsidiary gets a large cut of the corporation's global sales. Calibrate the deal correctly and profits can be shifted from places where taxes are high to places where taxes are low.

This allows multinational corporations from all countries, not just the United States, to avoid paying taxes on profits earned outside their home country. Under both the worldwide system, which was what the United States had before 2017, and the territorial system that is now the global norm, companies are supposed to pay taxes to the government of the country where those profits were earned. For American companies, avoiding the IRS is worthwhile only if foreign profits can also be moved out of the reach of the high tax rates in other major markets such as Canada, China, France, Germany, and Japan. Similarly, foreign companies selling to Americans have an equally strong reason to shift their profits from the United States to places without corporate income tax.

The results can be seen in the data. As foreign sales rose in importance and large U.S. companies got better at profit shifting, their effective tax rate dropped from a bit over 35 percent in the mid-1990s to about 30 percent by the early 2000s to about 26 percent by the mid-2010s. Although the tax law passed at the end of 2017 lowered the effective corporate tax rate below 20 percent and more or less replaced America's worldwide system of corporate taxation with a territorial system, it did not remove the incentives for profit shifting.[28]

These profit shifts have also done strange things to the official figures on trade and investment, especially as companies have transferred more and more of the value of what they produce into intangible assets. About 40 percent of all profits earned by multinational corporations outside their home markets are shifted from high-tax jurisdictions, such as China, France, Germany, Japan, and the United States, into low-tax jurisdictions, such as the Cayman Islands, Ireland, and Singapore. Exports from the high-tax countries are artificially depressed, imports are artificially elevated, and profits earned from subsidiaries in corporate tax havens are unreasonably large.[29]

Consider Apple. Each iPhone is assembled by Foxconn, a separate company, out of components Apple does not produce. Apple makes few goods itself—it mostly pays others to make them. Despite this, much of the value of each phone is captured by Apple either in the form of profits paid to shareholders or as wages paid to the American workers who developed the software, designed the finished product, and ran the company's business operations. The production of each iPhone should therefore generate exports for the countries that make the components (mainly Korea, Japan, and Taiwan), imports of those components for the country where it is assembled (China), exports of finished devices from the country where it is assembled (China again), and exports for the country that produced the operating system and other bundled software (the United States).

This is not what happens. Instead, much of the value generated by Apple's American operation is counted as an export from a corporate tax haven. While most of the value generated by Apple comes from its workers in the United States, much of the income Apple generates when it sells its wares abroad is officially paid to Apple's tax haven subsidiaries.

The exact mechanics are complicated and have likely evolved over time, but the simplified version goes something like this. First, Apple's Irish subsidiary pays a fee to the parent in Cupertino, California, to cover the cost of research and development. This counts as an export of services from the United States to Ireland. (Most of America's exports of R&D services go to corporate tax havens, while most of Ireland's imports of R&D services come from the United States.)

The next bit is tricky. According to an investigation published by the *New York Times* at the end of 2016, Foxconn's assembly plant in Zhengzhou, China—which put together about half of all iPhones—is technically not in China at all but in a special no-man's-land surrounded by a customs boundary called a "bonded zone." This lets Foxconn import components without paying Chinese tariffs. Even more important, the bonded zone lets Apple buy the finished phones from Foxconn before they have technically entered China, sell those phones to subsidiaries based in corporate tax havens such as Ireland, and then let those subsidiaries sell the iPhones to the rest of the world after adding its hefty profit margin.[30]

This allows Apple to book the bulk of its profits in countries where it pays the least tax even though the phones are shipped from Chinese ports. The result of all this is that Apple paid only about 18 percent of its pretax income in cash taxes in its 2017 fiscal year, although the company expected eventually to pay a tax rate of about 25 percent. (The 2018 data are not representative because of one-time provisions of the new tax law.)[31]

Apple is far from unique. Microsoft, for example, reports that its average effective tax rate in fiscal years 2015–17 was also about 18 percent. Part of the reason is that Microsoft managed to attribute only 12 percent of its total profits to sales in the United States, on average, during those three years. As the company itself notes, "Foreign earnings taxed at lower rates" shaved off about 19 percentage points from Microsoft's U.S. corporate tax rate. Google also paid an average effective rate of around 18 percent. Only some of this can be explained by the lower level of corporate tax rates in America's major trade partners. At least as important is the ability of these companies to report their profits in countries with effective tax rates close to zero.[32]

Creative Taxation

Software companies are not the only ones able to exploit the weaknesses of the global tax system. Pharmaceutical companies spend billions of dollars to research and develop new drugs. Once the drugs are approved, the cost of manufacturing them is often trivially low. The value comes from the labs that generate the patents rather than the plants where pills are made. Placing the patents offshore and manufacturing the effective ingredients in favorable tax jurisdictions can lower effective tax burdens. Johnson & Johnson, for example, paid an average effective tax rate of about 17 percent in the years before the 2017 tax law changes. "International operations" consistently shaved about 17 percentage points off the headline rate.[33]

Almost any multinational can use these tricks to lower its tax burdens with enough creativity. Starbucks had its subsidiary in the Netherlands collect 6 percent of all non-U.S. sales as payment for the right to use the company's "intellectual property." One result was that Starbucks's U.K. operation consistently lost money—or at least that was what the company said whenever it was asked to pay taxes on its profits to the U.K. Treasury. Even more impressive, the Dutch subsidiary collecting all that royalty income also claimed that it made no money even though it had no costs beyond some office space and a few dozen employees.[34]

Many American companies making money by selling goods and services overseas therefore generate foreign direct investment income from their operations abroad, rather than export earnings attributable to the United States. About two-thirds of this income officially came from seven tiny countries known to offer tax benefits to American multinationals: Bermuda, the Cayman Islands, Ireland, Luxembourg, the Netherlands, Singapore, and Switzerland. Until the 2017 tax changes penalized the practice, foreign companies made their American subsidiaries appear unprofitable to minimize their U.S. tax bill, often by having them borrow at high interest rates from their corporate parents. One result is that U.S. direct investments abroad consistently yield about 4 percent more than foreign direct investments in the United States. Another is that more than three-quarters of the net income earned by foreign subsidiaries of American corporations are now attributed to a handful of tiny tax havens.[35]

The counterpart to the hyperprofitability of American and European companies' foreign operations lies in the southwestern bit of the Republic of Ireland, which, officially, is one of the wealthiest parts of Europe. Cork is the largest city in the region and has been home to Apple's European headquarters since 1980. About six thousand people currently work there in functions ranging from logistics to manufacturing custom iMacs. Major pharmaceutical companies, including Pfizer, GlaxoSmithKline, and Johnson & Johnson, also have operations in Cork. Further north, Dublin is home to subsidiaries of Facebook, Google, and Microsoft.[36]

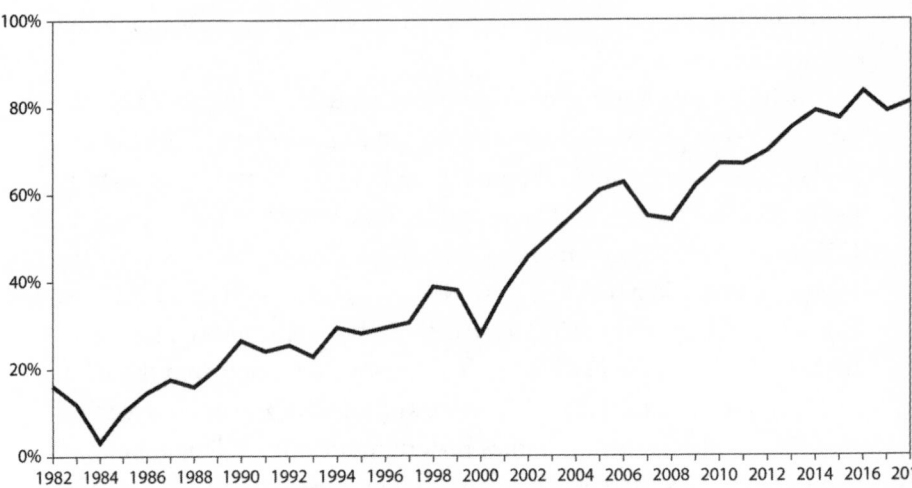

Fig. 1.2 Most U.S. foreign direct investment income is now booked in corporate
tax havens (share of net income attributed to subsidiaries in the Caribbean,
Ireland, Luxembourg, the Netherlands, Singapore, and Switzerland).
Sources: Bureau of Economic Analysis; Matthew Klein's calculations

There are many legitimate reasons for American companies to
have operations in Ireland: a highly educated English-speaking workforce, easy access to the vast consumer market of the European Union,
and short direct flights to most major U.S. cities. Until the 1990s, however, the Republic of Ireland was a poor backwater on the periphery of
Europe. It is confined to a mostly rural island and has a history of complicated relations with its main neighbor.

To overcome these disadvantages, the Irish government has long
used tax preferences to attract foreign investment. The official corporate
tax rate is just 12.5 percent. This is one of the lowest in the world and has
long been one of the main reasons why so many pharmaceuticals are
made in Ireland. But the low official tax rate is less significant to American companies than the ability of operations "registered" in Ireland to
be "tax-resident" in the Caymans or Bermuda, where the corporate tax
rate is zero. Combine a couple of these quasi-Irish subsidiaries together,
often with a Dutch one in the middle, then shift profits from high-tax
jurisdictions such as Germany to low-tax ones such as Ireland, and mul-

tinationals can engineer an effective tax rate close to zero on their international income.[37]

In 2018, the most recent year with comprehensive data, the Irish subsidiaries of American corporations generated about $53 billion in profits—roughly the same amount of profits generated by U.S. subsidiaries in Canada ($31 billion), China ($13 billion), and Japan ($13 billion) combined. Dutch subsidiaries of U.S. companies generated $87 billion in profits in 2018—about equal to the profits earned in Australia ($10 billion), Brazil ($4 billion), the United Kingdom ($47 billion), France ($2 billion), Germany ($7 billion), Hong Kong ($8 billion), and Mexico ($9 billion) together. This cannot be explained by real economic relationships; the explanation is instead profit shifting meant to minimize tax obligations. The seven corporate tax havens together were responsible for more than $324 billion in U.S. direct investment income in 2018.

Subpart F may have been rendered mostly useless by the Treasury's mistake in 1996, but until the 2017 tax law changed things, the Revenue Act of 1962 still meant that American corporations could avoid paying U.S. taxes on those foreign profits only if they were reinvested abroad. Dividends and stock buybacks were not allowed. Almost anything else, however, was acceptable. The result was that subsidiaries of American multinationals located in corporate tax havens accumulated trillions of dollars of financial assets in the past two decades. From 1998 through 2017, American companies operating in the seven corporate tax havens "earned" and then "reinvested" more than $2.1 trillion of profits. Over the same period, American companies operating in the rest of the world earned and reinvested less than $1.5 trillion in profits—a difference of roughly $640 billion.[38]

Most of this money ended up back in the United States as fixed-income investments even though it was considered foreign for tax purposes. Company reports are transparent about this. Apple's 2017 annual report describes how most of its financial assets are "held by foreign subsidiaries" yet invested in "dollar-denominated holdings." Microsoft's 2017 annual report says that its "investments are predominantly U.S. dollar-denominated securities" even though it also says that 96 percent of its financial assets are "held by our foreign subsidiaries and would be subject to material repatriation tax effect."[39]

Between the start of 2012 and the end of 2017, U.S. companies rein-vested about $1.2 trillion in the main corporate tax havens, according to the Bureau of Economic Analysis. Over that same period, the U.S. Trea-sury's regular survey of investors reports that the value of Treasury, agency, and corporate bonds owned by residents of the Caribbean, Ire-land, Luxembourg, the Netherlands, Singapore, and Switzerland in-creased by . . . $1.2 trillion. This is unlikely a coincidence. At the end of 2017, for example, Irish residents ostensibly owned more than $688 bil-lion in U.S. Treasury, agency, and corporate debt, up from just over $200 billion at the start of 2012. In that same period, Apple went from holding about $56 billion in "long-term marketable securities" to holding $195 billion, while Microsoft went from holding $63 billion in financial in-vestments to holding $133 billion. Although their exact financial arrange-ments are not known, it is possible that these two companies alone could explain nearly half of the total increase in reported holdings of U.S. bonds by Irish residents. These arrangements distort the trade and in-vestment data, especially when it comes to Ireland's own exports and imports (and, increasingly, its domestic business investment).

The passage of the 2017 U.S. corporate income tax changes meant that American companies could return as much of these offshore savings to shareholders through dividends and stock buybacks as they wished. So far, the impact has been relatively modest: American companies withdrew just $250 billion from their foreign subsidiaries in 2018. But the impact has been much larger in the corporate tax havens. There, withdrawals were worth $319 billion in 2018. The corollary was a $256 billion decline in the value of U.S. bonds held by residents of the major corporate tax havens between November 2017 and June 2018.[40]

Standard trade data are filled with misinformation for the un-trained analyst. The importance of international tax avoidance means that standard bilateral figures are deeply misleading. Fortunately, there is an alternative: the current account combines trade flows with asset income flows and cross-border remittances, effectively canceling out the impact of corporate tax avoidance in the data.

It may have once made sense to study trade independently, but it is no longer possible to understand the world economy without a com-prehensive understanding of how money moves across borders. That, in

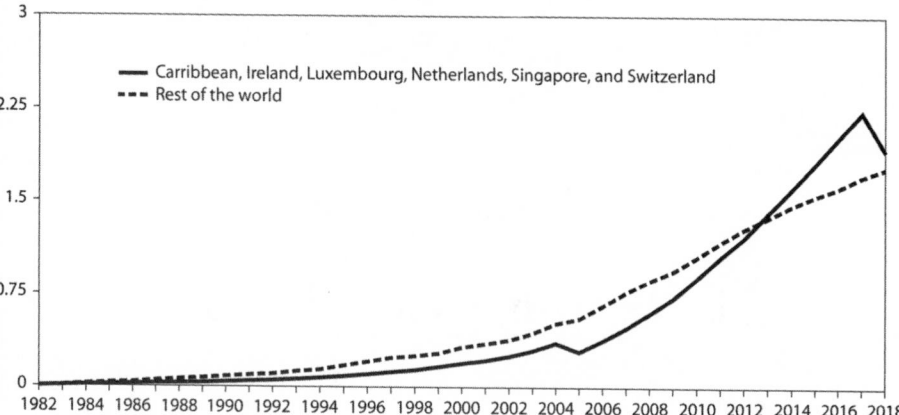

Fig. 1.3 The hidden stash (U.S. corporate profits earned and retained abroad, USD trillions). *Sources: Bureau of Economic Analysis; Matthew Klein's calculations*

turn, requires knowledge of how the international financial system has evolved into its current form. Whereas for much of modern history international capital flows consisted mostly of trade finance, and so mainly reflected trade imbalances, this is no longer the case. Financial imbalances now determine trade imbalances.

The Growth of Global Finance

Trade moves goods across space. This takes time and involves risk. Sellers might ship dud goods, pirates might steal the cargo, or bad weather might destroy the shipment. Buyers might back out of paying what they had agreed, or they might have made promises to sell imported goods they cannot keep if the products arrive late. Mere willingness to exchange is therefore insufficient to make trade happen. Finance, which moves purchasing power across space and time, is necessary. Trade and finance have been linked for thousands of years.

There are broadly three very different ways in which to think about this relation, however. Each mental model contains radically different assumptions about the sources and consequences of trade imbalances.

First, international flows can consist mostly of trade finance. In other words, the financial transactions are driven by relative production and transportation costs. Moreover, because the spread of international trade will be driven by Ricardian principles of comparative advantage, trade imbalances cannot become particularly large or persist for many years. In fact, they will be self-correcting because sustained deficits or surpluses will force domestic adjustments that eliminate the imbalances. Although there may be problems with the distribution of the benefits, the overall global economy unambiguously benefits from this type of trade.

Second, international financial flows can consist primarily of *rational* investment seeking out the most productive opportunities around the world. In this scenario, finance is likely to flow from rich, mature economies to rapidly growing developing economies, so trade imbalances are likely to consist of trade surpluses for the former and trade deficits for the latter. This roughly describes trade for much of the nineteenth century. Again, although there may be problems with the distribution of the benefits, the overall global economy unambiguously benefits from this type of trade and investment because it helps less productive economies to converge with societies at the technological frontier.

Alternatively, international financial flows can be driven by a wide variety of factors, including rational investment, speculation, capital flight, fads, panics, mercantilism, the desire for safety, and so on. If trade imbalances are caused by this combination of financial flows, however, any connection between rising trade and broader prosperity is only accidental. There is no longer any clear reason why the global economy would benefit. More precisely, to the extent that financial flows are driven by *anything* other than rational investors seeking out the most profitable opportunities, trade imbalances probably detract from global growth and distort the composition of many societies.

The third mental model is the one that bears the closest relation to reality. None of the main financial technologies—equity, debt, and insurance—are new. The massive scale of international finance, however, is a relatively recent phenomenon. As recently as 1855, the total value of cross-border financial claims was just 16 percent of one year of global economic output. By 1870, however, that figure had jumped to 94 percent. Today, it is over 400 percent.[1]

This growth occurred in cycles of booms and busts. Every international lending boom seems to be preceded and accompanied by the same economic phenomena. First, some structural change significantly expands the definition and amount of money, leading to a rapid credit expansion. In England, for example, regulatory changes led to aggressive bursts of bank creation in 1826–37, when the number of banks grew from 3 to 113, and in 1857–73, when the number of banks grew from 98 to 128. Both periods were characterized by major lending booms to de-

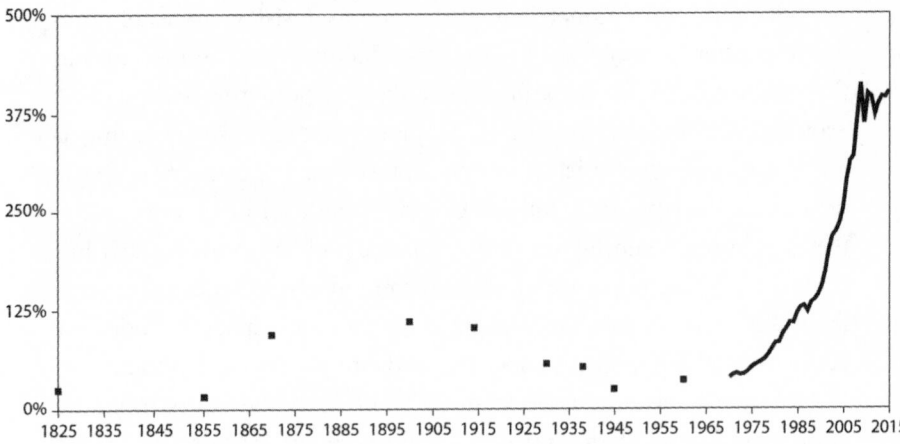

Fig. 2.1 The rise of cross-border finance (international assets and liabilities
as a share of world output). *Source: Bank for International Settlements*

veloping countries as well as bubbles in the high-tech ventures and other
risky projects of the time. Second, an asset boom in the domestic markets encourages increasingly risky behavior by successful investors, usually by borrowing more to make larger bets. As those bets pay off, investors make larger profits that they will want to continue investing in the
markets. Finally, some event sets off the fashion for foreign securities,
which causes money to pour across national borders, often into risky
developing countries.[2]

In each case, within a relatively short time, there is a huge expansion of lending and foreign investment to parts of the world that had
previously been excluded from it. The recipients of this new credit usually have little in common besides being remote from international financial centers. The boom typically ends when the sudden expansion of
lending ends even more suddenly.

Standard economic theory says that investments flow across borders
to take advantage of differences in growth prospects and that each country is evaluated separately. In this view, sophisticated investors continuously evaluate investment opportunities across a wide variety of countries and compare them to opportunities at home. Investors move their

money abroad only when the expected return of investing in foreign countries is high enough relative to expected investment returns at home.

There is an easy way to test whether this theory is correct: if foreign financial flows were driven purely by the relative attractiveness of different investment opportunities, the distribution of cross-border lending across countries should look random. There would be no synchronized credit booms from financial centers to countries on the periphery. After all, every country is unique and investors should be able to evaluate the effects of local political conditions, technological innovations, changes in demand or supply of an important locally produced commodity, and demographic shifts. Yet the history of the past several hundred years is replete with synchronized credit cycles.

This pattern is clearly visible in the relation between Great Britain and the United States during the eighteenth and nineteenth centuries, when the two economies had tightly linked business cycles. Part of the connection can be explained by fundamental ties: the United States was a major source of cotton for British textile mills and a major market for British manufactured goods, so what drove underlying economic growth in one often drove underlying economic growth in the other. More significant, however, is that these cycles were even more highly correlated with financial conditions in Great Britain. When the Bank of England was comfortable letting its gold reserves fall, both countries tended to expand and the flows of capital and goods between them also expanded. When the Bank of England was pulling gold back in from the rest of the global financial system, however, both countries tended to contract. Economic crises and panics in the United States, in other words, seemed to be linked more to British gold imbalances than anything else.[3]

When we look at the outcome of this process as it occurred during the international lending booms of the past two hundred years, the point is not simply to recount the history of cross-border finance but rather to confirm that changes in global financial conditions often matter far more than local growth prospects. What is striking is how institutional changes that led to increases or decreases in the global credit supply transformed investor perceptions of individual countries' real economic prospects. Sometimes this led to lending booms as capital

History of global financial cycles

Period	Major borrowers	Primary source	Outcome
1822–25	Spain, Naples, Denmark, Prussia, Greater Colombia, Mexico, Austria-Hungary, Chile, Russia, Brazil, Greece, Peru, Argentina	British	Major international defaults beginning in 1824, representing about 20–25 percent of total foreign investment
1834–39	U.S. states, Portugal, Spain, Mexico	Mostly British, some French	Major defaults beginning in 1837, mostly nine U.S. states following the collapse of cotton prices, representing about 20–25 percent of total foreign investment
1864–75	U.S., Russia, Ottoman Empire, Egypt, Spain, Austria-Hungary, Peru, Romania, Confederate States of America, Colombia, Tunisia	Mostly British and French, some German	Major defaults across the world beginning as early as 1867, representing about 25 percent of total foreign investment
1886–90	U.S., Australia, Argentina, Portugal, Brazil, Greece	British	Looms large because of the effect of the Argentine default on Baring Brothers, but a relatively minor crisis period beginning in 1890, with less than 5 percent of total foreign investment in the form of defaulted bonds

continued . . .

History of global financial cycles *continued . . .*

Period	Major borrowers	Primary source	Outcome
1905–19	Russia, Canada, South Africa, Argentina, various Balkan states, Ottoman Empire, Austria-Hungary, Brazil, Mexico, Cuba	British, French, and German, in that order, with some U.S.	Although defaulted debt represented over 20 percent of total foreign investment, war and revolution in Russia, the Ottoman Empire, and Mexico were to blame; otherwise high commodity prices caused by World War I ensured a very solid repayment record
1924–28	Germany, France, Argentina, Cuba, Chile, Peru, Australia, Canada, Brazil, Romania, New Zealand, South Africa, Yugoslavia, Greece, Austria, Colombia, Poland, Turkey	U.S. and British, in that order, with some Dutch	Major global default beginning in 1931 with defaulted bonds representing as much as 30–35 percent of total foreign investment
1970–81	Brazil, Mexico, Spain, Venezuela, South Korea, Argentina, Algeria, Turkey, Yugoslavia, Poland, Romania, Egypt, Indonesia, Philippines, Chile, Soviet Union	U.S., British, Japanese, German, French	Less-developed-country loan crisis and the lost decade of the 1980s
1991–97	Argentina, Mexico, Brazil, Korea, Russia, Turkey, Venezuela, Indonesia, Thailand, various CIS states, Colombia, Panama, Pakistan	U.S., German, French, Japanese, British	Asian Financial Crisis, Russian debt default, Turkish hyperinflation, Argentine crisis, and rise of precautionary saving

Source: Christian Suter, *Debt Cycles in the World Economy: Foreign Loans, Financial Crises, and Debt Settlements, 1820–1990* (Boulder, Colo.: Westview, 1992), 53, 66–67.

flooded out from the global financial centers to risky assets, both foreign and domestic. At other times, changes in financial conditions led to savage busts as savings retrenched from the periphery. These financial flows necessarily corresponded to trade flows, and large changes in the financial account were always accompanied by equal and opposite shifts in the trade account.

To put it differently, trade flows were determined by financial flows. The financial innovations that led to massive British capital outflows to Latin America in the early 1820s, for example, were directly connected to Britain's massive trade surpluses with Latin America during the same period. These trade relations cannot be explained by analyses of British manufacturing efficiency or the comparative advantages of Latin American producers. The better explanation is that financial flows across borders transformed economies and pushed them to adjust how much they imported and exported.

Finance historian Christian Suter has outlined what waves of capital outflow across borders from the great financial centers to "developing" economies looked like in the nineteenth and twentieth centuries (see table).

The First Global Credit Boom: The 1820s

As we explore these investment waves, we will see in each cycle that major capital flows do not seem to respond to changes in underlying trade conditions or even to underlying growth prospects. Instead, they are mainly the consequences of changing liquidity conditions associated with investment booms and collapses in the financial markets of the major banking economies.

Take England in the early nineteenth century. After winning the Napoleonic Wars, Britain began a period of rapid economic growth and technological progress. Following decades of wartime uncertainty and hardship, rich English savers were once again eager to find profitable investment outlets. The resulting frenzy eventually spread to some of the most far-fetched projects in remote corners of the earth—including at least one loan to a country that did not exist. The resulting international lending boom represents the first global credit boom followed by a global financial crisis. Friedrich Engels, writing in the late 1870s, called its collapse the "first general crisis."[4] It is a useful template for evaluating subsequent lending booms and is therefore worth discussing in detail.

There were at least four important changes in British financial conditions that set off the boom of the 1820s. The first was the seven-hundred-million-franc indemnity payment imposed on France at the second Treaty of Paris, which France was able to pay through the issues of *rentes,* French government bond obligations, arranged primarily by the London merchant bank Baring Brothers. (Postwar indemnity payments have often caused major changes in financial conditions.) Second, the British government announced in 1822 that it would convert its old perpetual bonds with 5 percent coupons to new bonds with 4 percent coupons. Investors were permitted to sell the old bonds back to the government and receive principal and accrued interest in the form of cash. This put nearly £2.8 million into the hands of British investors.

Third, also in 1822, Parliament allowed provincial banks to print money to fund their interest-bearing loans. This was highly profitable. According to one commentator, the banks "swamped the whole country with paper money, which found a ready outlet at that time in rising prices and universal speculation." Finally, the end of the wars meant the end of Napoleon's Continental System blockade and the recovery of European export markets. Combined with the collapse in military spending, the result was an extraordinary expansion of bullion reserves at the Bank of England from just under £4 million in 1821 to £14 million by late 1824.[5]

The change in British financial conditions occurred during a period of good news about Britain's underlying economic prospects: victory over Napoleon and a boom in technological innovation centered on trains, steamships, gas lighting, and textiles. Investors were enthusiastic about the opportunities for growth that came out of the combination of technological change and the sudden opening of new parts of the world. They were particularly enthused by the new Latin American countries, with their gold, silver, mineral resources, and, above all, populations just entering, with the defeat of Spain in their wars of independence, into liberal forms of rule and the global economy dominated by England.

Economic strength, military victory, and loose financial conditions led to a burst in confidence and a frenzy of speculative investing on the part of English capitalists and rentiers. It was also accompanied by a 30 percent increase in the level of consumer prices between 1822 and 1825.[6] An observer sixty years later described it like this:

> At the beginning of 1824, therefore, instead of grumbling and discontent, murmurs of satisfaction and gleeful anticipations of enhanced gains were heard from the capitalists on every side. . . . Business was exceedingly brisk. Everybody was making haste to get rich. Speculation of the most reckless character far outstripped the limits of the most adventurous trading. . . . [There was] an accumulation of money in the banks as well in London as in the provincial centers. A superabundance of capital sought employment of the riskiest of ventures. Projects of every kind for the construction of canals, tunnels, bridges, tramways, roads, and so forth, were eagerly entertained and accepted.[7]

One result seems to have been a significantly increased willingness on the part of British investors to take on risk. The Latin American revolutions were not secure until the final defeat of Spain at the Battle of Ayacucho on December 9, 1824—news of which did not reach England for another two months—and yet a Latin American loan frenzy began in 1822 with the £2 million loan to the new republic of Colombia.[8]

Negotiated in London by patriot-turned-villain Francisco Antonio Zea, this loan was singularly unsuccessful for Colombia. Approximately half of the issue was immediately exchanged at a 20 percent discount against inflated claims on the Colombian government incurred during the war of independence from Spain, while much of the balance was used to pay underwriting expenses and sales commissions or suffered deductions for interest and principal amortization prepayments. The republic received very little cash and had to return to the market fairly soon thereafter.

The loan was a great success for investors and the capital markets, however, and the newly emerging international loan market subsequently took off. Bankers made very large profits on limited risk. British investors receiving 4 percent on their own government's perpetual bonds were eager to purchase fixed income with 6 percent coupons at initial prices ranging from 80 percent to 84 percent of face value from a country that, as many promoters and journalists suggested, seemed really no different from the United States forty years earlier. The Colombian bond quickly traded up in the secondary market.

Thanks to the success of the 1822 Colombian loan, several other sovereign borrowers came to market that year. Chile issued £1 million in bonds, Peru issued £450,000, Denmark put in for £2 million, and Russia, which had been a major player in the defeat of Napoleon, raised a whopping £6.5 million. The most entertaining transaction was the £200,000 offering by the kingdom of Poyais. This was a fictitious Central American country whose self-appointed king, Sir Gregor Mac-Gregor, was a Scottish adventurer who had fought at the side of Simón Bolívar during the independence wars (and to whom a statue in Caracas is dedicated). After its issue the bond actually traded up before brokenhearted investors realized that there was no such country. MacGregor had invented his kingdom and fooled his bankers into underwriting and promoting the growth prospects for his imagined borrower.[9]

Over the next three years several other foreign loans came to market. Austria and Portugal issued £5 million between them in 1823. Colombia, Mexico, the kingdom of Naples, Brazil, the Argentine capital Buenos Aires, Greece, and Peru sold nearly £15 million in 1824. In 1825, the biggest and last year of the boom, Denmark, Mexico, Brazil, Greece, Peru, the Mexican city of Guadalajara, and the country of Guatemala—all repeat borrowers except the last two—collectively issued more than £15 million of new bonds. In addition, more than fifty stock companies were organized in 1824 and 1825 for the sole purpose of operating in Latin America. Their authorized capital was more than £35 million, although most of this had not yet been put up when the crash came.[10]

At first things went well for both investors and borrowers. The lending, investment, and silver booms combined to pump fuel into the newly emerging economies of Latin America, the United States, southern Europe, and elsewhere. In Latin America they strengthened the hands of the new governments, which believed that the combination of independence, republicanism, and integration into the world economy would allow the region to grow as rapidly as the United States had. Latin American consumption grew strongly, while imports from England by 1825 were double their levels of only four years earlier.

By 1825 problems were already beginning to lay themselves out in a pattern that would later become familiar. It became clear, for example, that many of the investments were of very questionable value, a common problem whenever a small country attempts to absorb large financial inflows. There are simply not enough productive opportunities available. Instead, the excess credit invariably finances boondoggles, surging imports of consumer goods, or, as was often the case in the 1820s, imports of weapons to fight one of the many civil wars that immediately broke out after independence from Spain.

None of this seemed to affect outbound investment flows until the Bank of England began to tighten monetary policy to bring gold reserves back into the country. Britain's postwar economic boom had led to a surge in imports that was partly paid for by exporting gold. At the same time, gold was being shipped out of Britain because of the foreign lending boom. The combined effect was that the Bank of England's bullion holdings fell from £14 million in 1824 to £2 million by late 1825. Bank officials responded by raising the discount rate to bring gold home from the rest of the world. By 1827, reserves had stabilized at around £10 million.[11]

The rise in interest rates increased the financing costs of holding commodities and put selling pressure on hoarders. As prices declined, several English banks that had lent against coffee, tin, iron, sugar, and cotton began to experience problems with their loans. By October 1825, both domestic and foreign loan markets were trading poorly in London. A number of failures among cotton trading firms in November caused the Bank of England to tighten credit further in order to protect its liquidity position. (The idea that the central bank should increase its lending to offset changes in private risk appetite would not be invented until the 1870s.) This worsened overall economic conditions and caused further asset price declines. In mid-December, two major London banks that acted as agents for dozens of provincial banks, mostly in the Yorkshire textile region, collapsed. This set off the general panic.

Over the next few weeks, as panic selling hit commodity prices, several more London banks and more than 60 provincial banks were forced to close. Altogether, 76 of the 806 banks in England and Scotland closed their doors permanently during the crisis period. Walter Bagehot, Britain's leading economist in the second half of the nineteenth century, wrote that the Bank of England itself was nearly forced to suspend payments. The remaining banks began calling in loans and raising liquidity as rapidly as they could to protect their balance sheets, which forced industrial companies to cut back production and lay off workers.[12]

By the summer of 1826, the crisis had spread to Berlin, Amsterdam, St. Petersburg, Vienna, Rome, and Paris. The effect on those who had borrowed during the boom was nearly immediate. First, the collapse of European demand depressed commodity prices and crushed Latin American export revenues. At the same time, the raft of bank failures caused global financial conditions to tighten dramatically, with even the surviving banks desperate to hoard gold. From the middle of 1825 through the end of 1828, there were no new foreign loans in the British market.

Deprived of income and unable to raise new funds, the new republics of Latin America could not make interest and principal payments on their debts. Beginning in 1826, payments were halted on one loan after the other. By 1829, every Latin American borrower except Brazil had defaulted, although even Brazil, in 1829, required an emergency new money loan of £800,000 to make its interest payments. The losses to British investors were huge, and the pages of the British financial press were soon filled with anger and recrimination.

In retrospect, the lending boom in Latin America and Europe can be understood as a classic speculative bubble. Many commentators at the time thought differently, however, insisting that investment decisions reflected real underlying economic prospects. They believed that rational investors were attracted by the change in political conditions—independence and republicanism—which would supposedly lead to greater international trade and faster growth. Instead, revolution and war led to decades of instability. The brutal end of the boom demonstrated just how misplaced investors' hopes had been. It would take a full generation before Latin American borrowers could regain full access to the international markets.

The 1830s and the Second International Lending Boom

It did not take long to unlearn the lessons of the 1820s. Just ten years after the Latin American frenzy, the British capital markets were afflicted by another speculative international lending fever—this time, to the United States. Unlike most other global lending cycles, the boom and crash of the 1830s and 1840s was driven by tight links between a single lender (Great Britain) and a single borrower (the United States).

By 1830 England had begun to recover from the 1825 collapse. Bumper harvests in the early 1830s relieved Britain's grain shortage and began driving down grain prices. That lifted the purchasing power of the majority of Britons who were not farmers. This fundamental driver was amplified by a change in liquidity conditions: the Bank Act of 1826 had permitted the creation of new banks with the power to issue notes worth at least £5.

The initial impact was small, thanks in part to the preceding financial panic. Until 1833, just thirty-four banks of issue had been created under the new law. Between 1833 and 1835, however, thirty-four more banks were created, while forty-two new banks of issue were established in 1836 alone. At the same time, changes in the discounting procedure of the Bank of England and a significant expansion of its branches vastly increased the quantity of paper credits in circulation. The rapid creation of money was accompanied by an increase in asset and commodity prices, including the price of cotton.[13]

The United States, meanwhile, was living through an economic boom of its own that had been amplified by loosened financial conditions. Before President Andrew Jackson was elected in 1828, the Second Bank of the United States had maintained monetary discipline by regularly buying banknotes issued by other banks and redeeming those notes for gold. This effectively limited how much money the smaller banks could print by tying their note issuance to the fixed supply of metal.

After Jackson took office, however, he began shifting the federal government's deposits from the Second Bank to politically connected "pet" banks. Flush with new deposits, those banks grew rapidly. The effect was compounded by the Second Bank's loss of deposits, which forced it to cut back on its purchases of other banks' notes. The combined result was rapid expansion of the overall banking system. The number of state banks had already grown from 329 in 1829 ($110 million of capital) to 506 in 1834 and 788 by 1837 (over $500 million of capital).[14]

At the same time, the federal government had been selling huge amounts of public land and depositing the proceeds in the pet banks. This encouraged speculative purchases of public land with borrowed money, which further loosened financial conditions by effectively converting unimproved land into mortgages. Credit creation drove up asset prices in both Britain and the United States. Rising collateral values boosted bank profitability and encouraged the creation of even more banks.

British investors responded to reports of feverish economic activity and skyrocketing markets by embracing the U.S. growth story, pouring huge sums of money into American loans and investments. Recipients included several U.S. state governments, which were considered, in those pre–Civil War times, to be quasi-sovereign borrowers. Money also poured into railroads and canals. Industrial activity drove up the prices of cotton and other commodities used as inputs for manufacturing.

The resulting influx of funds drove a U.S. import boom. America's trade deficit ballooned from an average of $2 million per year from 1823 through 1830 to an average of $24 million per year from 1831 through 1836. As in the previous decade, changes in British financial conditions led to a rapid increase in spending power, a local stock market boom, rising commodity prices, and, ultimately, a huge increase in overseas lending.[15]

Things changed on both sides of the Atlantic in the middle of 1836. In July President Jackson required that all land purchases be paid for in physical gold or silver. Paper notes were no longer acceptable. Bank lending against property was suddenly limited to the actual bullion deposits on hand. Jackson's "specie circular" effectively eliminated the credit expansion that had fueled the land boom. Around the same time, the Bank of England decided to raise its discount rate from 4 percent to 4.5 percent to reverse the outflows of its gold reserves. In August, it raised its discount rate again to 5 percent.

At first the increase in rates and reduction in deposits in the private banking system had little effect because English banks increased their own money creation to compensate for the Bank of England's tightening. They simply made more loans and issued more notes and currency relative to their fixed supplies of gold reserves. Once news of the specie circular reached England, however, the Bank of England's directors decided that they would no longer lend to British banking houses with "excessive" American exposure. Their ham-fisted announcement precipitated a global credit contraction fairly quickly thereafter.[16]

First, British banks with U.S. business sold their cotton inventory to cover withdrawals. As a result, the price of America's principal export dropped by 30 percent in the beginning of 1837. That meant that U.S. debtors had less income to service their obligations, and American banking houses in New Orleans and New York began closing in 1837. The British, beginning to suffer from their own economic slowdown, cut off all further lending. Ironically, the panic pushed Britain's private banks to pull their gold holdings from the Bank of England. The Bank of England had wanted to rebuild its reserves but instead continued to lose them. Eventually, it had to apply for an extraordinary £2 million gold loan from the Bank of France. Even with the loan, reserves dropped as low as £2.4 million.[17]

British investors had never lent to the U.S. federal government, which had paid off the entire public debt in 1835. Instead, the loans went to a variety of private borrowers and to several state governments. The states were the most burdened, particularly since tax revenue was generally low and most revenues consisted of land sales—now sharply reduced because of the specie circular—and various forms of import revenues, now on a collapsing import base.

When these borrowers were simultaneously faced with lower import earnings, slowing economic activity, and a standstill in refinancing, they were wholly unable to raise enough gold to make the required payments. The result was predictable. By 1842, at the bottom of the depression, Pennsylvania, one of the richest states and heaviest borrowers, suspended interest payments. By then, Arkansas, Florida, Illinois, Indiana, Maryland, Michigan, and Mississippi had already defaulted along with much of the U.S. banking system. Pennsylvania eventually resumed interest and principal payments, but Mississippi, Arkansas, and Florida, with "carefully rationalized arguments," simply repudiated the debt outright.[18]

The international loan crisis was not exclusively an American crisis, but given its huge wealth, promise, and the amounts lent, it was perceived primarily as a U.S. crisis. States, just by themselves and excluding private borrowers, defaulted or rescheduled $120 million of loans.[19] Europeans were outraged. By the end of the decade James Mayer de Rothschild, the head of the French branch of the House of Rothschild, was reported to have told a visiting representative of the U.S. Treasury, with characteristic pomposity, that "you may tell your government that you have seen the man who is the head of the finances of Europe, and that he has told you that you cannot borrow a dollar, not a dollar." The fury and sense of betrayal of English investors led to an outpouring of hatred and scorn for the American rascals, and English literature is the richer for the many scathing diatribes that followed.[20]

The "First Global Financial Crisis": 1873

Europe entered a long expansion in the late 1850s that lasted throughout the U.S. Civil War and the various wars of German and Italian unification. Until 1873, imports and exports more than doubled in the United Kingdom, the United States, France, Austria, and Belgium. Investment boomed in the high-tech industries of railways, steamships, and telegraph cables, while the United States led a revolution in the production of agricultural commodities.

The strong growth in the real economy coincided with another burst of financial innovation. In the United States, Treasury secretary Salmon P. Chase marketed bonds to middle-class Americans in the North to finance the Civil War with the help of banking newcomer Jay Cooke & Company. France under Emperor Louis Napoleon created the first universal investment banks: Crédit Industriel et Commercial (1859), Crédit Lyonnais (1863), and Société Générale (1864). These developments radically improved the banking system's ability to collect and channel middle-class household savings into new investment projects. By the mid-1860s, Paris was beginning to rival London as a market for new international loans.[21]

Financial innovation was not limited to France and the United States. Germany also saw a similar expansion of its banking system and in the creation of joint-stock corporations. So many joint-stock companies were created in 1866–73 that still exist today that the period is known in Germany as the *Gründerzeit*, or founders' era. Most of the new German banks had been created in the 1850s, but in a financially backward and fragmented market, it took nearly two decades for them to develop and unify the provincial money and credit markets. In Austria, similarly, bank capital, which had amounted to 190 million gulden in 1866, had exploded to 508 million gulden by the end of 1872. In the first three months of 1873, fifteen more banks were established with additional paid-up capital of 72 million gulden.

Perhaps the most important trigger for the bubble that followed was the 5-billion-franc indemnity imposed on France after losing the 1870–71 Franco-Prussian War, which France was able to pay off in just three years. The reparations payment resulted in a transfer of wealth from France to Germany equal to roughly 20–25 percent of either country's gross domestic production (GDP).

The global lending boom was reinforced by the need to finance rising trade between the European powers and the peripheral nations. European demand for Peruvian guano (used for fertilizer) boosted export revenues and restored investor confidence, allowing Latin American governments to return to the capital markets in the 1850s to refinance or restructure older defaulted debt. By the 1860s, the Latin American governments had finally worked out their loan problems and their creditworthiness was bolstered by booming commodity prices.

Meanwhile, gold booms in California and Australia expanded both international gold holdings and human migration. Workers and miners traveled in huge numbers from Europe, the East Coast of the United States, Chile, and East Asia to the gold mining centers. Asset prices rose steadily during the 1860s, particularly toward the end of the decade, as the long, largely uninterrupted economic boom that began in the 1850s solidified confidence. The Dutch and Germans, and to a lesser extent the English, had bought huge amounts of low-priced U.S. government bonds during the Civil War. The victory of the booming, self-confident North made those investments very successful and whetted global appetite for further adventures in international lending.

Market behavior accelerated during the 1860s until, between 1870 and 1873, the markets seemed to change and speculative activity stepped up markedly. Global commodity prices, which had been rising but were generally steady over the previous decade, suddenly shot up. In Germany and Austria, a sudden explosion of new banks dedicated to the mortgage market, funded by French reparations, helped finance a construction boom that, combined with the frantic run-up in securities prices, plunged the country into a series of notorious stock swindles that came close to bringing scandal to Otto von Bismarck's government.[22]

In the United States, the New York Stock Exchange was engulfed in a speculative frenzy surrounding railway stocks and bonds. Stock market operators like Jay Gould and "Diamond" Jim Brady quickly became leading players and notorious figures in what had become a deeply dishonest market. In England the stock market skyrocketed, and British investors, after buying £57 million of Latin American bonds during the whole of the 1860s, scooped up £59 million in the first three years of the 1870s. The Mexican economic historian Carlos Marichal writes that during this period "all the Latin American states were besieged by the European moneylenders, who urged them into the financial fray. Under the circumstances, it is not surprising that few politicians or bankers took precautions to deal with a possible abrupt change in the international economic climate."[23]

Once again, rapid European money creation led to a burst of speculative activity in distant markets, followed by an expansion of international lending, followed automatically by soaring trade imbalances. Among the worst afflicted in trade was the newly established German Empire, which saw its trade account thrown into massive deficit as its increasingly valuable currency drove manufacturers out of global markets. At the time, weakness in manufacturing was more than made up for by strength in the property and financial markets, as well as in the booming service industries, so no one seemed especially worried by the surging imports of foreign goods.

The 1873 crisis began in Vienna with a stock market crash on May 8. In New York, the news unnerved investors in American railway bonds issued during the preceding boom. Speculators used these securities as collateral for loans to buy even more railway bonds, which made them sensitive to relatively small declines in price. On September 18, in a tre-

mendous shock to confidence, the house of Jay Cooke & Company—
America's largest private bank and the financial agent to the U.S. gov-
ernment—was forced to close because of its holdings of Northern Pacific
Railway bonds.[24]

The news of Jay Cooke's closing was enough to break the New York
exchange. Sellers poured into the market. Speculators who had borrowed against assets such as land and railway bonds were forced to sell
their holdings at low prices to raise cash and repay their debts. Shortly
thereafter, banks around the country suspended payments to depositors. The New York Stock Exchange closed and did not open until the
end of the month. The United States subsequently entered five years of
what was then called the Great Depression.

In October, the crisis returned across the Atlantic as the German
markets crashed. England was hit in November. The Bank of England
fended off the rush for gold by raising its discount rate, exacerbating
the downturn. Russia and the Scandinavian countries were sucked into
the panic soon after. France was the least affected because its loss in the
Franco-Prussian War and subsequent reparations payments had helped
it avoid the market boom.

Banks collapsed around the world, while the survivors sold their
assets and hoarded gold. Once again, global credit contraction prevented
international borrowers from raising the funds necessary to make debt
payments. Middle Eastern and European countries defaulted on their
loans. Chile was able to avoid defaulting on its foreign bonds only at the
cost of liquidating its banking system and losing all its gold. In 1878, the
country declared that its currency would no longer be convertible into
bullion.

The Baring Crisis and the First Lending Boom
of the Twentieth Century

Although Argentina had borrowed from the London markets in the
1820s and 1860s, it was economically insignificant for most of this period. It had also escaped the 1873 crisis relatively unscathed. Moreover,
by the late 1870s, Argentina had emerged as a major exporter of wheat,
leather, and chilled meat to the European market. By 1881, the country

had reformed its currency and banking sector and, under the leadership of General Julio Argentino Roca, began to borrow heavily to pay for infrastructure investments and military spending. The subsequent economic boom made it one of the wealthiest countries in the world and the darling of international investors. By 1889, between 40 percent and 50 percent of all British funds invested outside the home market were invested in Argentina.[25]

By the end of the 1880s, however, Argentine president Miguel Juárez Celman's inflationary policies were generating political opposition and undermining the sustainability of the currency in the eyes of British investors. The biggest sign of impending trouble was when Baring Brothers, Argentina's lead banker, arranged a large £2 million offering for the Buenos Aires Water and Drainage Company and was able to place only £150,000 with investors. The rest had to be held by the bank itself.

To assuage the concerns of its foreign creditors, the Argentine government converted the peso-denominated *cedulas* (mortgage bonds that were the largest component of foreign financing) into gold-denominated *cedulas*. Tying domestic debt to gold was supposed to signal the government's commitment to maintaining the exchange rate. Regaining the confidence of foreign creditors was supposed to lower borrowing costs and make it easier for Argentines to raise new funds to roll over maturing debts.

This is a popular strategy—Mexico did something similar in 1994 by converting some of its peso debt into dollars, for example—but it is always risky. If borrowers cannot repay their debts, they will eventually default—regardless of how painful it may be. As it happens, Argentina's gambit failed. Part of the problem was the Bank of England, which raised its discount rate from 3 percent in the beginning of the year to 6 percent by October in an attempt to discourage gold outflows. Lending from London duly slowed, and Argentina found it increasingly difficult to raise new money to support its currency. New loans declined from £23 million in 1888 to £12 million in 1889 and to just £5 million in 1890.

Argentina also had its own domestic problems. In July 1890, Argentina's finance minister resigned because of his opposition to President Celman's inflationary monetary policies and precipitated the feared exchange rate crisis. The drop in the currency led to a spike in inflation and forced up the cost of servicing the gold-denominated *cedulas*. Later that month, an attempted military coup forced President Celman to flee. It took time for news of the devaluation, the political crisis, and Argentina's inability to make interest payments to reach Europe. Once it did, the price of Argentine securities eventually dropped below 40 percent of face value.

By November, losses on Argentine bonds—including the ones it had been unable to sell to outside investors—nearly bankrupted Baring Brothers. The Bank of England responded by assembling a consortium of private banks to rescue Baring because of fears that its collapse would bring down the British financial system. (Something similar occurred in 1998 when the Federal Reserve Bank of New York organized a bailout of the hedge fund Long-Term Capital Management after Russia's sovereign default.) The intervention was insufficient to prevent a broader financial panic, however. British lenders responded to the Argentine crisis by slashing foreign lending, which contributed to a series of international panics around the world for the next three years.[26]

The Argentina crisis was eventually resolved, and international lending to Latin America resumed until World War I. It was in the 1910s, after all, that U.S. commercial banks established their first overseas branches, including in Argentina. Unusually, this became one of the only major international lending booms that did not end in large-scale defaults, because the war needs of the belligerents led to a rapid increase in export revenues by borrowers that could be used to service old debts. The only countries that did default—Russia, Mexico, and the Ottoman Empire—did so after revolutions, foreign invasion, or both.

During the war, Americans lent to Europeans, who used the money to pay for imports of U.S. food and manufactures. After the war, America's initial priority was getting the money back. Those efforts failed, however, so the new strategy was to provide new loans to the former belligerents in the hope that they would be able to rebuild more quickly and eventually pay off the old loans. Americans lent to Germans to pay reparations to France to service debts to the United Kingdom, which in turn owed the United States. This circular lending strategy seemed to work well after the Dawes Plan of loans to Germany in 1924. Americans became increasingly comfortable lending abroad, and the international loan market took off. In Latin America, this rapid expansion of new lending was called the "dance of the millions." The subsequent investing frenzy drove up the prices of assets as diverse as Latin loans, ships, major commodities, and of course U.S. stocks.

The stock market crash of 1929 and the subsequent collapse of the U.S. banking system brought the 1920s international lending boom to an abrupt end. There was a sudden temporary explosion of international lending in the first half of 1930, but it was too little to help. Unable to raise new money in the United States and unable to earn much in the way of export revenues thanks to the depressed demand for commodities, smaller countries at the periphery of the financial system found themselves incapable of making payments on their debts. Once again, the result was massive defaults.

The Less-Developed-Country Lending Boom

The Great Depression, World War II, the start of the Cold War, the introduction of capital controls, and the success of the Marshall Plan delayed the start of the next major lending boom until the 1970s. That boom had its roots in the 1950s, when the Soviet Union began moving its dollar deposits to Swiss banks to protect them from confiscation. Over time, European and Japanese banks lent these so-called Eurodollars to borrowers outside the United States, creating a separate dollar-denominated financial system that was connected to, but distinct from, the regulated one based in New York.

The Great Inflation was a major impetus for the growth of the Eurodollar market and its cousin, the money-market mutual fund. Since the 1930s, U.S. banking regulations had limited how much interest banks could offer to attract deposits. The theory was that limiting competition would make banks less risky and prevent crises. American banks and their depositors did not mind this arrangement when deposits yielded more than inflation. By the late 1960s and early 1970s, however, accelerating inflation meant that savers were losing money by leaving it in checking or savings accounts. American and international banks came up with an elegant solution that allowed them to sidestep banking regulations: they would sell short-term debt (commercial paper) to mutual funds that would then replicate the features of typical bank accounts. These money-market funds offered savers much higher yields and allowed European—and later Japanese—banks to access dollars for making loans.

The appeal of these offshore dollars became apparent after the price of oil rose from $2 to nearly $40 a barrel over the 1970s. (Among the causes were soaring demand, dwindling production in the continental United States, and supply disruptions in the Middle East.) The oil exporters generated enormous revenues and were flooded with dollars. Despite trying their best, they could not spend the money quickly enough and ended up depositing much of their windfall in the Eurodollar market. The accumulation of dollar deposits in the world's major banks funded a lending boom to Latin America, the Soviet bloc, and even North Korea. The initial loans were very successful, and after surviving the difficulties of the first oil price hike, less-developed countries (LDCs) responded to the influx of credit with faster economic growth and a surge in consumer goods imports. Within a few years, many of the world's largest banks had lent multiples of their equity to developing countries.

As in 1825, the LDC lending frenzy of the 1970s was killed by a sharp and deliberate monetary contraction—this time engineered by the Federal Reserve System in 1980–82 in an effort to end the Great Inflation of the 1970s. Interest rates soared to the point that West German chancellor Helmut Schmidt famously said that real interest rates were at their highest levels "since the birth of Jesus Christ." That caused debt servicing costs to soar at the same time that commodity export revenues collapsed. Banks became unwilling to finance new loans as they lost Eurodollar deposits. The result was predictable—at some point the net outflow of funds was too great for the LDCs to maintain, and beginning with Mexico in August 1982, they began asking their creditors for debt relief.[27]

The European Banking Glut and the Crisis of 2008

The most significant financial development of the past two decades was the launch of the euro in 1999. At a stroke, a dozen separate currencies were replaced with a single currency. To many observers, foreign exchange risk had been eliminated, even as default risk remained un-changed. European banks that had been confined to operating mostly in their home market were suddenly liberated to lend across the conti-nental monetary union. French banks could access Dutch and German savings to make loans to borrowers in Italy and Greece, Spanish banks could borrow from French and German savers to make loans to Por-tugal and Italy, Italian banks could borrow from Austrians to lend to Germans—the possibilities were endless. European banks were able to borrow and lend far more than they ever could before.

One consequence was a massive boom in cross-border borrowing within Europe. Debt owed by euro-area residents to residents of other countries increased by more than €8 trillion between 2002 and 2008. At least as important, however, was the expansion of European banks out-side Europe, particularly to the United States. By 2007, more than 40 percent of all bank credit to the U.S. nonbank private sector came from lenders headquartered outside the United States, mostly from Europe.

The European banks had effectively become American banks. They borrowed dollars by issuing short-term debt to Americans and used the proceeds to make loans and buy mortgage bonds in the United States. The flows of money from Europe to the United States, from the United States to Europe, and from European countries to each other were all much larger than any of the other major cross-border financial flows before 2008.

The result was a genuinely transatlantic financial system. Many of the biggest investment banks involved in creating so-called private-label American mortgage bonds were European. Deutsche Bank underwrote more subprime mortgage bonds than Goldman Sachs, Bank of America, Citigroup, J. P. Morgan, or Countrywide. European investors owned about 20 percent of all the U.S. asset-backed securities outstanding on the eve of the crisis. During the panic of 2008, most of the Federal Re-serve's emergency loans went to banks based outside the United States, mainly in Europe. Writing in 2011, the economist Hyun Song Shin ob-served that, globally, "the U.S.-dollar denominated assets of banks out-side the United States are comparable in size to the total assets of the U.S. commercial banking sector, peaking at over $10 trillion prior to the crisis."[28]

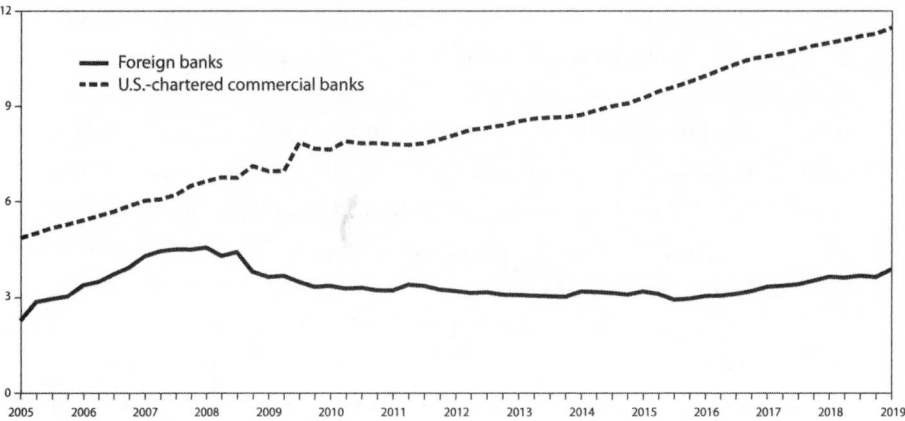

Fig. 2.2 Foreign banks played a major role in the U.S. credit boom and bust (bank credit provided to the U.S. nonfinancial sector, by nationality of bank, USD trillions). *Sources: Bank for International Settlements; Federal Reserve Board; Matthew Klein's calculations*

From one perspective, this system is radically different from what existed in the 1820s. Back then, it would have been ludicrous for a British bank to have funded a large proportion of its lending to Colombia by borrowing from Colombian savers. Yet in some ways the story of the 2000s demonstrates how the essential drivers of cross-border financial flows have stayed the same. A structural change in banking regulation led to a boom in lending that flowed from the starting market to the rest of the world. Changing financial conditions in Europe meaningfully affected financial conditions in the United States. Later, as U.S. mortgage defaults generated losses for holders of mortgage-backed securities (MBS), American conditions ended up redounding back to Europe. Together, finance and trade connect the world.

We have shown that we no longer live in a world in which international flows consist mostly of trade finance, even though its assumptions continue to guide much of the policy discussion on trade. We have established that international financial flows do not consist primarily of *rational* investment seeking out the most productive opportunities around the world but are primarily driven by changes in credit conditions and speculative sentiment. Next, we will show that to understand what drives international capital flows we must first understand what drives savings. Long-term growth is determined mainly by the growth of productive investment, which is necessarily funded by savings, but a country can have more or less savings than it needs for investment purposes, and so it must import or export the difference. As we will see, the savings rate of any country is determined not by cultural factors or attitudes toward thrift, but rather by how income is distributed domestically.

Saving, Investment, and Imbalances

Scarcity has defined most of humanity's existence. Until relatively recently, simply securing enough food to prevent starvation was a major challenge. During the long era of scarcity, people had to choose whether to use finite resources to invest in productive assets or to satisfy immediate needs (consumption). Historically, consumption won. Growing populations invariably consumed any additional output, which limited wealth creation and capped living standards. Back then, suppressing consumption (saving more) was necessary to generate a surplus of production above consumption to fund worthwhile investments.

When resources are abundant, however, trying to save by consuming less is wasteful and counterproductive. People who could be working are left idle even as desires remain unfulfilled. Fields lie fallow as the hungry starve. Factories and machines deteriorate for lack of use. Rather than generating a surplus that can be invested, cutting consumption simply leads to lower production. Moreover, the resulting excess capacity discourages new investment and ultimately leads to lower living standards.

Globally, all economic output is either consumed or used to develop productive assets. For the world as a whole, saving and investment are equal by definition. In most countries, however, saving and investment are not equal. Some places produce more than they use domestically, while other countries produce less than they need. These differences are reconciled through trade: excess output is exported to places where domestic demand (consumption plus investment) is greater than domestic production (GDP). Surpluses and deficits are the result.

This can be represented with the following set of simple equations:

Global demand = Global production

Demand = Consumption + Investment

Production = Consumption + Savings

Domestic demand = GDP + Imports – Exports

Exports – Imports = Domestic saving – Domestic investment

Trade imbalances allow gluts in one society to compensate for shortages in another. In the right circumstances, these surpluses and deficits make everyone better off compared to a world full of closed economies. Countries with few attractive domestic investment opportunities, perhaps because of their demographics and their position at the forefront of technological development, ought to be net exporters. Without export markets, those countries would be stuck in permanent slumps caused by the imbalance between their abundant productive capacity and their weak domestic demand. The natural recipients of those exports are countries bereft of needed capital goods and infrastructure. Without access to foreign production, investment in the deficit countries would have to compete for limited resources with domestic consumption. It is not a coincidence that two of the worst famines in modern history—the Soviet Union in 1929–33 and China in 1958–62—were perpetrated by authoritarian regimes committed to rapid industrialization while cut off from the rest of the world.

At other times, however, trade imbalances can make people worse off. Instead of relieving shortages, imports simply crowd out domestic production. This has been the defining problem of the past few decades: people in certain countries are spending too little and saving too much. This is not because their households are especially thrifty or because their governments are unusually prudent. It is not even because their businesses are rationally responding to the dearth of attractive opportunities. Rather, it is because of choices made by elites within those countries that transfer wealth and income away from people who would spend more on goods and services, such as workers and pensioners, to those, such as the rich, who would instead use extra income to accumulate additional financial assets. This imposes an untenable choice on the rest of the world: absorb the glut through additional spending (saving less) or endure a slump caused by insufficient global demand.

Two Development Models: High Savings versus High Wages

Societies raise living standards by putting more people to work, by making workers more efficient, and by expanding productive capacity. Investment is therefore essential for development. There are two basic ways to pay for this investment when domestic production is already running at maximum capacity: transfer resources from domestic consumers (the high-savings model) or transfer resources from the rest of the world by raising imports relative to exports (the high-wage model).

In other words:

$$\text{Investment} = \text{GDP} + \text{Imports} - \text{Consumption} - \text{Exports}$$

While most countries have relied on some combination of the two development strategies to pay for their industrialization, each approach has distinct implications for domestic politics and for international trade. High savings lead to trade surpluses because they raise production relative to domestic demand, while high wages tend to produce trade deficits because they raise domestic demand above existing productive capacity in an effort to attract foreign investment.

The high-savings model forces ordinary people to spend less so that the government and businesses can spend more. This in itself is not novel: elites the world over have repressed peasants and appropriated their agricultural surpluses for thousands of years. The innovation of the high-savings development strategy is that consumption is squeezed to pay for productive investment in infrastructure and capital goods, rather than to pay for elaborate monuments and the military. Done correctly, this investment raises ordinary people's living standards even as their share of economic output declines. The high-savings model is therefore the original version of trickle-down growth.

Raising the national saving rate is usually regressive and typically requires an authoritarian political culture or a high degree of centralization to make it work. This was pioneered in eighteenth-century Britain. First, aristocratic landowners used the power of the state to evict subsistence farmers and consolidate their holdings into enclosed estates. That boosted agricultural profits at the expense of the peasants, who were displaced from the countryside and forced into the cities. Their rising numbers limited their bargaining power with urban employers, which kept real wages from rising despite rising output per hour. That in turn boosted the profits of manufacturers, which reinvested those profits in developing additional capacity.

In 1740, just 4 percent of British production was saved rather than consumed domestically. By the 1820s, the national saving rate had grown to 14 percent and Britain had become an industrial superpower that was exporting its excess manufacturing output to the rest of the world, especially its imperial colonies and the rapidly growing United States. Forced saving enabled productive investment that generated additional output that was then used to create additional investment. Saving by itself did not create wealth, but it was instrumental to the process of wealth creation because it could be used to fund investment.

Britain did not pay for the first wave of its industrialization exclusively off the backs of its landless peasants, however. It also developed using elements of the high-wage model. While they became increasingly underpaid relative to the value of what they produced during the Industrial Revolution, British workers nevertheless continued to command higher pay than workers in much of the rest of Europe. Their high productivity and the favorable business climate pulled in capital from abroad, which allowed investment spending to consistently exceed national saving until after the end of the Napoleonic Wars. The difference was covered by the Dutch, who are estimated to have paid for about a third of Britain's total investment in the eighteenth century. The Dutch were willing to do this because British policies—including protective tariffs and what nowadays would be called intellectual property theft—had made investments in Britain more attractive than investments in the Netherlands and because at the time the Netherlands had a more mature economy with lower investment needs.[1]

Like Britain, the United States used elements of both development strategies when it industrialized in the nineteenth century. Before the Civil War, the South used an exceptionally cruel form of agrarian feudalism to produce copious volumes of cotton, tobacco, and other cash crops. Southern agricultural output was an essential input for British manufacturers and generated the bulk of America's export earnings. The South's social system—extreme wealth and income inequality reinforced by the brutal subjugation of the enslaved labor force—also crushed consumption.

Despite generating high saving rates, the planters had little interest in economic development. Instead of buying capital goods, they spent their surpluses buying additional enslaved workers and land. Southerners nevertheless contributed to America's industrialization because they were trapped behind high tariff barriers and were therefore forced customers of goods manufactured in the North. Southern agricultural exports generated by slave labor therefore helped pay, indirectly, for northern imports of advanced European technologies and machines that were then used to boost the North's manufacturing capacity.[2]

Far more important to America's economic development, however, was the North's use of the high-wage model to fund its industrialization. Outside the slave states, abundant land, liberal institutions, and Yankee ingenuity meant that American workers consistently earned the highest pay in the world and enjoyed rapid increases in living standards. At the same time, high birth rates and high immigration made the U.S. domestic market the most impressive growth story in human history. The U.S. population grew from 4 million people at the time of the 1790 census to 40 million by the 1870 census and to roughly 80 million people by 1900. Protective tariffs biased that market in favor of American goods over imports.

The combined result was that investments in America's economic development were incredibly attractive for European savers, especially the British. Foreign saving was therefore able to supplement domestic saving to pay for American imports of capital goods and lift U.S. investment without depressing U.S. consumption. Until the end of the nineteenth century, the United States consistently imported more goods than it exported even as its manufacturing output soared.

Like the Anglo-Dutch economic relationship in the eighteenth century, the Anglo-American economic relationship in the nineteenth was based on the transfer of excess output from a smaller but more advanced society to a larger one undergoing rapid industrialization. The same forces attracted millions of immigrants to come to America from Europe. After they arrived, many of these migrants started businesses using advanced technologies and skills from their home countries. Economists estimate that the value of this human capital inflow was worth several times the value of conventional foreign investment throughout the nineteenth century. The North's victory in the Civil War and the subsequent westward expansion of America's land borders solidified America's commitment to the high-wage model and increased its industrial potential even further. Rising inequality in the North in the decades after the end of the Civil War eventually depressed consumption relative to production, which meant that more investment could be funded internally. By the beginning of the twentieth century, America had become a net exporter.[3]

America's achievements attracted admirers and imitators, particularly in Germany and Japan. Friedrich List, one of the first theorists of the American System, had explicitly argued that America's internally vibrant but externally protected market was a model for what he hoped would be the unified German economy. A decade later, Erasmus Peshine Smith published his *Manual of Political Economy* (1853), which was perhaps the most important theoretical defense of America's developmental state. Like many in the antebellum United States, Smith saw abolitionism, protectionism, and mass immigration as part of a common program opposed to free trade and slavery. In his view, America's high wages—a product of high tariffs, abundant land, and, outside the South, human liberty—caused America's exceptional productivity. Expensive labor forced businesses to become more efficient and to invest in capital equipment. At the same time, rapid population growth expanded the domestic market and rewarded additional business investment.[4]

Smith's arguments found a ready audience in Japan. The shogunate had been unprepared when American naval ships arrived at Tokyo Bay in 1853 and was forced to accept disadvantageous commercial treaties with the West. Those treaties had prevented Japan from levying tariffs on imports greater than 5 percent. Dissatisfaction with the ensuing economic dislocation and the regime's overall handling of foreigners led to an elite revolt premised on the restoration of the Meiji emperor as head of state in 1868. In 1871 Smith was invited to Tokyo to advise the new government on international law. He went to Japan and quickly became an influential adviser to the Japanese government. Although Japan was unable to adjust its tariffs until 1899, it nevertheless adopted several recognizable elements of the American System.

First, the government actively invested in internal improvements, especially roads and railroads. Second, echoing Alexander Hamilton's advice a century earlier, the government subsidized "model factories" for ships and military kit. The economic historian Kenichi Ohno observes that these factories "had strong demonstration effects on emerging Japanese entrepreneurs" and "also trained a large number of Japanese engineers who later worked in or established other factories." All of this government spending was paid for with new taxes on land and forced loans from rich Japanese—higher saving to support additional investment. The explicit goal was to develop an indigenous productive capacity that would eventually displace imports.

Until then, however, Japan also relied on foreigners for its modernization. As in the United States, the immigration of specialists, including Smith, transferred human capital from the West, while Japanese students were paid to go abroad and learn from Western universities. Japan also had a large trade deficit, importing more than it exported to the rest of the world. In addition to raw materials such as cotton, almost all advanced machinery, including railroad engines and electric generators, had to be imported.[5]

The most extreme iteration of the high-savings model was the Soviet Union under Joseph Stalin. The Bolshevik coup of 1917 and the subsequent repudiation of Russia's foreign debts had turned the USSR into a pariah state unable to access the rest of the world's savings. Moreover, the Soviets were opposed to opening their country to foreign investors on ideological grounds. The lack of capital imposed a severe constraint on a largely agricultural society: foreign goods could be obtained only by barter or theft. Yet Stalin was committed to rapid industrialization to secure "the independence of the socialist economy from the capitalist encirclement," as he put it. Like George Washington 150 years earlier, Stalin believed that the development of an indigenous manufacturing capacity was a national security imperative. Unlike the Americans, Stalin chose to develop that capacity without recourse to trade deficits funded by investments from abroad. The Soviets would therefore have to sell exports to pay for their substantial imports of advanced technologies and capital goods.

In the 1920s and 1930s, those exports were mostly base metals, gold, and grain. Mining metal in sufficient quantities without machines required many workers, which were supplied at low cost by the gulag system of forced labor camps for the regime's political enemies. Securing a surplus from the peasants was more challenging. While the Bolsheviks were fighting to control the cities after 1917, the peasantry had fought and won a separate revolution against the old landlords. The peasants' victory meant that they could keep the surplus they generated from working land they owned.

In the early 1920s, the Bolsheviks felt that they had no choice but to accommodate these new agrarian capitalists to preserve the success of their proletarian revolution in the cities. Vladimir Lenin likened the resulting New Economic Policy to the 1918 Treaty of Brest-Litovsk with imperial Germany, which had saved the Bolshevik regime at the expense of Russia's western frontier. Both were meant to be temporary expedients. By the end of the 1920s, however, Stalin had concluded that the correlation of forces had changed and violently enslaved the Soviet peasantry through a process called collectivization. Even though agricultural output was lower under state ownership, the government had total control of that output and was able to extract a substantial surplus by squeezing the peasants. Grain exports soared in the early 1930s even as tens of millions starved to death. By the end of the 1930s, the typical

Soviet subject got fewer calories from grain than in the prerevolutionary period, but far more calories from vodka.

This was a humanitarian catastrophe, but it did enable imports of industrial equipment from the Soviets' main trade partner: Nazi Germany. Ideological differences were insignificant compared to the complementary economic needs of the two societies. Both countries were international pariahs, which cut them off from global markets, and both were willing to circumvent the limits imposed by the West by trading with each other. Like the nineteenth-century relationship between imperial Germany and tsarist Russia, resource-poor Germany in the 1930s traded advanced manufactures in exchange for the raw materials it needed for rearmament. The Germans were willing to supply their technology to the hated communists because they thought that the Soviets would not be able to modernize quickly enough to become a military threat. The Soviets had the opposite view (and believed that the Nazis would focus on fighting the West), which made them happy to provide crucial supplies to the Nazis to pay for their own industrial transformation.

By the eve of World War II, Stalin had achieved his strategic objective of an indigenous industrial base. Had the Soviet Union remained a primitive agrarian society, it could not have defeated the Germans, who had outmatched Russia in World War I. But although Stalin had transformed his domain into a formidable military power, this had come at enormous (self-imposed) cost. Much of the Soviet population had been conscripted into providing forced labor. Tens of millions had died of starvation to supply agricultural exports to pay for Western manufactures. The Soviets had modern tanks and aircraft, but soldiers lacked such basic goods as boots and radios. Consumer goods were essentially unavailable. The Soviet Union's experience demonstrated both the triumph and the limitations of the high-savings growth model.[6]

Japan developed a more humane variant of the high-savings model after World War II. Workers, businesses, and the government agreed on a social contract that generated decades of rapid growth and economic convergence with the West. Workers agreed not to strike and to limit their requests for wage increases. Businesses agreed to reinvest profits aggressively in domestic capacity and technological improvements. The government agreed to support companies with cheap loans offered at the expense of regular savers, as well as regulatory restrictions on imports to protect the domestic market. Within Japan, a handful of conglomerates dominated the economy in an oligopoly at the expense of consumers.

Abroad, those same companies competed ferociously for market share against one another and against producers from the United States and Europe, which forced them to become efficient and innovative. Japanese workers, consumers, and retirees all subsidized industrial development by overpaying for goods and services, by taking home a lower share of national output than their counterparts in the West, and by using a financial system designed to transfer purchasing power from households to businesses. Japanese companies returned the favor by upgrading the country's manufacturing base, passing along productivity gains to workers, and refraining from excessive executive pay, while the government invested in top-tier infrastructure. Moreover, despite its rapid growth, Japan's exports consistently exceeded its imports from the rest of the world.

The Japanese development model created problems as the country converged to Western living standards. When a society has an abundance of educated and industrious workers but lacks sufficient physical capital and technology, there are many obvious worthwhile projects to invest in. Transferring purchasing power from workers to businesses and the state can therefore accelerate national development.

Unfortunately, Japan's institutional biases in favor of investment over consumption created pressure to keep investing even after the best projects had been completed. By the early 1980s, the mechanisms developed after the war to constrain household spending and subsidize corporations had outlived their usefulness. The incremental gains from each additional investment steadily fell while systematic constraints imposed on household spending exacerbated the decline in investment returns. Japanese society eventually adjusted in the 1990s and 2000s, but in an unnecessarily painful way: business investment plunged, unemployment rose, and the household saving rate dropped to zero to compensate for weak wage growth. This could have been avoided if Japan had abandoned its development model earlier.

Many postcolonial countries tried to modernize according to either the Soviet or Japanese variants of the high-savings model. After its division in 1948, Korea experienced both versions. Until the 1970s, the communist North appeared to be more successful than the more market-oriented South, which had copied many features of the Japanese model. As time went on, however, the Soviet system's main advantage—the rapid development of physical capital—was outweighed by the severe disadvantages of low productivity, an inability to innovate, and systemic malinvestment.

By contrast, South Korea's conglomerates, consciously echoing the experience of their Japanese models, had to upgrade their technology to compete in global markets. In 1970, living standards in South Korea were just a tenth of what they were in the United States. After Korea's financial crisis in 1997, its living standards were about half of U.S. levels. As of 2016, however, South Korean living standards had reached almost 70 percent of those in America—comparable to Japan, New Zealand, and France.[7]

In the nineteenth century, America's high-wage growth model was complementary to Britain's surpluses. Argentina, Australia, and Canada were also eager recipients of British savings. The world as a whole prospered from this arrangement because, with the exception of Argentina, the societies receiving resources from abroad were generally the ones able to make the best use of them. At the same time, excess production was coming from the richest and most advanced societies. By the end of the twentieth century, things had changed. Poor countries were often subsidizing the consumption of the rich—at the expense of both.

Excess Savings and the Great Glut

Scarcity stopped being a serious problem in the rich world sometime near the last quarter of the twentieth century. Making things has become easier and cheaper than ever before. Shortages have been replaced with gluts. The age-old tradeoff between consuming more today and producing more tomorrow is gone. Investment is now constrained by insufficient consumption, rather than by the old competition for resources. The modern condition is therefore defined by the perverse coincidence of abundant idle resources and unmet material needs. This has had profound consequences for the relations among savings, investment, and trade.

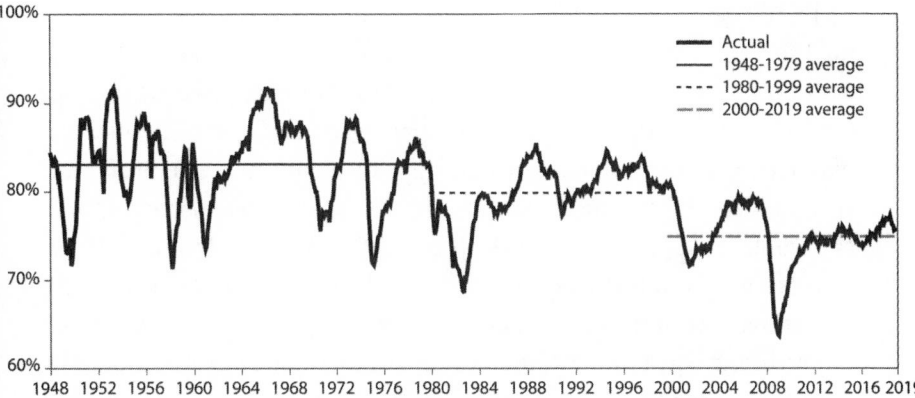

Fig. 3.1 The great glut (U.S. manufacturing capacity utilization rate).
Sources: Federal Reserve Board; Matthew Klein's calculations

There are two basic inputs to production: labor and capital. Both have been in abundance for decades. Unemployment rates across the rich world have been systematically higher since the 1970s than they were before. The situation looks even more extreme after accounting for the rise of part-time employment, which depresses the number of hours worked per job, and the steadily rising share of people of working age who neither work nor go to school. If there were more work to be done, people could easily be found to fill the jobs. The problem has been an absence of demand for their labor.[8]

A similar story can be told about the supply of productive capital. The Federal Reserve has tracked the productive capacity of the U.S. manufacturing sector and its relation to output since 1948. From then through the end of 1979, American manufacturers used 83 percent of their capacity to produce goods, on average. From the beginning of 1980 through the end of 1999, capacity utilization averaged 80 percent. Since the start of 2000, manufacturing capacity utilization has averaged just 75 percent thanks to the combination of excess capacity built in the 1990s and limited growth in domestic production since then. Manufacturing capacity has shrunk slightly since 2008, but output has shrunk even more.[9]

Corporate investment behavior is also revealing. Traditionally, the business sector is supposed to spend more expanding productive capacity than it generates in cash flow, with the difference covered by household savings. The additional investments are supposed to lead to higher cash flow that can help cover the cost of further expansion while also repaying savers. Although some companies, or even entire industries, may lack growth opportunities and opt to distribute their profits to shareholders rather than retain earnings to reinvest, the business sector as a whole is supposed to require others' savings to grow. In the past few decades, however, this mechanism has broken down. The business sectors of many countries now spend less than they generate in cash flow. The resulting corporate surpluses are either distributed to shareholders, as in the United States, or retained by the companies, as in Germany, Japan, and South Korea. Regardless, the implication is that there are far fewer worthwhile investment opportunities in the rich world than in the past. Those that remain are mostly infrastructure and housing, which are hampered by political constraints rather than by an excessive cost of capital.[10]

One consequence has been a steady decline in the prices of manufactured goods. Capital equipment prices in the United States have dropped by 30 percent since 1991 in absolute terms. The prices of durable consumption goods—mainly cars, appliances, and furniture—have dropped by more than 36 percent since the peak in 1995. The prices of clothing and footwear are lower now than in the mid-1980s. Since 1990, most inflation in the United States has come from higher prices for health care (including prescription drugs), housing, and education—all sectors where the government tightly regulates supply and heavily subsidizes demand. In the rest of the economy, prices have been flat.

Relative to the average American's disposable income, the cost of buying manufactured goods has collapsed by more than 90 percent since the late 1940s, with most of the decline occurring since the mid-1980s. Similar conditions can be found in Europe and Japan.[11]

Financial market data are also consistent with the great glut. Asset prices, like all other prices, are determined by the balance between supply and demand. Put another way, the valuations of stocks and bonds should reflect both the desire by businesses and the government to raise money to fund new investments (supply of assets) and the willingness

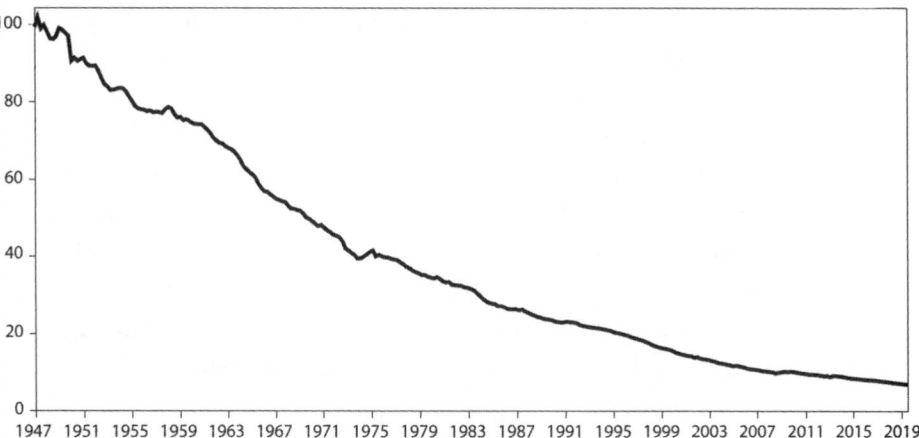

Fig. 3.2 The prices of manufactured goods have plunged relative to disposable incomes (manufactured goods price index divided by average disposable personal income, January 1947 = 100). *Sources: Bureau of Economic Analysis; Matthew Klein's calculations*

of households to consume less today in exchange for being able to consume more in the future (demand for assets). Low asset prices (high future returns for savers) represent the cost that companies must pay to attract funding when resources are scarce. When productive capacity is abundant, however, the expected return on additional investment should be low. Valuations would be high, and yields would be low.

As it happens, inflation-adjusted long-term interest rates have fallen steadily across the world since the abnormal increase associated with the disinflation of the early 1980s under the Federal Reserve leadership of Paul Volcker. For decades, real borrowing costs have been below long-term forecasts of real economic growth and remain around zero. Corporate valuations have steadily increased, especially in the rich world, while credit spreads have been exceptionally tight outside of the financial crisis period. By some measures, financial conditions in the rich countries over the past few decades are almost as loose as they have ever been. Commodity prices have steadily declined relative to average incomes. Private equity firms are burdened with trillions of dollars of funding that they have not been able to deploy. Covenants in bonds and loans have steadily loosened in favor of borrowers. The ability to make productive investments may once have been constrained by access to material resources, but that era ended decades ago.

The great glut has been so damaging in part because standard economics has such difficulty describing it. The textbook definition of "saving" is "not consuming"—think of the biblical story of Joseph and the Pharaoh preparing for the seven lean years by hoarding surplus grain during the seven fat years. Since all output is either consumed or used to develop assets, saving necessarily equals "investment." Although this identity is true by definition, it can nevertheless lead to serious misconceptions.

The biggest mistake is to think that higher saving *causes* additional investment. Yes, restricting consumption frees up workers, machines, and material inputs. In times of scarcity, saving more is therefore a prerequisite for investing more. And when there are many worthwhile investment opportunities, idled resources can be redeployed relatively quickly. But there is nothing automatic about this process. Rather, it is contingent on specific economic conditions. When those conditions do not apply, higher saving simply means lower living standards.

In many ways, it is better to think of the textbook formulation in reverse: more investment leads to more saving. By definition, worthwhile projects enable societies to produce additional output relative to labor and material inputs. Most of that output will get consumed, lifting overall living standards. But as long as some of the extra production is used to pay for further investment, total savings will have increased. Savings can grow even as consumption rises relative to production. By extension, total investment can rise even when the saving rate drops without generating trade deficits. Efficiency improvements—generating more output from the same set of inputs—allow societies to keep investing in additional capacity while raising the share of production that is consumed.

More important, the reverse is also true. Trying to promote additional investment through higher saving is often counterproductive. The simplest way to raise the saving rate is to spend less on consumer goods and services. Unless investment immediately rises to offset the decline in consumption, however, the result is less total production and lower total saving, which ultimately discourages new investment.[12]

Changes in the income distribution affect all of these variables and therefore have important economic consequences. While most people spend close to everything they earn on goods and services, the rich do not. There is only so much a person can consume, no matter how expensive his tastes. Give most people an extra dollar, and sooner or later it will get spent buying something that provides jobs and incomes to others. Give that same extra dollar to a rich person, however, and it will probably be used to accumulate additional assets.

For the world as a whole, rising inequality means the value of those assets is necessarily contingent on continued increases in spending by people who have progressively lower shares of national income. The only way to make this work is with rising debt. The economists Michael Kumhof, Romain Rancière, and Pablo Winant found an almost perfect relation between rising income concentration in the United States in the 1920s and rising U.S. household indebtedness in the years before the Great Depression.[13]

Marriner Eccles, Franklin Roosevelt's Federal Reserve chairman, understood that this was why the American economy was so fragile in the 1920s despite the apparent burst of postwar prosperity. To Eccles, the root problem was the shift in the U.S. distribution of income from the masses to the elites. "By taking purchasing power out of the hands of mass consumers," he wrote in his retrospective account, "the savers denied to themselves the kind of effective demand for their products that would justify a reinvestment of their capital accumulations in new plants." It is obvious that consumption cannot grow without investments to produce more of what people want. It is less obvious, but just as important, that those investments require rising consumption to be profitable. Building truck factories or apartment complexes or power plants is not "investing" in any meaningful sense if nobody ends up buying more trucks, living in the apartments, or needing the extra electricity. It is just waste.[14]

This explains how the world can be afflicted by a savings glut without having a high saving rate. The level of the saving rate by itself is meaningless. What matters is the amount of unconsumed output relative to the supply of worthwhile investment opportunities. Saving is excessive when real resources are diverted from the satisfaction of immediate human needs to develop wasteful investments. In many cases, of course, distinguishing "worthwhile" from "wasteful" is possible only in retrospect. But excess saving necessarily leads to wasteful investment because it encourages overbuilding and because suppressing consumption reduces the viability of otherwise worthwhile projects.

When a society—call it "Scroogeville"—increases its saving rate, it is, by definition, consuming less relative to what it produces. Because the world's consumption and investment together must equal global output, some combination of the following three outcomes must occur:

- The investment rate in Scroogeville rises.
- The investment rate in the rest of the world rises.
- The saving rate in the rest of the world falls.

These three possibilities are equivalent to the following four scenarios:

- Productive investment rises globally.
- Wasteful investment increases globally.
- Consumption outside Scroogeville rises.
- Production outside Scroogeville falls.

Two of those outcomes—higher wasteful investment and lower production outside Scroogeville—are unequivocally bad. Higher consumption outside Scroogeville could be good but could also be dangerous depending on how that additional spending is financed. While higher productive investment would be unequivocally good, it is also the least likely outcome in today's developed world. There is simply no evidence that the world's investment needs are unmet because of excessive capital costs. Rather, investment has been restrained by the lack of attractive opportunities—itself caused by weak global demand—and by irrational political constraints.

As it happens, the International Monetary Fund (IMF) reports that the world's saving and investment rates have been stable as a share of global output since 1980. Dramatically higher saving in some places— most notably China—has been offset by much lower saving elsewhere.

One implication is that, globally, there was no shortage of funding for worthwhile investment projects. Had there been a shortage, large increases in savings in one part of the global economy would have been matched by increases in global investment. That did not happen. Instead, places that squeezed consumption relative to production simply forced production to fall relative to consumption elsewhere. This had significant consequences for trade.[15]

China's investment rate has soared since the 1980s, for example, but not by enough to offset the even larger relative decline in consumption (rise in saving). Until 2008, the result was a surge in production relative to domestic demand, with the rest of the world forced to absorb the difference. China boomed, but the distribution of spending within the country created serious distortions for the rest of the world. Since 2008, China's surplus has shrunk because the investment share of GDP has increased. The consumption share, however, has not, except marginally in the past few years. The result is that China's saving rate is higher now than when it had trade surpluses worth 10 percent of its productive output.

By contrast, Germany's surplus is a function of weak growth in domestic demand. Domestic consumption and investment have grown sluggishly for almost thirty years. Total production has also been weak since reunification but has grown marginally faster than domestic demand. As in China, the difference has come from net foreign spending on German exports. Germany's saving rate and its investment rate are not unusual when viewed separately. The gap between them, however, is almost unprecedented for a country of its size.

In the United States, the situation has been the reverse: while domestic demand has been weak, as in Germany, output growth has been even worse. Foreign saving crowded out U.S. domestic production in the form of a trade deficit. By contrast, Spain's massive deficit was caused by an investment boom. There were no meaningful changes to its production or its consumption habits. The subsequent shift into surplus was caused more by the investment bust than by any change in the household saving rate. Greece also had an investment boom and bust, but unlike Spain, this was amplified by a consumption boom and bust.[16]

By definition, the experiences of some of these countries were connected to the experiences of others. There are only three possible explanations that link surpluses in some countries with deficits in others:

- Changes within China, Germany, and other surplus countries caused their domestic demand to fall relative to their domestic production, which forced the rest of the world to spend more relative to production through a combination of falling output, higher investment, and rising consumption.
- Changes within the United States, Spain, Greece, and other deficit countries caused their output to fall relative to their spending, which forced people in the rest of the world to produce more than they needed to satisfy their domestic needs.
- Hermes, the Greek god of commerce—or perhaps his Indian counterpart, Lakshmi, who controls wealth—has been extraordinarily busy spending all of his time managing trade, investment, and savings, country by country, with such precision that at every single point in time, by an astonishing coincidence, all the saving rates and all the investment rates in hundreds of more-or-less autonomous entities in the world balance out perfectly.

A close reading of the events of the past thirty years shows that the first option is the best explanation. Political and social changes within the surplus countries transferred purchasing power from workers, who spend most of their income on goods and services, to elites, who prefer to accumulate financial assets.

This has occurred in a variety of ways in different countries. The Chinese *hukou* (household registration) system deprives hundreds of millions of urban workers access to government benefits for which they pay tax, for example, while German companies refuse to invest domestically despite rising profitability and regular losses on their investments abroad. These choices mechanically suppress consumption and investment relative to production, which in turn forces the rest of the world to spend more than they produce.

The Balance of Payments

Savings travel internationally through financial markets. Countries with trade surpluses do not donate their excess production to the rest of the world but sell it in exchange for claims on future production. Those claims are serviced either out of income earned from trade surpluses or by issuing even more claims. The balance of payments tracks these transactions. The current account looks at trade flows and the cost of financing trade imbalances, while the financial account measures the purchases and sales of assets across borders, including the change in central bank reserves in countries that intervene in the currency markets. The net amount of money coming in or going out via the financial account must equal the net amount of money moving across a country's borders as recorded in the current account, although measurement difficulties sometimes create differences between the two figures.

A country's current account balance is simply the sum of the individual saving and spending decisions of the residents of that country. There are two kinds of people in the world: those who spend more than they earn, and those who spend less. Since all income ultimately comes from the spending of others, these individual differences always balance out at the global level. There is therefore no way to save without someone else *dis*-saving. Those who spend less than they earn have a surplus that has to go somewhere. It could stay in a bank account, it could be used to buy financial assets such as stocks and bonds, or it could get put into physical assets such as real estate, art, and precious metals.

These asset purchases would be impossible without willing sellers. While there may be some transactions in between, the ultimate asset-sellers use the proceeds to spend more than they earn. These could be people who own existing assets and want to transform some of their past saving into current spending, such as retirees gradually liquidating their holdings, or they could be people who want to raise money to buy things they cannot afford by issuing freshly minted assets. Households take out mortgages to buy new homes, businesses issue shares to finance capital investment, and governments sell bonds at auctions, for example. The savers and the dis-savers necessarily go together.

If people in a country collectively spend more than they earn, then the country as a whole has a current account deficit. In other words, the amount of money coming in from the rest of the world as income— exports, foreign investment earnings, remittances, and foreign aid—is less than the money going out in the form of imports, dividends and interest paid to foreigners, and transfers. By contrast, if a country's households, businesses, and government collectively spend less than they take in as income, then the country has a current account surplus. In that case, the combination of exports, foreign investment earnings, and transfer receipts brings in more money than goes out on imports, income paid to foreigners, and remittances.

The flip side of all this is the financial account. Any country where spending collectively exceeds income must cover the difference by raising money from selling assets. A country with a current account deficit by definition must have a financial account surplus: the total amount of money coming in from foreigners buying domestic assets must be greater than the total amount of money going out as locals buy foreign assets. Conversely, countries where people collectively spend less than they earn must be investing their current account surpluses abroad; more money is going out to buy foreign assets than is coming in from the rest of the world to buy local assets.[17]

The following equations may help clarify these relations:

Current account = Financial account + Statistical discrepancy

Current account = Household saving + Corporate profits + Taxes – (Household investment + Business investment + Government spending)

Financial account = Foreigners buying local assets – Locals buying foreign assets

Financial account = Private sector financial account + Change in central bank reserves

Large surpluses or deficits are not inherently good or bad. "Good imbalances" allow savers from richer surplus countries to earn healthy returns by financing development and rising living standards in deficit countries. This is what the United States did for much of the nineteenth century, when it imported mainly British capital to boost domestic investment to levels much higher than it could have otherwise achieved without squeezing American workers. More recently, except for a brief period in the late 1980s, South Korea consistently imported more than it exported in the decades from independence in 1948 until the Asian Financial Crisis in 1997. Korea is also one of the few countries to transition successfully from poor to rich.

Norway, which was once one of the poorest countries in Western Europe, imported massive amounts of foreign savings in the form of large current account deficits in the 1970s to pay for the development of its offshore oil and natural gas fields. Once those fields began producing, Norwegians were able to repay their obligations and eventually amass a large stock of foreign assets purchased from their hydrocarbon profits. Had Norwegians been constrained in their ability to spend more than they earned, those resources never would have been developed. Both Norway and the world as a whole would have been poorer.[18]

At the same time, surpluses can be bad. Savings have to go somewhere, but there is no guarantee that they will go into profitable investments. Germans, who have been such avid exporters of financial capital over the past two decades, are almost uniquely bad at investing abroad. Since the start of 1999, the German private sector collectively spent a little over €5.1 trillion acquiring assets in other countries. Yet over the same period, the amount of these foreign assets grew by only €4.8 trillion. The difference represents a valuation loss of 7 percent across nearly two decades thanks to such holdings as American subprime mortgages and Greek sovereign debt.

Even after accounting for dividends and interest income, Germany's foreign investments have done worse than the foreign investments owned by residents of almost every other rich country. A 2019 study by Franziska Hünnekes, Moritz Schularick, and Christoph Trebesch concluded that "Germany could have become about 2 to 3 trillion Euros richer [between 2009 and 2017] had its returns in global markets corresponded to those earned by Norway or Canada, respectively." Strikingly, Germans' poor returns have been caused almost entirely by their remarkable inability to pick the right stocks and bonds, rather than broader differences in asset allocation compared to savers in other countries.

This abysmal performance looks even worse compared to what could have been achieved by buying German assets. The same study concluded that "domestic returns were significantly higher than the return earned abroad." Between 1999 and 2017, German assets have returned about 2.4 percentage points more each year on average than Germany's foreign assets. Since 2009, the gap has widened to a staggering 5 percentage points. For perspective, while €1 million invested in a representative collection of German assets in 1999 would have generated roughly €2 million of interest, dividends, and capital gains by 2017, the same amount invested in a representative sample of Germany's actual foreign assets would have returned less than €1 million.

Another way to see this is to compare how German residents have fared on their foreign investments compared to how foreigners have fared on their investments in Germany. From the start of 1999 through the end of 2018, Germans invested €2.6 trillion more abroad than non-Germans have invested in Germany. Yet Germany's net foreign asset position grew by only €1.9 trillion, which implies a net loss of 29 percent. Germans would have been far better off had they invested more at home or spent more on goods and services they actually wanted.[19]

Two things determine whether an imbalance is healthy or dangerous: how the money is raised and how the money is spent. Ideally, richer countries make direct equity investments in poorer ones with lots of potential, as in the case of South Korea. In the past few decades, however, surplus countries have been lenders, rather than shareholders, while deficit countries have often been mature economies that lack useful projects in need of outside funding. The result has been debt booms wasted on boondoggles. People in both the surplus countries and the deficit countries have lost out from this exchange.

Although some of this can be blamed on insufficient regulation in the countries on the receiving end of these financial flows, the bigger problem is that the flows are too large and go to the wrong places. Popular antipathy to trade therefore stems from the failure of international capital to go where it is needed in forms that are useful. This in turn can

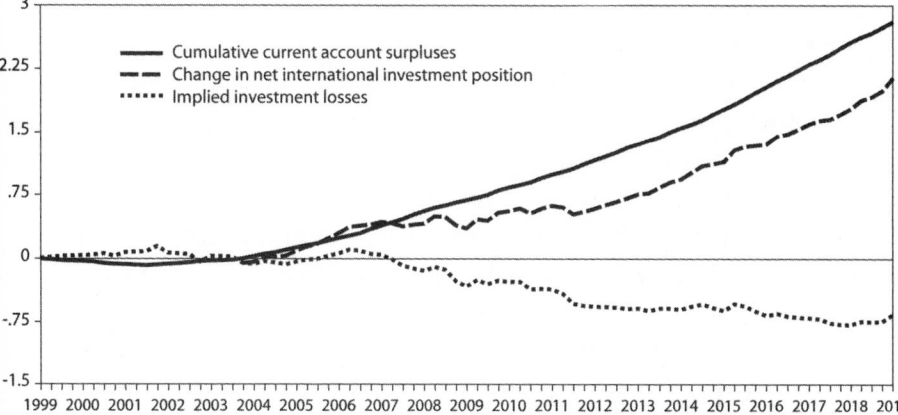

Fig. 3.3 German investors have lost almost 30 percent on their foreign investments (components of net international investment position, EUR trillions). *Sources: Eurostat; Matthew Klein's calculations*

be blamed on policies in surplus countries that steadily transfer income and wealth from workers to elites. Because the rich have higher saving rates, the effect has been to shift purchasing power away from goods and services to financial assets. Not finding enough additional financial assets to buy in their home country, the rich invest their additional wealth abroad. Everyone else is deprived of income they could have used to buy additional imports. The result is that inequality within countries can cause imbalances between them.

The Two Causes of Imbalances: Pull versus Push

Surpluses require deficits elsewhere and deficits require surpluses. One cannot happen without the other. The current account surplus or deficit of any individual country must balance out the sum of the current account surpluses and deficits of every other country. Sometimes finance is "pulled" in by people who want to spend more on consumption and investment than they earn. In this case, the countries with current account deficits are ultimately responsible for the imbalances. At other times it is "pushed" by people who choose to save regardless of whether there are good investments available. In that case the imbalance originates in the surplus countries.

Neither cause of imbalances is necessarily better than the other. Countries with good investment opportunities may try to pull in foreign capital, but so will countries eager to fund unsustainable consumption booms or dubious projects. Countries on the receiving end of money indiscriminately pushed in their direction can sometimes turn the unexpected inflows into a windfall, but most fail to do so, particularly when the inflows are extremely large.

There is no guaranteed way to identify the origin of an imbalance, but market prices can provide clues. After all, pulling money in from skeptics in the rest of the world is difficult. The trick is to pay them: foreign investors will commit capital anywhere if they can get returns that provide fair compensation for the risks of inflation, default, and currency devaluation. Although determining what is fair is a challenge, it is easy to tell when investors think they need more compensation for the risks they are taking: asset values go down. Rising real interest rates, collapsing equity multiples, and a falling currency are bad for existing owners but make new investments comparatively attractive. The current account deficit country is therefore the likely source of the imbalance if its interest rates rise (or the international value of its assets goes down) as its external financing need rises.

This is a frequent phenomenon for countries on the periphery of the international financial system. Consider Turkey over the past few years. Between 2010 and 2018, the country went on an investment binge funded by borrowing from abroad. Turkey's current account deficit was consistently worth about 6 percent of its domestic income. This boosted output at the cost of rising debt. Attracting foreign money to cover this excess of spending over income required persistent currency depreciation beyond what would have been implied by differences in inflation: the real value of the Turkish lira fell by half between 2010 and the middle of 2018. Unsurprisingly, foreign savers grew increasingly skeptical of Turkey and mostly lent in debt that could only be repaid with U.S. dollars, not Turkish lira. (Think of Argentina's nineteenth-century gold-backed debts.)

Interest rates also had to rise. The cost of a dollar-denominated business loan rose from about 4 percent in 2010 to 6 percent by the second half of 2018. Over the same period, interest rates on lira-denominated business loans soared from 9 percent to 28 percent. Eventually, foreign revulsion with Turkish assets slashed Turkish spending power, which in turn forced Turks to cut their consumption and investment to the point that they moved into a current account surplus by the middle of 2019.[20]

Things look different when unneeded capital is pushed in from abroad. Instead of rising, interest rates in the deficit country stay stable—or even fall—as the imbalance grows. This is what happened to Spain after committing to join the euro. In the mid-1990s, Spaniards spent roughly as much as they earned, so the current account was nearly balanced. Meanwhile, benchmark interest rates were over 5 percent after subtracting inflation.

From then until 2008, Spain's current account deficit steadily widened to roughly 10 percent of GDP. Yet over the same period, Spanish real interest rates dropped below 0 percent. Spain is a member of the euro area, so its currency could not move relative to its main trading partners in the rest of Europe. But Spanish wages and prices rose faster than in Spain's neighbors, so its real effective exchange rate rose by 18 percent during this period. By every possible measure, Spain's cost of capital was plunging even as Spaniards borrowed more and more from the rest of the world.

Spaniards were not trying to pull money in—far from it. Rather, Spain was overwhelmed by a flood of foreign investment into its banking system, its bond market, and its real estate. (After stagnating throughout the 1990s, Spanish house prices more than doubled between 2001 and 2007.) These inflows increased the purchasing power of Spaniards far more than it increased their incomes. The difference was covered by a debt and investment binge nearly without precedent. As long as new money kept coming in, Spain appeared to experience a growth miracle that was the envy of Europe. Once foreigners stopped pushing their unneeded capital into Spain, however, Spanish spending was forced to rapidly contract below Spain's incomes. The current account eventually reversed into a substantial surplus, but only at the cost of crushing unemployment.[21]

Why It Is Better to Give Than to Receive:
The German Empire in the 1870s

Spain's experience was not unusual or unrepresentative. Lottery winners often do worse in life than if they had bought a losing ticket. The sudden infusion of money acts like a hit of cocaine and distorts behavior in similarly unhealthy ways. Something similar happens to countries on the receiving end of unsolicited financial inflows. Few societies have been able to absorb sudden, large sums of capital from abroad without experiencing soaring debt, asset bubbles, and economic crises. It is an almost inevitable consequence of a rapid and unexpected increase in real purchasing power. The experience of the new German Empire in the early 1870s presents one of the most striking examples of how the lottery of financial inflows affects recipients in broadly similar ways regardless of cultural and institutional differences.

For most of its history, Germany had been divided into many small states with distinct identities, political forms, and religious traditions. By the nineteenth century, German nationalists were dreaming of unification. One state would have to force the others to submit to joint rule. The obvious candidate was the kingdom of Prussia, the second-most populous state in the post-Napoleonic German Confederation. (The Austrian Empire was much bigger but had far fewer Germans.) Prussia began to realize the nationalists' dream by provoking and then winning short wars, first against Denmark in 1864, which "liberated" Schleswig-Holstein, and then against Austria in 1866, which gave Prussia an excuse to annex its hostile neighbors in northern Germany and create a new North German Confederation alongside its docile allies. Combined, these changes made Prussia the dominant power in Europe.

By the 1860s, Prussia's biggest rival was the Second French Empire, led by the nephew of Napoleon Bonaparte. Afflicted by gallstones and a weakness for mistresses, Louis-Napoléon was prone to strategic errors and presumptuous pronouncements. Anticipating an Austro-Prussian conflict, he had tried to negotiate secret treaties in 1865 and 1866 with both belligerents that would guarantee additional French territory on the Rhineland. Otto von Bismarck, the wily Prussian minister president, was able to use this information to convince the defeated southern German states (secretly) to ally with the North German Confederation in a mutual defense pact after the war.

Louis-Napoléon persisted in his territorial quests, trying to buy Luxembourg from the Netherlands and then proposing—in violation of France's treaty commitments—to annex Belgium. Things came to a head when, in 1868, Spanish republicans deposed Queen Isabella II. By 1870, the republican revolution had failed, and Spain needed a new monarch. France and Prussia each proposed alternative candidates. Although the Spanish never seriously considered Prussia's Hohenzollern suggestion, the idea nevertheless drove the French to make unreasonable demands and eventually declare war on Prussia in July. Bavaria and the other south German states immediately declared their support for Prussia. Within six weeks, Louis-Napoléon had been captured after the Battle of Sedan. The Third French Republic continued the war after his capitulation, but it too was eventually forced to yield to the superior opponent.

Prussia had won a resounding victory in battle. It had demonstrated its power to the other German states, which promptly joined the new Prussian-dominated German Empire, and to the rest of Europe. The challenge was to postpone a rematch. The French were eager to avenge their humiliation and nursed dreams of reclaiming the German-speaking territory of Alsace-Lorraine. Prussia, however, needed time to build its new political union, and it needed peace to recuperate from nearly a decade of warfare. Somehow, France had to be kept down long enough for Germany to become secure. The proposed solution was an indemnity: German armies would occupy much of France's industrial heartland until the Third Republic paid 5 billion gold francs to the Reich—a payment equal to roughly a quarter of France's economic output in 1870. The burden would be so high, it was hoped, that it would cripple French reconstruction and ensure a pacific western neighbor for generations. The other side of the transaction was a transfer to the German economy equal to around a fifth of its domestic production over three years.[22]

Despite the apparent magnitude of the indemnity, the French government found it relatively easy to raise the money, and the German government received the full amount ahead of schedule in 1873. French savers, it turned out, had ample resources to draw on. For years they had collectively accumulated assets abroad and used the income to cover the

French trade deficit, gold imports, and purchases of additional foreign assets.

After the war, France stopped importing gold, moved into a trade surplus, and stopped investing abroad, all of which freed up income to buy billions of francs' worth of French government bonds. This alone covered about half the indemnity payment. The rest was covered by French sales of foreign assets to buy domestic bonds, foreign demand for French assets (especially from German savers), and French gold sales. To the great surprise of the Germans, this was not bad for France. While the French economy struggled immediately after the war, the new debt did not cripple it for long because France was easily able to manage the interest payments on its perpetual bonds.

Part of the reason, according to the financial historian Charles Kindleberger, is that the French indemnity had expanded the global money supply. The German money supply obviously grew as gold flowed from France into its banking system, but this had not been offset by an equal reduction in France's money supply. The debts the French government issued to finance the indemnity created a huge, highly liquid, and highly credible debt instrument—something very similar to money. The transfer of money from France to Germany therefore resulted in a sudden and substantial increase in the global supply of moneylike assets.[23]

The transfer, counterintuitively, ended up being harmful for Germany. Over three years it absorbed a financial inflow worth about 8 percent of GDP each year. Much of the money was allocated to military costs, ranging from debt repayments to new fortifications on the border with France to the establishment of a pension for veterans. This spending boosted German purchasing power, which raised the trade deficit through a boom in imports. Meanwhile, rising wages—German coal miners in the Ruhr saw their hourly pay jump 60 percent between 1871 and 1873, for example—and prices made German exports uncompetitive in global markets. Gold began flowing back from the Bank of Prussia to the Bank of France. One way or another, the balance of payments always balances.

At least as damaging as the impact on the trade balance was the impact on Germany's financial markets. The government knew it could not immediately spend the entire indemnity on infrastructure investment and military armament, because those projects take time. While it waited, the indemnity was invested in financial assets, including bonds issued by the German states and railroad bonds. Ludwig Bamberger, a German parliamentarian and a cofounder of Deutsche Bank, had warned of what this would do to financial conditions in Germany, and suggested the government hold the unspent funds in gold or foreign assets.

His advice went unheeded, however, and Germany engaged in a frenzy of investment at home and abroad in which a substantial share of the inflows from France was wasted. The economist Arthur Monroe writes that the government's investments "released on the German market, within about two years, a sum nearly three times as great as the total monetary stock of the country and considerably greater than the combined debt of all the German states, including debts incurred for railroad building."

The German economy responded to French financial inflows in essentially the same way that other economies have responded to large financial inflows before and since. The German economy grew rapidly in the immediate postwar period, growing more than 6 percent each year on average. After 1874, however, the country shrank for three straight years. Similarly, there was a short-lived banking boom in Germany and Austria, followed immediately by a bust once the reparations inflows stopped. The supply of German banknotes grew more than 12 percent a year from 1871 to 1874 and then shrunk by 10 percent each year until 1878.

By 1876, the economic situation was so dire that a coalition of German manufacturers began pushing the government to adopt protective tariffs to compensate for the changes in the terms of trade wrought by the indemnity; these were eventually adopted in 1879. Economists and politicians throughout Germany blamed the indemnity for the country's economic collapse. Some, especially in France, even believed that Berlin might send the money back.[24]

Navarro's Error: Why Bilateral Flows Obscure the Sources of Imbalances

Another valuable lesson can be learned from the Franco-German experience of the 1870s: while the flow of gold from France to Germany ultimately pushed Germany into a trade deficit and France into a trade surplus, this was not matched by a corresponding change in the trade balance *between* France and Germany. Germans spent more on imports from all over the world while their exports to the rest of the world stagnated. France imported less from the rest of the world and exported more. The bilateral financial flow affected trade between France and Germany, but the effect on their bilateral trade balance was insignificant compared to the broader impact. In general, the dynamics of surpluses and deficits cannot be explained by focusing on bilateral trade and financial relations.

This means that countries that spend more than they earn are not responsible for the current account deficits of their trade partners, regardless of what the bilateral data may indicate. America's persistently large bilateral surplus with Australia, for example, does not explain Australia's overall current account deficit, because Australians and Americans both spend more than they earn. Australians happen to import more from the United States than they export to it, but this does not change the fact that both countries are in the same basic situation. Money earned from U.S. exports to Australia gets spent on gadgets or solar panels from China, which generates income to buy coal and iron ore from Australia. As it happens, Australia's trade deficit with the United States is more than offset by Australia's trade surplus with China. That bilateral surplus is not enough to prevent Australia from having an overall current account deficit with the rest of the world, nor is it enough to prevent China from having a large surplus. The global relation is what matters.[25]

Similarly, the United States consistently reports large bilateral current account surpluses with the Netherlands and with Singapore. We have shown that this can be explained by the combination of corporate tax avoidance strategies and by the misreporting of U.S. goods exports that land in major ports before being transshipped elsewhere. Despite these bilateral surpluses, both the Dutch and the Singaporeans consistently spend far less than they earn—both in absolute terms and relative to their incomes. They are both among the largest contributors to global imbalances today and are therefore among the biggest contributors to America's current account deficit. If they saved less and spent more on imports from other countries, the extra income would eventually flow through to additional demand for U.S. exports, regardless of whether this affected their bilateral balances with the United States.

The same perspective applies to the financial account. Bilateral balances in the financial account provide no insight into *which* countries are spending more or less than they earn. In fact, bilateral financial account balances are unrelated to the bilateral balances in the current account. Moreover, there is no reason why a country's bilateral trading relations *should* mirror its bilateral financial relations. Homebuyers rarely get mortgages directly from sellers, for example. German banks making loans to French banks that lend to their Greek subsidiaries that then buy Greek government bonds issued to pay for German-made submarines were ultimately financing trade between Germany and Greece, even though the bilateral financial flows were from Germany to France and then from France to Greece. It is also difficult to determine the true nationality of people buying financial assets when they use custodial centers to remain anonymous or route their purchases through tax havens. (This is analogous to the problems with bilateral data on trade and profits earned from foreign investments described earlier.)

Peter Navarro, the Harvard-trained economics professor and trade adviser to Donald Trump, disagrees with this analysis. Navarro believes that bilateral trade deficits matter, and he also seems to believe that these bilateral trade balances necessarily map onto corresponding bilateral financial flows. In a 2017 column in the *Wall Street Journal,* for example, he wrote that the problem with China's bilateral trade surplus with the United States is that it enables China to "[buy] up America's companies, technologies, farmland, food-supply chain—and ultimately [control] much of the U.S. defense-industrial base."[26]

As it happens, the data imply that Americans have invested about $46 billion into China between the beginning of 2015 and the beginning of 2019, while Chinese residents have sold a total of $380 billion of U.S. assets. In other words, a total of $430 billion in net financing went *from* the United States to China. If bilateral financial flows mirrored bilateral trade flows, as Navarro seems to believe, the United States would have experienced a large current account *surplus* with China over this period. Instead, America had a bilateral *deficit* with China worth a bit over

$1.5 trillion. Even if the official data wildly understate Chinese investment into the United States in those years because of custodial relationships and surreptitious financial flows, it still seems unlikely that direct Chinese financing of U.S. spending was enough to cover the difference between American exports to and imports from China.

Savers in Europe likely helped cover the funding gap. From the start of 2015 through the beginning of 2019, the total difference between foreign savings coming into the United States and American savings going out to the rest of the world through the financial account was about $1.5 trillion. Over the same period, residents of the euro area invested about $976 billion more in the United States than Americans invested in Europe. About two-thirds of the total U.S. financial account surplus, in other words, has come from residents of the euro area. Yet those funds have not been returned directly to Europe: the total bilateral *current account* deficit from the start of 2015 through the beginning of 2019 has been just $116 billion. About $860 billion in funding therefore went from Europe to the United States, only to be spent in China and elsewhere.

Ironically, Navarro would have been on firmer ground criticizing China if he had abandoned his focus on bilateral balances and adopted a global perspective. China has a current account surplus with the rest of the world because Chinese residents invest more abroad than non-Chinese invest in China. At the same time, the United States has a current account deficit because non-Americans invest more in the United States than Americans invest abroad. These facts are both more relevant and more compelling than the bilateral relations.

Navarro's flawed analytical framework leads to even larger errors when considering the case of Mexico—a frequent target of the Trump administration. The United States consistently runs large trade deficits with Mexico. Americans also pay Mexicans to work in the United States, while many people living in the United States send remittances to their relatives in Mexico. Add it all together and the cumulative bilateral current account deficit from the beginning of 2015 through the beginning of 2019 was about $350 billion. In the same *Wall Street Journal* column from 2017, Navarro claimed that if "America successfully negotiates a bilateral trade deal this year with Mexico in which Mexico agrees to buy more products from the U.S. that it now purchases from the rest of the world" then this "would show up in government data as an increase in U.S. exports [and] a lower trade deficit."[27]

There is no reason to believe this. If, as Navarro implies, Mexicans were to pay for additional U.S. exports by buying fewer exports from the rest of the world, their total spending would not change. At best, Mexico's shrinking bilateral surplus with the United States would be exactly offset by rising U.S. deficits with the rest of the world as those countries collectively lost income by selling fewer exports to Mexico. The likelier outcome is that Navarro's proposal would *increase* the U.S. aggregate current account deficit. Mexicans presumably have good reasons, such as price and quality, to buy goods and services from non-U.S. producers. If they were compelled to switch vendors, they would probably have to spend more money than before just to get the same amount of satisfaction. They might instead choose to cut their spending and save more.

Penalizing Mexican exports would also be counterproductive. Losing access to the U.S. market would make Mexico less attractive to foreign investors while increasing the relative attractiveness of American manufacturing assets. The result would be a global shift in financial flows from Mexico to the United States that would boost American purchasing power and depress spending in Mexico. The net effect would be a narrower bilateral U.S. trade deficit with Mexico at the cost of a wider overall American trade deficit.

Navarro fails to understand that Mexico absorbs excess global savings and manufactured products that would otherwise have increased the U.S. trade deficit. America's bilateral current account deficit with Mexico *cannot* contribute to America's overall deficit because Mexicans, like Americans, spend more than they earn. After all, Mexico consistently runs one of the world's largest current account deficits in absolute terms, consistently worth about 2 percent of its GDP. Mexico's large bilateral trade surplus with the United States is mainly a consequence of its location next to the world's largest consumer market. American, European, and Japanese manufacturers have spent decades establishing factories in Mexico to build components and assemble products to ship north. Only about 60 percent of the value of U.S. imports from Mexico comes from Mexico.[28]

There is only one thing Mexicans could do to try to increase total

U.S. exports: increase their spending and widen their own current account deficit. Mexicans would end up producing extra income for the rest of the world, some of which might eventually turn into heightened demand for American-made goods and services. Even this might fail, especially if the surplus countries save their windfall from additional Mexican spending, rather than use the money to support extra consumption and capital investment that would eventually flow back to the United States. In that scenario, extra spending by Mexicans would simply increase current account surpluses elsewhere rather than contribute to a narrower American deficit.

This strategy would also be extremely risky for Mexico, since it sits somewhere between the United States and Turkey in its ability to attract foreign savings. If Mexico were pushed to borrow more to support extra spending on U.S. exports, the result would likely be a temporary boom followed by a crisis. The subsequent decline in Mexican spending would more than offset any short-term benefits to either the United States or Mexico.

If Navarro truly wanted to understand the development of America's trade deficit over the past several decades, he would do better to focus on why people in the major surplus economies have consistently spent less than they earned. He would also do well to study why the world's savers have long preferred to store their excess wealth in the United States and what that has meant for Americans. As we will explain, starting with China, the answers have nothing to do with cultures of thrift or profligacy. Instead, they have everything to do with the distribution of income and the structure of the global monetary system.

From Tiananmen to the Belt and Road

Understanding China's Surplus

T he Chinese economy has grown at a breakneck pace for four decades. Initially, this was because Maoism had been replaced with the moderate reformism of Deng Xiaoping and his colleagues after they took over the leadership of the Communist Party in 1978. After nearly a century of war and repression, the latent entrepreneurial energies of the Chinese people were finally allowed to flourish. This produced significant gains in living standards in the decade or so after the start of the 1978 reforms. It also produced difficult political problems that were subsequently suppressed in exchange for a new model that generated rapid growth at all costs. That new model, combined with China's unique political model, has been responsible for China's subsequent rapid growth as well as its sustained imbalances.

The Chinese government started implementing its distinctive, but familiar, developmental model in the early 1990s. As in Britain centuries earlier, workers have flowed from the countryside to the cities, in part thanks to new opportunities and in part because local governments confiscated or appropriated their land as urban centers expanded dramatically. These new urban workers are systematically underpaid relative to the value of what they produce, which generates a substantial surplus that has been used to fund investments in physical capital. Investment was always prioritized above consumption.

Meanwhile, like the Americans in the nineteenth century, China attracted modern technology and expertise by promising foreign businesses high profits and access to a large domestic market. Like Japan and South Korea, China funneled household savings to preferred companies through a state-controlled banking system. Also like its Asian neighbors, China uses discriminatory regulations and moral suasion to favor so-called domestic champions over non-Chinese producers.

For many years, this approach appeared to work reasonably well for China, even if it created significant environmental problems at home. Unfortunately for China, the high-savings growth model has long outlived its usefulness, with increasingly difficult consequences for China and the rest of the world.

The reason is that investments are worthwhile only if they satisfy unmet consumption needs. Otherwise they are just wasteful misuses of resources that could have been better deployed elsewhere. Funding investment at the expense of consumption is therefore self-defeating if the result is excess capacity and impoverished workers—precisely the situation in China since the early 2000s. As China's then-premier Wen Jiabao put it in March 2007, "There are structural problems in China's economy which cause unsteady, unbalanced, uncoordinated and unsustainable development."[1]

Until the financial crisis, the costs of this strategy were effectively passed on to the rest of the world through rising trade surpluses and massive financial outflows. In the mid-2000s, Chinese residents, mostly affiliated with the central government, were buying more than $700 billion in foreign assets each year. These outflows were absorbed by the United States and other rich countries at the cost of falling manufacturing capacity and rising household indebtedness. (We will explain the mechanism in more detail later.)

During the financial crisis, collapsing demand in China's main export markets—most notably the United States—caused a sharp contraction in the country's current account surplus, forcing the Chinese government to choose between allowing domestic production to fall (which would cause unemployment to rise) and spending more domestically to lift internal demand. Lifting demand was clearly the better option, but that could mean either higher investment or higher consumption.

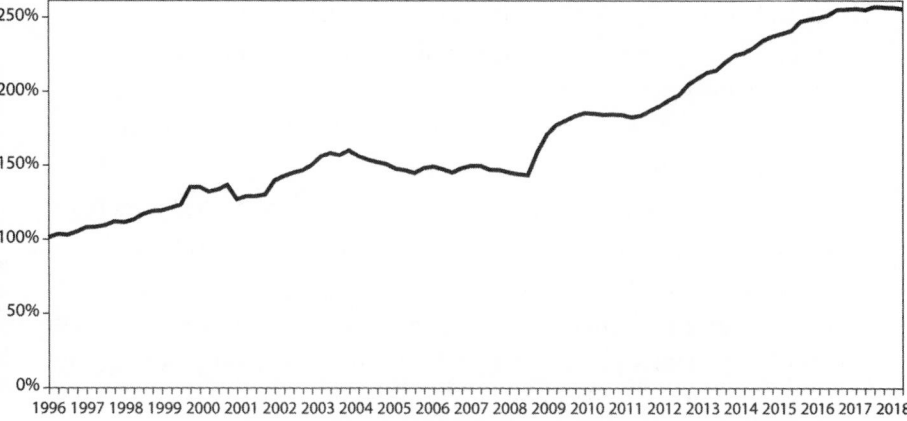

Fig 4.1 China's imbalances come home (total debt owed by nonfinancial sector as a share of GDP). *Source: Bank for International Settlements*

With investment levels so high and already being misallocated on a massive scale, the central government might have preferred higher consumption. But China's myriad institutional constraints, which we will discuss in more detail later in the chapter, meant that consumption could not have grown quickly enough except through a surge in household borrowing. Unsurprisingly, given what the Chinese leadership had just seen occur in the United States, there was no interest in a similar experience.

That is why the government chose to focus on boosting investment. The most straightforward response to the global financial crisis was a massive boost in infrastructure and housing investment to offset the decline in foreign spending. This simultaneously magnified China's long-standing imbalances while shifting them inward. China was able to sustain growth even as its current account surplus fell at the cost of a nearly unprecedented surge in Chinese indebtedness. Unproductive investments have failed to pay for themselves.[2]

The danger is that the Chinese government, having reached the limits of its ability to generate rapid growth through debt-funded investment, will once again attempt to shift the costs of its economic model to the rest of the world through trade surpluses and financial outflows. The only way to prevent this is to rebalance the Chinese economy so that household consumption is prioritized over investment. That means reversing all of the existing mechanisms transferring purchasing power from Chinese workers and retirees to companies and the government—reforms at least as dramatic and politically difficult as the reforms implemented by Deng Xiaoping beginning in 1978.

Unfortunately for China, the choices of the past few decades have become politically entrenched. It is easy for an antidemocratic authoritarian regime to suppress workers' rights and shift spending power from consumers to large companies. Stalin did it, after all. The problem is that years of state-sponsored income concentration creates a potent group of "vested interests"—Premier Li Keqiang's preferred term—that will fiercely resist any reforms that would shift spending power back to consumers. Any successful adjustment process will require a new relationship between the government, the people, and the elites.[3]

Although the Chinese government has made some genuine efforts to improve the well-being of ordinary Chinese people in recent years, including environmental protection, financial reform, and health insurance provision, these have not been nearly enough to reverse the long-term trend since 1989. The great unanswered question for China is whether the Communist Party can reform this system for the benefit of the Chinese people without losing its political monopoly.

To understand why China got into this situation and why it has been so hard to reverse this process, it is necessary to understand China's growth trajectory over the past four decades. One of the biggest mistakes analysts make in their understanding of China's development is to conflate the nearly four decades since Deng Xiaoping began his historic reforms into a single, consistent growth model from whose success we can draw conclusions about the policymaking process. It is much more useful to think about this period as consisting of four very different stages, the last of which, with great difficulty, we are just beginning.

The First Stage: "Reform and Opening Up"

The first stage began in crisis. By the end of the 1970s, decades of Maoist policies had severely constrained the productive capacity of the Chinese people to the point that the economy had been contracting even as the population swelled. Average living standards had plunged to less than 8 percent of the levels in the developed world. Worse, this had happened during the baby boom of the 1950s and early 1960s. That boom would raise the working-age share of China's growing population by roughly 20 percentage points between the early 1970s and the mid-2000s. While this demographic shift subsequently became an important source of China's extraordinary economic growth, it would have proven politically and socially devastating had China's economy continued along the earlier path.[4]

To prevent collapse, the Chinese economy had to be transformed in a way that eliminated the many constraints on economic productivity that had developed over the preceding decades. Deng Xiaoping's reforms did just that and, what is more, were immediately successful. Between 1950 and 1977, real output per person in China grew at an average yearly rate of just 2.5 percent. (By comparison, real output per person in Japan, which was also recovering from wartime devastation, grew at an average yearly rate of 7 percent over the same period.) After 1977 and until this decade China has experienced only three years in which yearly GDP growth came in below 7 percent: in 1982, when China grew by 5.2 percent; in 1990, when it grew by 4.0; and in 1991, when it grew by 3.8 percent.[5]

Under Deng Xiaoping's program of "reform and opening up," the government relaxed laws preventing unplanned economic activity, reduced the role of central planning in favor of localized planning, and allowed farmers to keep their surplus food after selling a minimum quota to the state. "Big push" investment projects and expensive military budgets were abandoned in favor of a "go slow" approach that favored domestic consumption. Credit allocation was gradually decentralized by an explosion of new local banks that within three decades left roughly 60 percent of all new lending in the hands of local provincial institutions, up from roughly zero when the reforms began. These reforms unleashed an explosion of economic activity that generated tremendous wealth creation.

Deng's challenge was reforming the rigid institutional character of the Chinese economy without undermining the rule of the Communist Party or fomenting internal opposition to his leadership. Because his reforms necessarily eroded the bureaucracy's ability to constrain and direct economic activity, they met with powerful elite resistance almost from the beginning. Almost by definition, liberalizing reforms harm entrenched interests for the sake of raising overall productivity, which is why, throughout history, reforms have always generated political opposition from powerful groups that benefit from the existing economic model.

Deng's solution was to adopt a gradualist approach to economic liberalization that kept many of the old elites in positions of power. This meant that the planned economy and the nascent market economy interacted in unpredictable ways. Some prices were regulated and set by the state according to production quotas, while others were allowed to float freely according to supply and demand. Because it was considered more strategic, heavy industry was liberalized more slowly than farming and light manufacturing, which created imbalances between the rural and urban economies.

One consequence was rapid food price inflation in the late 1980s that lowered living standards in the cities. As the economist Barry Naughton describes, this produced "a sense that the government was failing to honor a kind of implicit social compact with urban residents." In an environment that had been characterized by increasing openness, many Chinese workers and students across the country expressed their discontent by demanding greater political rights and participation, most famously in Tiananmen Square, at the center of Beijing and at the edge of the Great Hall of the People, China's main legislative and ceremonial center. Although some Chinese leaders had sympathy with those goals, the Communist Party violently suppressed the prodemocracy movement on June 4, 1989.

Deng's opponents felt vindicated by the prodemocracy movement, which they believed was a symptom of liberalization. Over the next two years, the orthodox communists attempted to reverse the reformist program. Not coincidentally, the Chinese economy grew at its slowest rate since 1978 in the years immediately after Tiananmen. Weak growth eventually undermined their claims to leadership and gave Deng and his allies in the ruling Standing Committee the chance to reinvigorate liberalization—this time with a harder political edge. Even as late as 1992, however, opposition persisted, and Deng's famous Southern Tour was organized primarily to overwhelm continued elite resistance.[6]

Stage Two: The Chinese Development Model

At this stage, we can now usefully speak about the Chinese growth model. After the repression of 1989, the government shifted from merely seeking to eliminate growth constraints to actively implementing new policies to generate rapid growth. In the absence of political reform, the Communist Party would command popular legitimacy by presiding over remarkable increases in living standards. These new policies would also begin to generate imbalances, the most important of which became the extraordinarily low share of national income retained by ordinary Chinese households.

This was not an accident. Developing countries, the Ukrainian-born economist Alexander Gerschenkron argued in his 1951 masterpiece essay "Economic Backwardness in Historical Perspective," have historically faced two key constraints. First, perhaps because of uncertain property rights, noncredible legal systems, and unstable financial and political systems, they do not generate enough domestic savings to fund investment. Second, for many of the same reasons, the private sector fails consistently to direct investment into productive projects.

Gerschenkron's conclusion was that these constraints could be overcome by government intervention. According to Gerschenkron, the state can accelerate development by amassing resources from the private sector and using those resources to build badly needed infrastructure and manufacturing facilities. Household consumption would be suppressed so that investment could rise. In practice, this means that workers and retirees are taxed directly and indirectly to subsidize investment directed by central authorities—a development strategy naturally suited to authoritarian regimes that do not need to be held accountable to their voters.[7]

Nearly every investment-driven growth miracle of the past century has followed this prescription. The Soviet Union under Stalin industrialized using the Gerschenkron model in the 1930s. Maoist China attempted—but failed—to achieve something similar during the Great

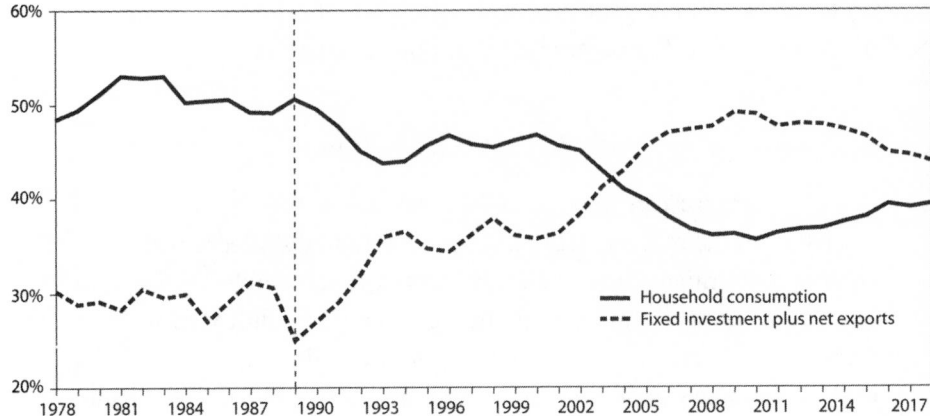

Fig. 4.2 China's imbalances began after 1989 (shares of GDP).
Sources: China National Bureau of Statistics; Matthew Klein's calculations

Leap Forward of 1958–62. (Brazil's military dictatorship had mixed results with the model during the 1960s and 1970s.) Japan is the only major democracy to have implemented this model in the decades after World War II. Its iteration, which was later adopted by South Korea during its military dictatorship, has been the most successful.

Starting in the early 1990s, the Chinese government, having learned from these experiences, began to implement a variety of mechanisms to transfer spending power from ordinary Chinese for the sake of subsidizing domestic investment and foreign consumption. China's rapid growth helped hide the scale of these transfers from ordinary Chinese workers and retirees. Household income grew rapidly even as Chinese households consumed smaller and smaller shares of the Chinese economy's output. This had a profound impact on China's economic relations with the rest of the world, at least until 2008. During the 1990s and 2000s, the decline in Chinese consumption relative to GDP was substantially larger than the rise in investment, with the result that China's internal transfer mechanisms generated a massive current account surplus that reached roughly 10 percent of China's national output by 2007–8.

One mechanism was the currency. China had been steadily devaluing its managed exchange rate against the U.S. dollar since the early 1980s, but this was mainly because the old official price had been arbitrarily high and limited the government's ability to manage financial outflows. In 1994, the government abandoned this policy and devalued the yuan by a third, from 5.8 yuan per dollar to 8.7 yuan per dollar. By the middle of 1995, a new hard peg had been established at 8.3 yuan per dollar. This exchange rate would be rigidly maintained until the middle of 2005.

The result was that the yuan became progressively undervalued relative to economic fundamentals. China had tied its currency to the dollar even though productivity was growing far slower in the United States than in China, or much of the rest of the world. This made Chinese exports increasingly cheap for foreign consumers and simultaneously deprived Chinese consumers of the ability to buy everything their labor had earned. It was a transfer from China's consumers that subsidized the profits of manufacturing operations in China—including the joint ventures established by American, European, and Japanese companies. This transfer helps explain why China went from having a current account deficit in 1993 to increasingly larger surpluses by the 2000s. By the time China allowed the yuan to begin gradually appreciating against the dollar in 2005, the country had a current account surplus worth 6 percent of GDP.[8]

The People's Bank of China (PBOC) had to spend trillions of dollars to maintain its exchange rate during the years of the peg and to limit the rate of yuan appreciation after 2005. The reason is that every country's current account and financial account have to balance. Income flowing in (or out) must be matched by savings flowing out (or in). China had a large and growing trade surplus, which normally would have corresponded with large and growing financial outflows by Chinese savers. China's government, however, for reasons relating to both political and financial stability, restricted the ability of Chinese to move money out the country. For all intents and purposes, there were no financial outflows from the Chinese private sector. At the same time, foreigners were eager to invest in China. Instead of balancing out, the (private) financial account and the current account were reinforcing each other.

Normally, exchange rates adjust to prevent this. A rising yuan would have made Chinese assets less affordable for foreign investors, and it would have lowered China's exports and lifted China's imports by raising the consumption share of GDP and reducing the savings share. It is important to understand exactly how this works. Nearly all households are directly or indirectly net importers, and so benefit from a stronger currency. A rising yuan would effectively force a transfer of income from the manufacturing sector to households, and as this transfer raises household income relative to national income, it also raises household consumption relative to domestic production, or (which is the same thing) it reduces savings relative to investment.

The interaction of those forces would have kept the financial account and the current account in balance. Preventing this outcome required the PBOC to generate an offsetting financial outflow equivalent to the gap between China's private-sector financial account and its current account. Between the start of 1998 and the end of 2008, for example, China had a cumulative current account surplus worth just under $1.4 trillion. Excluding the interventions of the PBOC, China also had a cumulative financial account *surplus* worth $500 billion. The balancing term was the growth in China's foreign exchange reserves, which rose by $1.9 trillion over that period. Those assets represent an equivalent transfer of wealth from Chinese households to the owners of Chinese export manufacturing.

By itself, manipulating the currency below its fundamental value should not have had an impact on the trade balance for very long, if at all. Heightened demand for Chinese exports boosts Chinese production, which should lead to higher wages and prices at home, especially if workers want to be compensated for the high cost of foreign goods. Rising wages in China should have raised the cost of Chinese exports for foreign consumers while lowering the cost of imports for Chinese consumers. Regardless of the exchange rate quoted by currency traders, the real value of the yuan should have appreciated, nullifying the impact of the PBOC's interventions on the current account balance. Inflation, in other words, should have offset the initial distributional impact of the central bank's reserve buying.

According to estimates from the Bank for International Settlements, however, China's inflation-adjusted exchange rate depreciated by roughly 20 percent between 1998 and the end of 2007. By this measure, the yuan did not consistently surpass its 1998 level until 2011.[9]

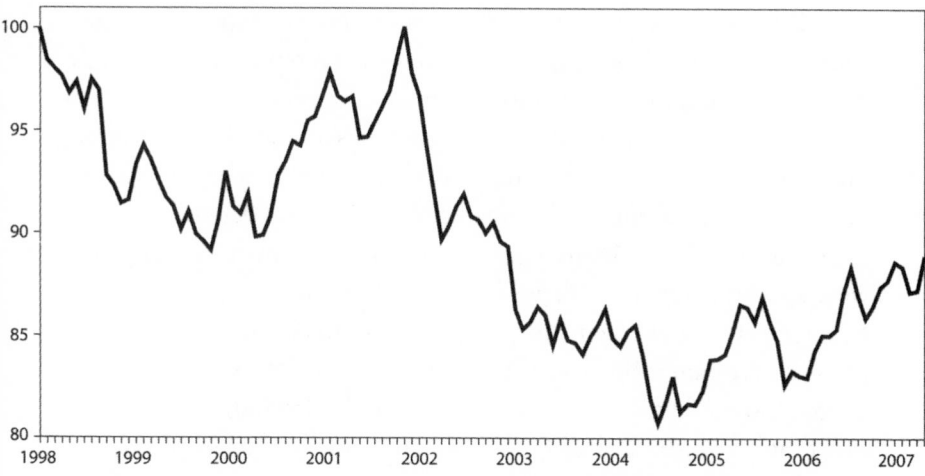

Fig. 4.3 China's current account surplus developed when its currency was undervalued (real trade-weighted value of Chinese yuan, January 1998 = 100). *Sources: Bank for International Settlements; Matthew Klein's calculations*

Inflation, of course, is a measure of consumer prices, and the Chinese government was already committed to suppressing consumption to support additional investment and exports. Those other measures were even more important than currency manipulation at generating the massive trade surpluses during this period.

Many of these measures are regulatory. Property rights are often ignored, which allows local governments to seize valuable land from Chinese households to sell to developers. Expropriations were encouraged by the central government's incentive system for local party officials. Those incentives, which often prioritized reported output growth above all else, also encouraged local governments to ignore pollution and environmental degradation to attract business investment. Ordinary Chinese had their wealth and health taken from them to benefit elites. Their living standards grew far less than China's domestic production. The share of Chinese GDP consumed by Chinese households fell by 15 percentage points between the late 1980s and the bottom in 2010. As of 2018, Chinese households still consume less than 40 percent of Chinese output—a lower ratio than in every other major economy in the world, by far.[10]

One of the least-appreciated mechanisms for suppressing consumption, and the most important, was financial repression. (Tellingly,
however, the gradual elimination of financial repression over the past
few years has only partially reversed China's domestic imbalances.)
There were few ways in China to save other than holding deposits in one
of the government-run banks. Interest rates on those deposits were set
at extraordinarily low levels, especially relative to growth. Lending rates
were also far below what they would have been in a market-based system but were high enough above deposit rates to generate a guaranteed
profit for the banks. Borrowing was limited by regulators and credit was
steered toward favored borrowers, who were able to enjoy cheap financing at the expense of ordinary savers and borrowers who lacked political
connections.

The financial system, in other words, produced a massive and sustained transfer from the Chinese people to large manufacturers, infrastructure developers, real estate developers, and provincial and municipal governments. The transfer was worth about 5 percent of Chinese
GDP each year between 2000 and the start of interest rate liberalization
around 2013. With such cheap capital, it is not surprising that entities
with privileged access to loans embarked on a massive investment spree,
often with little concern about the quality of the projects they were
financing.[11]

The Chinese government is also able to suppress consumption to
subsidize investment using what the Chinese historian Qin Hui has
called the "comparative advantage of lower human rights." This gives
bosses an edge in bargaining over wages and benefits. Labor organizing
and adversarial unions are illegal in China. Those who try to help improve working conditions, whether they are lawyers or students, are often
arrested for threatening the social order. Political prisoners are either
unpaid or underpaid workers for private companies in everything from
shoemaking to electronics assembly.[12]

The Chinese government's distinct attitude to worker protections
also extends to its treatment of hundreds of millions of migrants moving
from the countryside to the cities. Thanks to China's *hukou* system, these
workers are effectively illegal immigrants in their own country. Originally meant to keep workers on farms in the Maoist era, the *hukou* sys-

tem limits the rights of Chinese to move and settle anywhere in China outside of where they were born.

Local governments have declined to enforce the laws preventing rural migrants from holding jobs in cities because it has been good for business. Yet these workers remain under constant threat of eviction, especially in the largest and richest cities, which makes for a relatively compliant workforce. The result of all this is that workers at nonfinancial corporations in China are paid only 40 percent of the value of what they produce. In most other countries, by contrast, the labor share of corporate value added is closer to 70 percent.

The *hukou* system further functions as a regressive tax. Regardless of where they live, workers are required to pay into the national social security system, which covers health, education, pension, and other benefits. Chinese are only eligible to receive those benefits, however, if they are resident where they were officially registered. This has curtailed social spending for hundreds of millions of poor Chinese even as they pay taxes to support relatively rich local governments. Even without these distortions, China's official tax system is regressive. The personal income tax system collects only about 1 percent of GDP, compared to taxes on consumption and social security taxes, which together take in 14 percent. The perverse result is that low earners often face higher tax rates than the rich.[13]

Subsidizing production at the expense of workers and savers necessarily suppressed consumption and forced up China's saving rate to the highest level ever recorded in history. This was not because these transfers caused household savings to rise but because they shifted income from higher-consuming households to lower-consuming sectors of the economy. These savings financed a massive program of investment in infrastructure and manufacturing capacity directed by central authorities. When it works, this is a powerful development model. It results in such rapid growth that even with substantial direct and hidden taxes and transfers, living standards nonetheless soar, as they clearly did in China.

This process also transformed the relation between the central government in Beijing and the country's elite. Because central authorities collect national resources and allocate them into favored projects, a powerful new group emerged that benefited disproportionately from these economic growth policies, in large part because they were the direct beneficiaries of the measures used to subsidize investment by constraining the growth in household income and consumption. This group strongly supported government policies and competed actively to accomplish the objectives set out by Beijing. The more successful they were, the more they were rewarded in the form of indirect subsidies, with access to extraordinarily cheap credit quickly becoming the most valuable asset in China.

Stage Three: From High Investment to Overinvestment

There are always limits to the effectiveness of any unbalanced growth model. The third stage of Chinese growth began at the end of the 1990s. As before, China's underlying economic potential continued to expand rapidly thanks to rising productivity, high investment, and the continued migration of workers from the countryside to the cities. Unlike the earlier periods, however, actual Chinese output grew much more than this underlying potential. Until 2008 or so, the difference was absorbed abroad through rising trade surpluses. After the global financial crisis, the Chinese government responded to the collapse in external demand for Chinese manufactures by ramping up domestic investment even further. Without a commensurate increase in profitable investment projects, however, the result was simply a sharp increase in the domestic debt burden.

To understand why, it is necessary to comprehend the importance of China's GDP growth targets, and for that, it is necessary to understand the difference between GDP growth as a system output and GDP growth as a system input. In most economies, GDP is a measure of output generated by households, businesses, and the government, all of which face constraints on how much they can spend. Official statisticians measure the relevant changes in activity, which are reported as the amounts by which GDP expanded or contracted during the period.

But this is not what happens in China. In China, the GDP growth rate is an input into the system. It is set early in the year as the GDP growth target for that year and represents the amount of growth needed to accommodate social and political objectives, among which of course is the desire to keep unemployment low. As such it modifies the standard economic constraints, allowing local governments to generate enough economic activity that, together with the economic activity of the private and real estate sectors, add up the GDP growth target.

This creates powerful—and dangerous—incentives. China's provincial and municipal governments control most of the credit creation within the banking system, and Chinese banks rarely have to write down loans for projects that cannot service the debt. The easiest way for officials to hit their targets is therefore to tell the state-run banks to lend to favored companies to invest in as much infrastructure, manufacturing, and real estate as necessary. Whether the investments are worthwhile is irrelevant. All that matters is that the quantity of spending generates enough reported GDP to meet the central government's objectives.

At least until the mid-1990s, this incentive system was not a problem for China because the shortage of infrastructure and manufacturing capacity was so large. The only important constraint on productive investment was the pace at which savings could grow. Almost any investment increased productivity by far more than the cost of the project. Under these circumstances, the best financial system was the one that expanded most rapidly, which necessarily means the one that was the least discriminating in choosing projects. Anything and everything would get funded if it conformed to the party's basic political objectives. This is the financial system China got. It was not a sophisticated steward of capital, but it was extremely successful—thanks to government regulations—at capturing the surge in China's domestic savings and lending cheaply to every conceivable investment project.

There are two major differences between the Chinese economy and most other economies that allow local governments to meet the growth target quarter after quarter and year after year with such precision. First, local governments are not subject to hard budget constraints—that is, they can engage in near-unlimited amounts of nonproductive economic activity unconstrained by the need to remain solvent. This is possible because local governments control most credit creation within the banking system. Second, because the loans are directly or indirectly guaranteed, banks do not have to write down loans made into projects that cannot service the debt. This allows them to extend as much new credit as is required by local governments to fund the activity needed to achieve the GDP growth target.

By the late 1990s, however, years of extraordinarily rapid investment growth had made it increasingly difficult to identify obviously productive investments. The long-standing defects in the Chinese banking system became a serious constraint. Cheap credit from captive household savings subsidized investments that added less economic value than they truly cost. China had reached a saturation point past which its investment boom became increasingly unproductive.

This may seem surprising, since China is still a lower-income country and was a truly poor country back in the late 1990s, when its GDP per capita was comparable to that of Honduras or Zimbabwe. In 2012, economists at HSBC Global Research estimated that the total value of China's capital stock per worker was just 6 percent of the level in the United States. They concluded from this that "China needs to invest more, rather than less." Their implicit assumption was that China should invest as much as possible until it reached the level of capital deepening in the world's most advanced economies.[14]

It is much more useful, however, to assume that every country has its own optimal investment level based on its domestic institutions and that it is meaningless to compare investment levels per capita in rich countries with those in poor countries. Risky long-term projects make sense only in particular social and institutional contexts where the risk of expropriation is low, financial markets are stable, regulations are unobtrusive, contracts are honored, and the rules of the game are unlikely to change unexpectedly. Countries with these conditions should naturally be able to absorb far higher levels of investment per person than countries without these conditions.

The capital stock should therefore be much higher in places where governments are accountable to the people and constrained by laws and a strong civil society. By contrast, high rates of corruption, vague regulations, and arbitrary rule are natural obstacles to productive investment. Technical factors also matter. America's relatively forgiving system of bankruptcy, with its focus on giving borrowers a fresh start, has helped foster an entrepreneurial culture of innovation compared to more hide-bound European societies. Similarly, the treatment of patents and the ease (or difficulty) of moving from job to job or place to place within a country can make a substantial difference to a society's prosperity. Even unquantifiable cultural characteristics, such as the importance of education and the overall willingness of people to trust others they are not related to, have a large impact on the optimal level of physical investment.[15]

Not all economies, in other words, can absorb equal amounts of investment productively. Societies are not poor because they lack buildings, machines, and other forms of physical capital. Rather, they usually lack capital because they are poor, and they are poor because their institutions prevent them from absorbing investment and labor as productively as they otherwise might.

The few societies that have genuinely suffered from shortages of physical capital are the exception rather than the rule. They often are countries recovering from natural disasters or wars, such as Europe, Japan, and Korea in the 1940s and 1950s. Less common, but also notable, are advanced societies experiencing rapid population growth through a combination of high birth rates and immigration, such as Australia, Canada, and the United States in the nineteenth century. The rarest exceptions are societies experiencing rapid transformations in their domestic institutions that sustainably increase their optimal investment level. The best examples are likely in Central and Eastern Europe after abandoning communism, but even they have had far lower investment rates than China. Moreover, they were relatively prosperous before the world wars and communist occupations.

Where does China fit in? China clearly experienced a meaningful transition in 1978 when Deng Xiaoping and his colleagues came to power and began the process of economic reform. Those reforms coincided with the first sustained period that China was able to enjoy relative domestic and international peace in nearly a century. All of this should have increased the country's optimal level of physical capital. It is unlikely, however, that these changes have been sufficiently meaningful to warrant the substantial increase in investment over the past two decades. In fact, the economist Harry X. Wu estimates that China's underlying productivity has not improved since the early 1990s. Output has

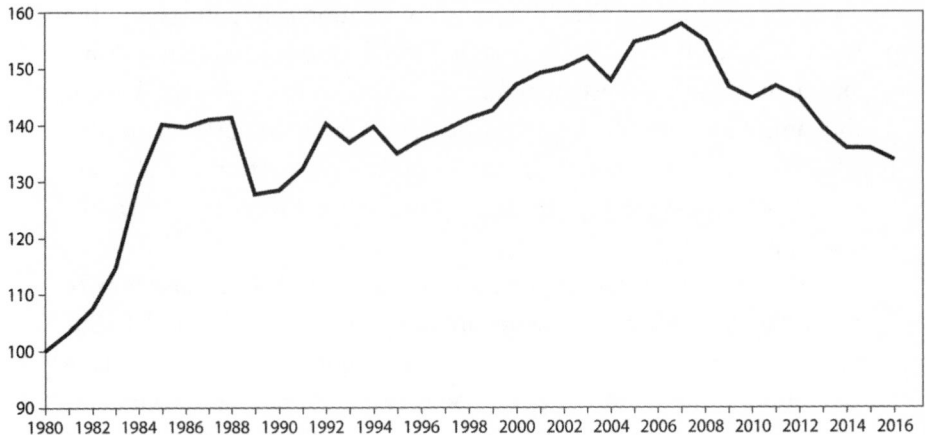

Fig. 4.4 China needs more productivity growth (estimate of underlying productivity, 1980 = 100). *Source: Harry X. Wu*

increased only because more machines and workers are being used to make more stuff. That would explain why the Chinese economy has been unable to grow without relying on either foreign demand or rapid increases in domestic indebtedness.[16]

Unfortunately for China, the financial system remained designed to expand domestic investment as rapidly as possible, regardless of whether any individual project is economically justifiable. The costs of investing in infrastructure or manufacturing capacity were so heavily subsidized by hidden and explicit transfers from households that there was no mechanism to constrain, or even to identify, wasted investment. Anyone in China who could plausibly claim to be satisfying the central government's development objectives could get access to cheap credit. As they continued to borrow and build, these vested interests became increasingly powerful politically and increasingly determined to maintain their access to low-cost loans to fund further growth. China's politics distorted its economy, which has distorted its politics even more.

Reversing these imbalances will be challenging. It would have been better for China to have revised its investment-led growth model as soon as it became apparent that the economy was suffering from widespread investment misallocation, but had that happened, China would have been unique in history. Instead, what typically happens is that the vested interests who benefit from that growth model delay meaningful adjustments, and this is what happened in China. And as in every historical precedent, the necessary adjustment was postponed long enough for debt to become a serious problem. China has not been an exception. Premier Wen Jiabao admitted in early 2007 that it was time to change and to rebalance demand, yet things continued to get worse until 2011–12.

More recently, however, China's central government has rightly begun to grapple with these problems. So far, it has focused on curtailing investment spending as quickly as possible by constraining credit growth. The PBOC's preferred measure is called "aggregate financing to the real economy." During the boom years, broad credit was growing by well over 20 percent annually. In 2016, it grew 15 percent. In 2018, total credit grew less than 10 percent. Similarly, the growth rate of fixed asset investment has slowed from roughly 26 percent each year in 2005–11 to 10 percent by 2015 to just 6 percent by 2018.[17]

This is real progress, but the growth in Chinese debt continues to exceed the growth in China's debt capacity. Even now, the government is building elaborate subway stations in desolate marshlands in order to sustain domestic spending rather than making policy changes to raise household income and create better incentives for small businesses. This poses a challenge to the rest of the world.[18]

Will China's Imbalances Shake the World Again?

Officially, China's annual current account surplus peaked at about $420 billion in 2008 and has since contracted to an annual rate of about $190 billion in the first half of 2019. Both in absolute terms and relative to China's economy, it would therefore seem as if one of the country's main imbalances has been resolved. But a closer examination suggests that China's external rebalancing is fragile and prone to reverse. Persistent transfers from workers and retirees continue to depress consumption. If investment spending slows without an offsetting increase in household spending, China's surplus will widen once again—to the detriment of the rest of the world.

The first thing to note is that China's trade surplus in manufactured

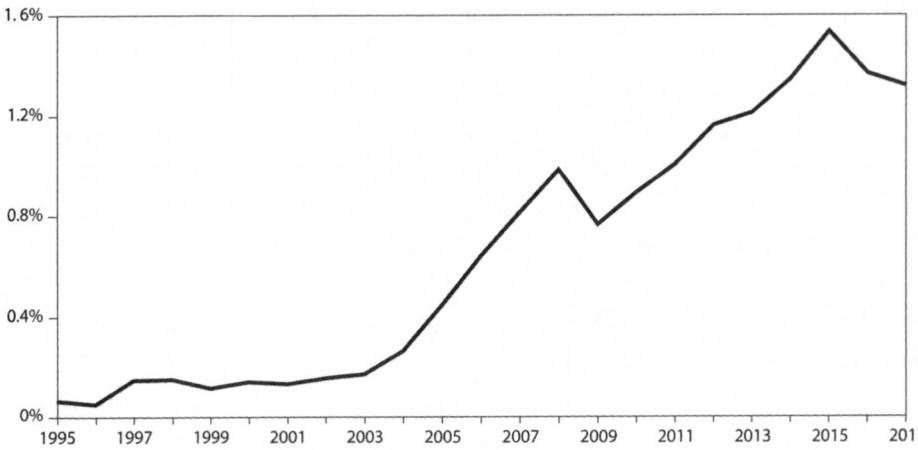

Fig. 4.5 The China glut (China's trade surplus in manufactured goods relative to the rest of the world's GDP). *Sources: International Monetary Fund; China Customs; Brad W. Setser*

goods is already far larger than in 2008, both in absolute terms and relative to the economic output of the rest of the world. In other words, the glut of excess Chinese production has only gotten worse and the burden imposed on China's trade partners to absorb this glut has only gotten bigger. From this perspective, there has been no rebalancing.

Surprisingly, this has occurred even as China's manufacturing exports have become decreasingly important to the Chinese economy. In 2007–8, Chinese exports of manufactures were worth about 30 percent of its GDP, while the figure now is just 18 percent. Part of the explanation is that China's overall share of global output continues to rise, so any change in China's trade or current account balance looks very different depending on whether the perspective is China's domestic economy or the rest of the world.

More important, however, is what has happened to Chinese spending on imports of manufactured goods. Like all countries, China imports manufactures for two reasons: to use them as components for finished goods that will eventually be exported to others and to satisfy domestic investment and consumption needs. Both kinds of imports have shrunk in importance, with the result that total imports of manufactures have shrunk from 23 percent of Chinese GDP in 2004 to less than 10 percent

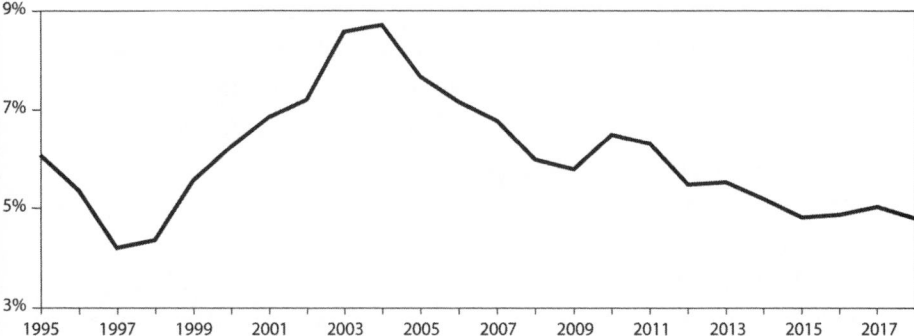

Fig. 4.6 China has embraced a strategy of import substitution (Chinese spending on manufactured imports for domestic uses relative to GDP). *Sources: International Monetary Fund; China Customs; Brad W. Setser*

of Chinese GDP today. This helps explain why China's overall trade surplus appears to have been unaffected by U.S. tariffs as of the middle of 2019.[19]

Part of the reason is that Chinese companies no longer need to import as many components to export finished products—domestic suppliers are increasingly up to the job. Two-thirds of the value of China's exports of advanced manufactured goods came from abroad in the early 2000s, but today, most of the value now comes from Chinese labor and capital. Stories about low-wage Chinese workers merely assembling advanced components made elsewhere are, at best, unrepresentative of the situation. At the same time, Chinese domestic capacity has gotten far better at satisfying China's domestic needs: imports of finished manufactured goods have dropped from 9 percent of Chinese GDP in 2004 to less than 5 percent today. The "Made in China 2025" agenda is explicitly aimed at accelerating this process of import substitution.

Import substitution has succeeded thanks in part to Chinese government policies that have systematically encouraged Chinese businesses to substitute foreign production for domestic production, even when this has raised costs for Chinese consumers. Since joining the World Trade Organization in 2001, China has scrupulously adhered to its WTO commitments and abided by the decisions of its judges. Yet the Chinese economy may be fundamentally incompatible with the spirit of any rules-based trading system because the Chinese party-state has enormous power to tell companies what to do. Communist Party cells are embedded in most Chinese companies, even the subsidiaries of non-Chinese firms. Executives at many large companies, including those without direct government ownership, are party members, which makes them eligible for promotions and favors—and vulnerable to party discipline.

Even those who are not party members often attempt to affiliate with Beijing's priorities. The legal academics Curtis J. Milhaupt and Wentong Zheng "identified ninety-five out of the top one hundred private firms and eight out of the top ten Internet firms whose founder or de facto controller is currently or formerly a member of central or local party-state organizations such as People's Congresses and People's Political Consultative Conferences." Regulators can and do bring in executives for interviews on any subject that concerns them. The Chinese financial system is dominated by state-owned entities, which gives the party leverage to help companies that promote its objectives and to punish those that do not. Milhaupt and Zheng note that private firms have "little autonomy from discretionary state intervention in business judgment" because "the state exercises significant extra-legal control rights over private firms."[20]

In this system, there is little need for tariffs to direct domestic demand toward domestic production. Executives can simply be told to pick Chinese suppliers over foreign ones. These tools have allowed the Chinese government to pursue a modernized version of Friedrich List's National System adapted for an age when explicit tariffs are considered outmoded. The result is that, unlike most other countries, imports have become less and less important to the Chinese economy since the mid-2000s.

Chinese manufacturing trade data are easy to compare with figures published by other countries that represent actual economic activity. The same cannot be said of China's overall current account surplus. China's reported imports of travel services have ballooned from $102 billion in 2012 to $277 billion in 2018, even as China's reported exports of travel services to the rest of the world have stagnated. Although many

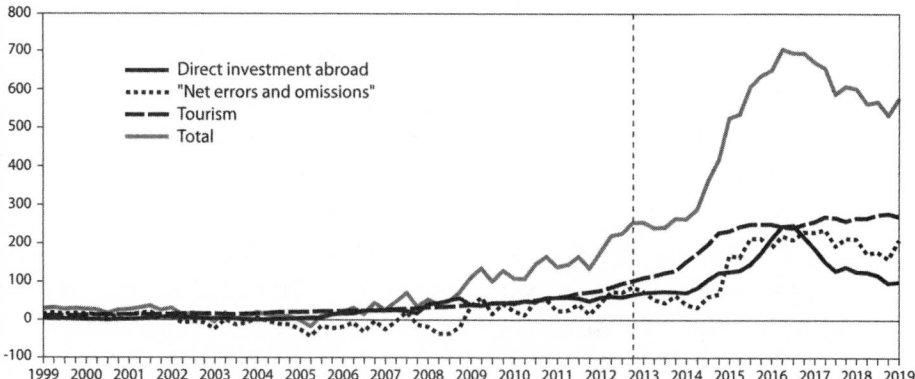

Fig. 4.7 The great escape (money leaving China, USD billions per year).
Sources: State Administration of Foreign Exchange; Matthew Klein's calculations

more Chinese students and tourists are traveling and spending money outside China now than a few years ago, the increase is not nearly large enough to match the change in the official figures. A 2019 analysis from economists at the Federal Reserve Bank of New York concluded that China's balance of payments data overstated the true trade deficit in travel services by "about $85 billion in 2018."

The likeliest explanation is that much of what is counted as travel is actually a form of capital flight. Visiting the United States to buy life insurance or housing—or to exchange high-priced jewelry for dollars—is not economically equivalent to going on a vacation and picking up a few souvenirs. Tellingly, the sharp increase in tourism spending occurred shortly after the start of Xi Jinping's anticorruption campaign. It is also correlated with other measures of Chinese capital flight, particularly the statistical discrepancy between the current account and the financial account, known as "net errors and omissions." The yearly value of these outflows peaked at $700 billion in 2015–16.[21]

The Chinese government accommodated these outflows with a mix of currency depreciation, sales of foreign reserves, and changes to its domestic monetary policy framework. Those measures eventually proved insufficient, however, which is why outbound capital controls were progressively tightened in 2016–17. Many of the Chinese executives who had demonstrated a particularly strong appetite for using their companies to borrow domestically to buy foreign assets have since been arrested, while others ended up dying under unusual circumstances.[22]

These data suggest that there is less to China's external rebalancing than meets the eye. Even so, Chinese really are spending more on imports of commodities—particularly soybeans, dairy, and meat—and they really are spending more on foreign travel and schooling. That is good for China and good for the world. The progress China has achieved is fragile, however, because of its legacy of excessive debt and overinvestment. While tightening credit is necessary for China's internal rebalancing, the danger is that this will end up strangling investment before complementary reforms have succeeded in lifting household incomes and boosting domestic consumption. The net effect would be to depress domestic demand.

That, in turn, would create two options. First, domestic production could fall to match the drop in domestic demand. Aggregate income would fall, likely through a combination of real wage cuts and much higher unemployment. China's political system might not survive that kind of social dislocation, and even if it could, the government has no interest in taking the risk of finding out. The likelier outcome is therefore that domestic production will fall by less than domestic demand, which necessarily means that China's trade surplus would expand through a decline in imports relative to exports. The Chinese government might choose to depreciate the yuan, for example, or find other ways to shift the burden of adjustment onto the rest of the world. Regardless of the specific mechanism, the global glut of excess production would get worse. From this perspective, China's "Made in China 2025" agenda can be understood as a preemptive measure to limit imports in preparation for the coming decline in domestic investment.

Similarly, the Chinese government's commitment to the Belt and Road Initiative (BRI) can best be understood as a way to manage the tradeoffs associated with its internal rebalancing, rather than as part of some strategic plan to gain territory or military bases. Recall that before 2008, the Chinese government dealt with overcapacity by exporting purchasing power and goods to Americans and Europeans. China avoided rising domestic indebtedness by accumulating trillions of dollars of U.S.

and European financial assets and financing rising debt in the rest of the world. That became unsustainable, however, once American and European borrowers reached the limits of their debt capacity. The Chinese government adapted by encouraging additional domestic investment even at the cost of rising domestic debt. As we have seen, this has also proved unsustainable, which is why the Chinese government has changed course again. Over the past few years, the priority, with some exceptions, has been to constrain domestic credit growth and limit domestic investment.

The real promise of the BRI, therefore, is that it will create new demand for Chinese exports of manufactured goods and construction services in Southeast Asia, South Asia, Africa, the Middle East, Eastern Europe, and Latin America. Chinese banks will lend to foreign governments and those governments will hire Chinese firms to build ports, railroads, electric grids, coal plants, telecoms, and more. So far, the BRI has been successful at generating demand for Chinese companies and Chinese workers outside China. But this has come at the cost of exporting many of the downsides of China's domestic development model to much of the rest of the world. Chinese lenders have little incentive to do due diligence, which has led to a raft of bad debts incurred by recipient governments. Chinese firms have little concern for the environmental impact of their projects. Political and cultural insensitivities have led to frictions between Chinese companies and host countries. Even if those problems could be overcome, the total addressable market of the BRI countries is far smaller than North America and Europe. It is therefore difficult to imagine China using the BRI to substitute for the loss of its traditional export markets.[23]

All this has implications for how the ongoing trade war could affect the Chinese economy. China's reported GDP growth—which measures economic activity whether or not this activity is wealth enhancing—will be unaffected by trade war, no matter how severe, as long as China has debt capacity and the government is willing to use it. Losing access to export markets will affect the sustainability of the Chinese economy, however, because the government will likely respond by encouraging additional borrowing to finance increasingly unproductive investment, or possibly household debt. This makes the Chinese economy more vulnerable to a trade war than would be implied by its apparently low reliance on exports. So far, China has responded to U.S. tariffs by accelerating its import substitution, depreciating the yuan, and (modestly) accelerating domestic credit growth, including household debt.[24]

Stage Four: The Spirit of '78

In the end, Beijing must choose among three difficult options: rising debt, rising unemployment, and wealth transfers from elites to ordinary households. To make matters more difficult, it will have to manage these tradeoffs at a time when its trade surplus is under stress, which puts further upward pressure either on debt or on unemployment. No matter what happens outside China, the government can continue to prop up growth as long as China's banks can continue to finance additional investment spending. There is some point, however, past which China will no longer be able to trade rising domestic indebtedness for lower unemployment. The sharp increase in private financial outflows after 2013 is a warning. Whether or not it is a deliberate process managed by the government, Chinese credit growth, and, with it, investment growth, will continue to slow.

The consequences have already been felt in some of China's provinces. The economists Wei Chen, Xilu Chen, Chang Tai-Hsieh, and Zheng Song found in 2019 that officials across the country, particularly Liaoning, Inner Mongolia, and Tianjin, have systematically overstated the amount of capital investment occurring within their borders since 2008. Rather than use cheap credit to boost spending, which would have been standard practice, they preferred to lie about the numbers. The authors note that "local leaders in these three provinces were recently arrested in corruption crackdowns, and one of the official accusations was that these leaders had overstated local GDP." The positive implication is that the Chinese economy may have rebalanced toward consumption further than the official data imply. The bad news is that China's debts are probably closer to 300 percent of national income, rather than the official ratio of 250 percent, which means the quality of past investments must be even worse than previously believed. That, in turn, means that China is likely even closer to reaching the limit of its debt capacity.[25]

The challenge for the Chinese government is to ensure that this inevitable outcome does not lead to a collapse in GDP and a surge in unemployment. The only sustainable solution is to reduce the economy's reliance on investment spending by raising domestic consumption. That means radically altering the distribution of wealth and income so that Chinese households can afford what they produce. What was taken from China's workers and retirees must be restored. China must implement a second round of liberalizing reforms in the spirit of Deng Xiaoping.

There is at least one major difference, however, between the reforms of the 1980s and the reforms needed today. Although both sets of reforms should lead to an immediate improvement in real productivity growth, it is unlikely that China's adjustment will result in spectacularly high GDP growth rates the way Deng's reforms almost immediately did. The reason has to do, perhaps not surprisingly, with debt. When Deng began his reforms, Chinese debt levels were low, unlike today. As he eliminated the institutional constraints and distorted incentives that prevented Chinese from productive activity, the resulting increased productivity showed up immediately as higher growth.

But high debt levels change the impact of more productive behavior in three important ways:

- First, high levels of debt create uncertainty about how the costs of default and repayment will be distributed. Although this is well known in corporate finance, it is not part of traditional macroeconomics. The important point is that everyone in the economy changes their behavior to avoid bearing the costs of bad debt, and these changes in behavior undermine growth. The rich try to take their money out of the country, businesses cut investment, workers become uncooperative, middle-class savers pull their money out of the banking system to buy hard assets, and so on. Chinese debt levels are high enough that many of these financial distress processes have already started. Until debt is written down, reforms aimed at unleashing productivity will result in less wealth creation than otherwise.

- In the past, Chinese provincial governments hit their GDP targets by borrowing in excess of the real growth capacity of the economy. Without the ability to borrow so cheaply, GDP would have grown much slower. This means that growth rates will slow significantly once debt levels stabilize. Moreover, China's debt levels are already so high that the priority should be reducing debt, rather than simply stabilizing it. Except in an economy in which all resources, including labor, are fully and productively used, increases or reductions in debt show up as changes in the growth rate. What had been a growth impulse must now move into reverse, which means that GDP will grow even slower than otherwise.

- Last, because the Chinese banking system has not recognized the economic losses its lending has generated, China's GDP has been substantially overstated by the amount of bad loans. Investments are worthwhile only if they support future consumption and production capable of justifying the cost of the investment. The corollary is that the loans used to finance the investment are repaid at a competitive rate of interest. Many investments in China fail to meet that standard. Instead of increasing long-term growth, they reduce it by adding bad debt to the financial system that cannot be repaid without additional subsidies extracted from workers and retirees. The costs of these bad loans and bad investments will eventually be amortized over the adjustment period, however, and will necessarily lower future reported GDP by the amount that past reported GDP had been overstated.

There is a pretty broad consensus on what reforms are needed, with the Chinese Communist Party's Third Plenum meeting from October 2013 providing at least part of the blueprint. China has made important progress in many areas, including interest rate liberalization, environmental protection, health insurance, and the one-child policy. Household consumption has even begun to rise relative to total production, although it remains far below where it was as recently as the early

2000s as a share of Chinese economic output. The next step, and the crucial one, will be to transfer substantial wealth and income from elites—particularly China's provincial and municipal governments and state-owned entities—to households. This means land reform, *hukou* reform, tax reform, privatization, the legalization of unions, and other measures so that household income can continue growing quickly even if GDP growth slows substantially.[26]

The only safe prediction is that over the next decade or two, China's imbalances will have been reversed, which means household income growth will substantially exceed GDP growth. But there are many ways this can happen. Progressive wealth transfers would make it possible to maintain the rapid growth of Chinese living standards even as investment growth slows to zero, or even turns negative. Chinese household income and consumption might grow at a vibrant 5–6 percent annually while average GDP growth would slow to 3–4 percent.

If, however, opposition to transfers forces the government to use credit growth as a substitute for reform, the risk is that China hits its debt capacity constraint. In that scenario, growth would slow much more dramatically, and the economy might even shrink. China would still rebalance because the drop in household income would be much lower than the drop in GDP. During the U.S. rebalancing from 1929 to 1933, total production fell about 26 percent and household consumption dropped by 18 percent. The relatively better model for China would be Japan after 1990. There, government debt soared while GDP growth slowed to almost zero, but household consumption grew at a solid pace of just under 2 percent thanks to a steady decline in the household saving rate.[27]

The point is that one way or another China will rebalance its economy—all imbalances eventually reverse themselves—but that the specific path depends on how the political system interacts within several competing constraints. As China's economy continues to slow, the central government in Beijing will necessarily forge a new relation with China's various elite groups. New institutions will be created that will determine the nature of Chinese economic growth over the rest of the century. What that new relation and those new institutions will look like is anyone's guess. The best outcome is that income shifts from the elite to ordinary households: this is the rebalancing that should in principle reduce China's need to force its deficient domestic demand onto the rest of the world.

One thing is certain, however. The adjustment period that has followed every growth miracle has always overturned expectations, especially the most seemingly obvious and widely accepted ones, and has always been far more difficult economically than even the greatest pessimists had feared. It is safe to assume that this will happen again.

The Fall of the Wall
and the *Schwarze Null*
Understanding Germany's Surplus

More than four thousand miles away from the Chinese Communist Party's violent assertion of its authority against the prodemocracy movement in June 1989, a distinctly different chain of events was playing out in Central and Eastern Europe. By the end of that year, more than a hundred million people had been liberated from communist regimes and the grip of the Soviet Union. Their integration into Western Europe's capitalist economy transformed German society and politics—with profound consequences for Europe and, ultimately, the world.

Although many in the former communist bloc eventually benefited from convergence with their richer Western neighbors, the period after reunification proved traumatic for many Germans in both the East and the West. Poverty and insecurity rose, especially for Germans with jobs. Workers at the top saw rapid income gains even as most other Germans experienced outright wage cuts. National income shifted from workers to the owners of capital. Tax cuts for high earners, the absence of a meaningful inheritance tax, and weakened social benefits all heightened the impact. The combined effect was to shift Germany's purchasing power toward entities—rich households and the businesses they control—that spend far less than they earn. Despite following a radically different path than China, Germany ended up in a surprisingly similar place. Class wars were won by the rich at the expense of everyone else.

Like China, Germany was therefore unable to absorb all it produced. This generated a surplus that had to go somewhere. Before 2008, Germany's excess savings went to borrowers in the rest of Europe, mostly in the form of loans from German banks to banks elsewhere. By exporting excess savings to its European trading partners, rich Germans forced people in Spain, Greece, Italy, and elsewhere to borrow more than they could reasonably afford. That turned out badly for both the creditors, who have lost hundreds of billions of euros on bad assets, and for the debtors, who have since suffered levels of unemployment unprecedented in modern European history.

Germany's net financial outflows have persisted since 2008 because policy choices have reinforced weakness in domestic spending. The most important of these has been the government's fanatical opposition to public borrowing, epitomized by the *Schuldenbremse,* or debt brake. Increasing fiscal rectitude has more than offset the gradual rebalancing of the inequities within the German private sector in the past few years. At the same time, the German government's zeal in imposing its economic model on its neighbors has magnified Germany's enormous surplus into an even bigger European surplus.

The End of Communism in Europe

The revolution began in Poland. In 1980, workers at the Gdansk Shipyard had formed an independent labor union called Solidarity. As in China, Poland's communist government considered any independent mass movement to be a threat to the party's monopoly on power, and it imposed martial law in 1981. Unlike in China, repression failed. By 1988, waves of strikes and growing popular support for Solidarity forced the Polish government to negotiate. On April 5, 1989, the Round Table Agreement legalized independent trade unions and scheduled free elections in which Solidarity could compete against the Polish United Workers' Party (PZPR) and its allies.

In one of history's great coincidences, Poland's first free legislative election since 1928 took place on June 4, 1989—the same day the Chinese army suppressed the prodemocracy movement in Tiananmen Square. Even though 65 percent of the seats in the Sejm (the lower house of the parliament) had been reserved for incumbents, Solidarity dominated the vote, winning all but one seat in the newly formed Senate and the full 35 percent of contestable seats in the Sejm. By August, Solidarity had convinced some of the satellite parties that had previously supported the PZPR to switch sides, and together they formed Poland's first democratic government under Prime Minister Tadeusz Mazowiecki. The new regime immediately began rolling back the country's authoritarian institutions and reforming the economy under the slogan of "shock therapy."[1]

It was Hungary, however, that decisively broke the communists' domination of Eastern Europe. Compared to the rest of the Soviet bloc, Hungary's Communist Party was relatively liberal, having legalized independent labor unions, some forms of market activity, and travel to the West. Nevertheless, it was afflicted by the same economic forces in the 1980s as its neighbors. The government's budget had come under enormous strain thanks to the cutbacks in subsidies from the Soviet Union and the burden of having to repay dollar-denominated debts borrowed in the 1970s during a period of extreme dollar strength.

For both ideological and cost-cutting reasons, the Hungarians decided to stop monitoring their border with Austria in 1988. (The electronic signaling system required parts that had to be imported from the West and hard currency was scarce.) East Germans, who were free to travel to other communist countries but not the West, began to escape through Hungary to Austria and then to West Germany. After progressively dismantling the border, the Hungarians officially announced on September 10, 1989, that they would no longer catch and return East Germans to the Stasi, the East German state security service, which precipitated an exodus. Hungary's government remained controlled by the communists (renamed "socialists") until May 1990 but left peacefully after losing free parliamentary elections.[2]

Mass emigration quickly undermined East Germany's dictatorship. The government's first response to the opening of the Hungarian border with Austria was to outlaw travel to Hungary, which prompted protests each Monday that grew every week. Moreover, the initial crackdown failed to prevent East Germans from continuing to escape to Hungary via Czechoslovakia. The regime therefore closed the border with its neighbor and ostensible ally in October 1989. Erich Honecker, the long-running dictator of East Germany who had criticized both the Soviets and the Hungarians as being too soft, ordered the military and the Stasi to crush the protest scheduled for October 9. Instead, they refused to fire and Honecker was forced out in favor of a less bloody-minded communist.

Honecker's ouster encouraged more protests, which grew to nearly half a million people at a time. By November 1, the East Germans had removed their border controls with Czechoslovakia, which a few days later removed its border with West Germany. At that point, the East German government figured that it would not make much difference if East Germans could travel directly to West Berlin. The announcement of the policy change on November 9, 1989, encouraged hundreds of thousands of would-be emigrants to gather on the eastern side of the Berlin Wall. Once again, the military refused to fire, and the wall was breached. By December, the ruling Socialist Unity Party of Germany had begun negotiating with the opposition and had officially abandoned Marxist-Leninism.

The revolutions in Central and Eastern Europe succeeded in large part because the Soviet Union lacked both the resources and the will to intervene. Unlike 1956 (Hungary), 1968 (Czechoslovakia), and 1979 (Afghanistan), the Soviets did not invade their satellites in the late 1980s to preserve their puppet regimes. The Soviets' reluctance can be partly explained by changes in their financial fortunes. Despite the Cold War conflict, the USSR depended on grain imports from Europe and the United States. It paid for those imports with hard currency earned by selling energy exports and, occasionally, its gold reserves. In the 1960s, the price of oil and gas rose by more than 50 percent relative to the price of wheat. In the 1970s, energy prices quadrupled relative to wheat prices. The Soviets' growing international purchasing power enabled their aggression, helped compensate for the internal weaknesses of the communist system, and encouraged the government to rack up large dollar-denominated debts from Western banks to pay for additional imports.

From 1980 to 1988, however, the oil price collapsed by two-thirds relative to both the wheat price and the dollar. The gold price also plunged. That made it increasingly difficult for the Soviets to sustain their military posture in the West, pay the ongoing costs of the war in Afghanistan, and service the foreign debts incurred in the 1970s. Any additional spending would have required a brutal squeeze of the home front. Crushing living standards to support the military was possible— Stalin had done it, after all—but it would have required domestic repression on a scale that Mikhail Gorbachev, who had ascended to the top of the party's leadership in 1985, was uninterested in, and probably incapable of, imposing. Instead, Gorbachev's priorities were softening the authoritarianism of his regime and repairing relations with the West. This gave the Central and Eastern Europeans their window of opportunity.[3]

Germany Restored

When the Berlin Wall fell in November 1989, it was not immediately obvious that the two Germanys would reunite as quickly as they did. The biggest hurdle was diplomatic: the division of Germany had prevented the finalization of the peace treaty to officially end World War II. Reunification, however, would have established "a government adequate for the purpose" of negotiating a settlement with the original Allies. Moreover, many West Germans were reluctant to pay the costs of reunification. Living standards in the East were less than half what they were in the West. Reaching anything near parity would be a generational challenge.[4]

At the same time, some Easterners wanted to maintain an independent identity and political culture. The incumbent Socialist Unity Party quickly rebranded into the Party of Democratic Socialism (PDS), which promised a gentler form of leftism. It was led by a reformist leader who opposed the authoritarian repression of his predecessors. Party leaders hoped that they could do well enough in free elections to have a legitimate claim to rule.

Things did not work out that way. On November 28, less than three weeks after the Berlin Wall was breached, West German chancellor Helmut Kohl presented the Bundestag with a ten-point plan for closer integration between the two Germanys. Most important was point num-

ber five, which stated that the West was prepared "to develop confeder-
ative structures between both states in Germany, with the aim of creating a federation" if East Germany were willing to become a democracy.
While the Americans were quick to support Kohl's push for reunification, the British, the French, and the Soviets were all unhappy. Decades
of peace had not dulled their fears of German nationalism. Ultimately,
however, there was little that they could do, considering the changes
taking place within East Germany.

Those internal changes were partly motivated by financial concerns. Like the other Eastern bloc countries, East Germany had too
much foreign currency debt that it could not afford to pay, especially if
emigration continued. Worse, it needed ongoing financing to cover the
imbalance between its exports and its imports. West Germany offered
help, but only if the East undertook radical reforms. (This may sound
familiar.) As Kohl said, "Assistance can only prove effective if fundamental reforms of the economic system follow." West German taxpayers
were not going to pay "to stabilize conditions that have become untenable." To get the money for needed imports, East Germany would have
to change.[5]

It did. The rapid liberalization of the political system led to East
Germany's first—and last—free elections on March 18, 1990. Thanks
to the active support of Kohl and the West German government, the
center-right Alliance for Germany won just under half the seats in parliament. Lothar de Maizière, the new prime minister of East Germany,
had campaigned on a program of rapid reunification. (He quit politics
by the end of the year after being accused of having informed for the
Stasi.) The PDS won barely a sixth of the popular vote, with the rest
going to other opposition parties. The Alliance for Germany, the Social
Democrats, and the Liberals formed a coalition of national unity and
immediately began formal negotiations with West Germany on the terms
of reunification and with the Allied powers to settle World War II claims.
On October 3, 1990, East Germany officially ceased to exist, and its con-
stituent states were admitted into an enlarged Federal Republic (West
Germany).[6]

The economic transition began even sooner. On June 17, 1990,
West Germany took over the recently established Treuhandanstalt, which

was charged with administering and eventually privatizing East Germany's roughly twelve thousand public enterprises. These collectively employed about four million people. The Bundesbank, West Germany's big commercial banks and industrial firms, and other Western European businesses were all represented on the supervisory board. Initially, the hope was that much of East Germany's industry would become financially sustainable with the help of Western managerial expertise. Profits from asset sales were supposed to be more than enough to pay for the Treuhandanstalt's operations and provide support to people who lost their jobs as enterprises were restructured. By the end of June, the two Germanys had eliminated all barriers to migration, trade, and investment between them.

On July 1, the Western deutschmark replaced the East German mark. While wages, pensions, and other contracts would be carried over from before, choosing the exchange rate between the two currencies proved contentious. Before the fall of the Berlin Wall, the black market exchange rate had been closer to 10:1, although economists believe that this reflected demand for specific Western consumer goods that were heavily taxed in the East more than anything else. The Bundesbank believed that an exchange rate of 2:1 would prevent undue inflation in West Germany and preserve East German industry. Kohl, however, felt that it was necessary for political reasons to convert Eastern marks into deutschmarks at a 1:1 rate for most purposes.

His decision was dictated partly by the desire to discourage migration from the East. Half a million Germans had already crossed the border since the fall of the wall, and more were still coming. These Easterners tended to be younger and more educated than the people they left behind, and their continued departure would cripple the East German economy. Setting the exchange rate too low could have exacerbated this trend. "If the deutschmark doesn't come to us, we go to it" had already become a popular slogan in East Germany.

Setting the exchange rate too high, however, could crush the East's economy and force an outflow of jobless Germans to look for work in the West. To staunch that potential flow, West Germany extended its social security and tax systems to the East. Among other reasons, the hope was that generous jobless benefits, early retirement, state pensions, health care, and other welfare payments paid by the federal government would obviate the desire to move west. These ultimately became the main instruments for transferring income to the new states of the Federal Republic. Subsequent debates about the sustainability of the social security system were implicitly about the willingness of West Germans to support displaced workers in the East.

The German economist Peter Bofinger presented a cogent defense of the 1:1 exchange rate at the time. East German workers were paid much less than their Western counterparts, and the Bundesbank's analysis justifying the 2:1 exchange rate had assumed that East German employers would not contribute to the federal social security system. After accounting for those payments, the gap in labor costs at the 1:1 exchange rate was close enough to the gap in worker productivity that any differences could be made up in "future wage negotiations." As Bofinger put it, "the real income of East Germans and the real income differential between East and West Germany will remain essentially unchanged immediately after the [German monetary union], with real net incomes in the East about 50 percent lower than in the West." Moreover, any other exchange rate "would have strongly increased the movement of workers from East to West Germany" because living standards in the East would have collapsed by more than half.[7]

The problem was what happened during those "future wage negotiations" after reunification. West Germany's labor unions wanted to prevent their employers from relocating factories to the East, so they pushed for aggressive wage hikes there, with the goal of parity between East and West by the mid-1990s. East Germans were willing to go along with this since they had no stake in the profitability of their enterprises and assumed that the West German executives put in charge through the Treuhandanstalt knew what they were doing. Those executives, meanwhile, were happy to accommodate the demands of Western labor unions at the expense of East German industry because it would buy them goodwill in their home market and because the government would ultimately bear any costs. By 1991, the result was that labor costs in East Germany—as measured by hourly pay divided by hourly output—had soared more than 50 percent above the level in West Germany.

Unreasonable wage hikes immediately after reunification had

doomed the East's industrial enterprises to a brutal restructuring. American economists at the time judged that "firms employing only 8 percent of the labor force were 'viable' after union, in the sense that they could earn sufficient revenue to cover short-run variable costs." East German manufacturing output accordingly collapsed by two-thirds between the end of 1989 and the beginning of 1991. By 1992, almost half of unified Germany's unemployed were in the newly absorbed Eastern states, despite accounting for less than 19 percent of the country's total population. Ironically, the job losses precipitated the westward migration the high-wage policy was meant to prevent: fully 6 percent of the East German population had moved to the West by 1994.[8]

This created problems for the Treuhandanstalt. Initial optimism about East Germany's assets quickly vanished as it became clear that most were worth only "their real-estate or scrap value." Instead of generating revenue, the privatization program ended up costing the government hundreds of billions of deutschmarks. West Germany was not interested in paying subsidies indefinitely, which pressured the agency to sell assets quickly, often at markdown prices. By 1995, almost all the companies owned by the Treuhandanstalt had been sold or parceled out to separate agencies, while the unrealized losses were officially absorbed by the federal government. About half of all workers in East Germany worked for businesses owned either by West Germans or foreigners. About 20 percent worked at companies founded after reunification. (Most of the rest had lost their jobs.)[9]

Many workers in the East became dependent on handouts or were forced to switch to low-paying jobs after their old employers were restructured. Some—disproportionately women—moved to the West, while those they left behind—disproportionately men without advanced schooling—became increasingly resentful at the lack of jobs and their inability to find marriage partners. At the same time, economists estimate that West German living standards ended up about 8 percent lower than they otherwise would have been by the early 2000s thanks to reunification.[10]

Despite these substantial costs, reunification has largely been a success. Thanks in part to ongoing transfers from the rest of the country, living standards in the former East Germany have almost completely converged to levels in the West, most notably in terms of life expectancy. The remaining gap in incomes between East and West Germany is trivial compared to the gaps between northern and southern Italy, northern and southern England, or the former Confederacy and the rest of the United States. Unemployment has plunged. Manufacturing output in the East has more than doubled since the early 1990s. Lower living costs have even attracted artists and others to migrate from the West to some cities in the East.[11]

The Sick Man of Europe

The costs of reunification, especially for the West, were not initially apparent. In fact, the initial reaction was a spending boom: the West German economy grew at an average annual rate of 5.7 percent from the beginning of 1989 through the start of 1991. Those gains, however, were short-lived. From the start of 1991 through the end of 1997, the unified German economy grew at an average yearly pace of just 1.3 percent. It was the worst sustained slowdown since the 1950s.

There were several reasons for this disappointing performance, but the most obvious was the government's austere policy stance. Thanks in part to the reunification boomlet, German inflation accelerated from about 1.5 percent per year in the mid-1980s to roughly 5 percent by the early 1990s. The Bundesbank responded by raising its discount rate from 2.5 percent at the end of 1987 to almost 9 percent by the middle of 1992— the highest level since the creation of the postwar central bank in 1948. Monetary tightening was soon followed by fiscal retrenchment. The German government scrupulously adhered to its Maastricht Treaty (1992) commitment to keep a lid on the budget deficit by cutting spending on infrastructure investment and maintenance by nearly 20 percent between 1992 and 1998.

This choked off inflation at the cost of throttling growth. High interest rates and tight budgets were particularly painful for the construction sector. After hitting its peak in 1994, building activity fell relentlessly for more than a decade. Overall investment spending in Germany was essentially flat from the early 1990s until 1997. The one relative bright spot was consumption spending, which grew almost 2 percent per year

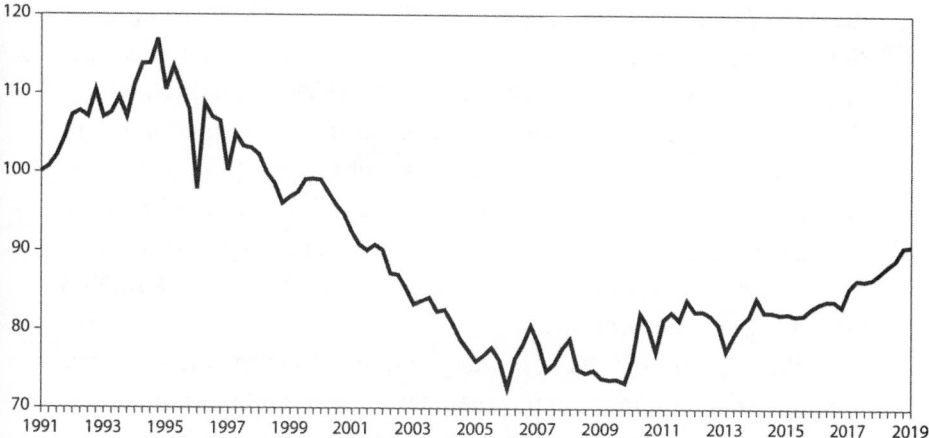

Fig. 5.1 The big bust (German construction activity, January 1991 = 100).
Sources: Deutsche Bundesbank; Matthew Klein's calculations

above inflation during this period. That, however, was possible thanks only to a large drop in the household saving rate.[12]

The downturn in domestic investment was exacerbated by the mixed blessing of the liberation of Eastern Europe. A hundred million new customers were welcome news for Germany's industrial enterprises, but their freedom also meant that there were now tens of millions of low-cost workers on Germany's doorstep. Many of them were also fluent in German. The typical German manufacturing worker earned about nine times as much as the typical Slovakian manufacturing worker in the year 2000. That yawning difference in labor costs was far bigger than the differences in worker productivity. German companies responded by moving jobs and production to Central and Eastern Europe. The tension became more acute once the European Union agreed to begin the accession process for Germany's Eastern neighbors (and Cyprus) at the end of 1997. Most would join by 2004, with Bulgaria and Romania joining in 2007. Once inside the European Union, they faced no barriers to trade or investment with the rest of the German manufacturing supply chain.[13]

Although the number of motor vehicles produced in Germany has barely grown in nearly three decades, German car companies now make more than twice as many cars as they did immediately after reunification. In 1992, German companies produced about 4.9 million passenger vehicles in Germany and roughly 2 million vehicles outside Germany. By 2000, German companies had increased their total production of passenger vehicles to 10 million vehicles, but essentially all of that increase came from plants in other countries. Production in Germany itself had barely grown to 5.1 million units. As of 2017, German companies produced about 16.5 million passenger vehicles, of which 10.8 million were made outside Germany.

While some of the extra production comes from the United States, Mexico, and China, much of it comes from Central and Eastern Europe. In 2017, plants in Czechia, Hungary, Poland, Romania, Slovakia, and Slovenia produced about 4.1 million passenger and commercial vehicles. These figures understate the scale of the outsourcing because they do not count the imported parts used to assemble finish vehicles. About half of the value of German motor vehicle output now comes from imported components.[14]

The threat of relocation gave German employers a powerful tool for holding down wages at home: if German unions pushed for higher pay, businesses would simply move jobs and factories a few hundred miles to the east. After subtracting inflation, the median wage of manufacturing workers in the former West Germany grew just 5 percent in total between 1991 and 2000. These developments meant that unions were less useful to German workers than in the past, and membership plunged by a third in the 1990s. At the same time, industrywide collective bargains were watered down with so-called opening clauses that gave local union representatives the option to negotiate bespoke deals at the company level. By the end of the 1990s, most of the remaining German union members were working under these looser contracts.

The unions' priority was to preserve jobs at the cost of forgoing pay raises. They failed: between 1993 and 1997, German manufacturing employment fell by 15 percent. Unemployment in the West rose steadily from roughly 5 percent in 1991 to nearly 10 percent by the end of 1997. Across Germany, three million full-time jobs vanished while only one million part-time jobs were added. At the same time, most workers saw their real wages fall throughout the 1990s before plummeting in the

2000s. This was particularly painful for German men, who were disproportionately employed full-time and accounted for most of the lost jobs.
Combined, the drop in employment, the shift to part-time work, and the
lack of wage growth meant that the real value of money spent on pay and
benefits for German workers was essentially flat between 1995 and 2011.[15]

It was around this time that German and international commentators began referring to the country as "the sick man of Europe." This
was not disappointing—it was terrifying. On April 26, 1997, Roman
Herzog, the distinguished German president, made an unusual speech
warning that Germany was in danger of being left behind in "a great,
global race." The end of the Cold War, the rapid modernization of Asia,
and new advanced technologies from the United States meant that "world
markets are being divided anew, and so are the prospects for prosperity
in the twenty-first century." The problem, according to Herzog, was that
Germans "ask too much of the government" because they subscribe to
"the myth that its resources are inexhaustible." Dependence on the state
had made Germans lazy, uncreative, and afraid of change.

The solution, in Herzog's view, was "a new social contract for the
future." This would require changes, he said, to "all the social entitlements that have accumulated over the years—and I do mean all of them."
To Herzog, deregulation on business, cuts to jobless benefits, lower
taxes, and lower wages were all necessary to ensure Germany's national
survival. As he put it, "The world is on the move; it will not wait for Germany." Herzog's speech was an indication of what was to come. The surprise was that the most left-wing government in the history of Federal
Republic would be the one to implement his program.[16]

Germany's 1998 federal elections took place at a propitious time
for the Social Democrats (SPD). Since 1982, Germany had been gov-
erned by the center-right coalition of the Christian Democratic Union
(CDU), Christian Social Union (CSU), and Free Democratic Party (FDP).
Helmut Kohl had served continuously as chancellor for sixteen years,
making him one of the longest-lasting leaders of a democracy in modern history. Only Otto von Bismarck spent more time as the chancellor
of Germany. The economic catastrophe of the 1990s, however, made
Kohl vulnerable to an attack from the left. The CDU/CSU-FDP coalition
had already suffered badly in the 1994 federal elections, which shredded

their commanding majority of 60 percent of the seats in the Bundestag to just over half.

By 1998, things were worse. Gerhard Schröder, the leader of the SPD, dubbed Kohl "the unemployment chancellor." The campaign worked: the SPD had its best performance since 1972. In combination with their Green Party allies, the center-left coalition won more than 51 percent of Bundestag seats. The center-right parties managed to get only 43 percent of the seats, with the rest going to the successors of the former East German communists (PDS).[17]

The election happened to occur shortly after the start of a brief revival in German domestic investment. Spending on machinery and equipment grew by 10 percent a year between 1997 and 2000, more than triple the growth rate in the preceding three years. The slow-motion decline of the construction industry temporarily stopped in 1998–2000. Net fixed investment by the private sector grew by 50 percent. Consumption spending accelerated thanks in part to another drop in the household saving rate. The combined effect was Germany's best stretch of domestic demand growth since reunification. After years of stagnation, two million jobs were added in Germany between the end of 1997 and the middle of 2000. Herzog's appeal for radical change seemed less relevant as the economy finally began to grow.[18]

Unfortunately, the late 1990s boom was driven by Germany's version of the tech bubble. The same mania that afflicted U.S. businesses was just as potent on the other side of the Atlantic. The Frankfurt-based Deutsche Börse launched its Neuer Markt in 1997 as Europe's answer to the Nasdaq. The new exchange would be the home for fashionable high-growth businesses. During the bubble, shares listed on the Neuer Markt outperformed the Nasdaq-100 Index by a factor of four. At its peak in March 2000, the companies listed on the Neuer Markt were worth nearly €234 billion—tiny by American standards but large relative to the size of the total German stock market.

The bubble burst shortly thereafter thanks to scandals (including insider trading, stock-price manipulation, and falsified earnings), fundamental overvaluation, and the turn in the business cycle. By 2002, companies listed on the Neuer Markt had collectively lost 95 percent of their value. Deutsche Börse announced that it would shut down the exchange that September.[19]

A borrowing binge had magnified the nonsense in the stock markets. Debt owed by German nonfinancial corporations rose by 25 percent between the start of 1997 and the end of 2001. The current account deficit of these companies ballooned from 2 percent of the German economy in 1998 to 7 percent by 2000. Unfortunately, no investment opportunities had justified that kind of excess. After the bubble burst, the bleak outlook for profits meant that banks and the financial markets were unwilling to keep financing the large difference between German business investment and German corporate cash flow. Companies were forced to repay their obligations. By the end of 2005, the face value of loans and bonds issued by German companies had shrunk nearly 4 percent. Debt did not surpass its previous level until 2007.[20]

This had real economic effects. When the bubble was inflating, German corporate investment boomed. After the bubble burst, investment collapsed. The long-running construction bust, which had paused during the tech boom, resumed with a vengeance in the 2000s: building activity plunged by 23 percent between the middle of 2000 and the trough in 2006. Overall capital expenditures fell by 12 percent between the middle of 2000 and the trough in 2005. Business investment net of depreciation fell by more than 60 percent. Two million full-time jobs vanished, and the number of hours worked fell by 5 percent. Overall employment held relatively steady only because of a massive shift from full- to part-time work.

At the same time, average hourly pay and benefits grew by less than inflation. The result was a sustained reduction in real household income. Unlike in the 1990s, this was not offset by a decline in the personal saving rate. In fact, the German household saving rate rose by more than a percentage point, with the result that consumption did not grow at all between 2001 and 2005.[21]

In prior recessions, the German government could have offset the collapse in business investment and household spending by lowering interest rates, cutting taxes, and boosting public spending. It could not do so in the 2000s because of its membership in the euro area. The common currency, which officially launched on January 1, 1999, meant that member states shared a single monetary policy. The new European Central Bank (ECB) had to set interest rates based on what made sense for the euro area as a whole, rather than what was best for any individual country. While Germany was the largest single member of the currency bloc, its sluggishness stood in contrast to booming conditions elsewhere, most obviously Spain.

Monetary policy appropriate for the average European country was therefore far too tight for Germany (and far too loose for Spain). Real interest rates in Germany during the downturn of 2001–4 were just as high as they were during the brief boom of 1998–2000. Schröder repeatedly called for lower interest rates, but his requests went unheeded. When asked about the pressure for looser policy at a press conference in April 2001, Wim Duisenberg, the ECB president, quipped: "I hear, but I do not listen."[22]

At the same time, the budget limits agreed in the Maastricht Treaty (1992) and the subsequent Stability and Growth Pact (1997) meant that the government had limited space to borrow to boost spending. Germany's federal, state, and local governments had been collectively tightening their budgets relative to economic conditions ever since 2001, but these efforts were not enough to keep the deficit within the prescribed limit. The government was further constrained by the legacy of high interest rates on the debt incurred in the early 1990s to pay for reunification. The interaction of those old debts with Europe's fiscal rules effectively prevented the German government from borrowing more to deal with the severe downturn of the early 2000s. Ironically, it was German negotiators who had demanded those rigid rules years earlier.[23]

Germany's trade and current account surplus has its origin in this long period of domestic weakness. Real domestic demand fell about 3 percent from the peak at the end of 2000 to the trough in 2004. Total spending on consumption and investment did not return to its previous level until the end of 2006. Slow growth relative to the rest of the world meant that foreign spending on German exports rose by more than German spending on imports.

The result was a massive shift in the current account balance. Throughout the 1990s, German residents spent slightly more than they

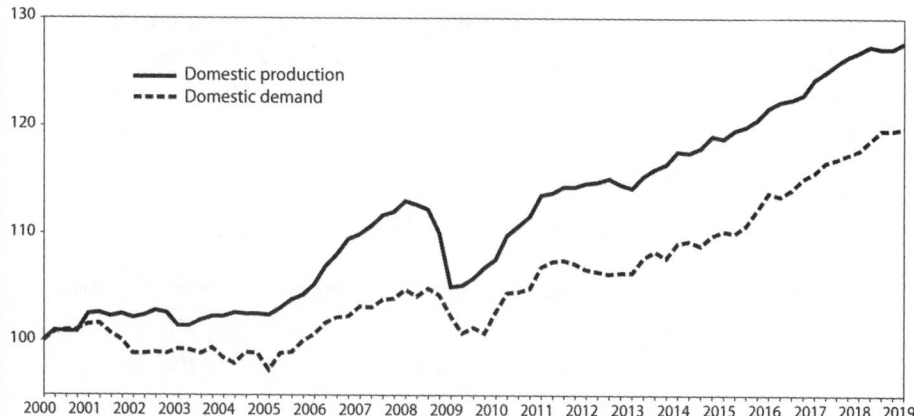

Fig. 5.2 Germany's surplus is a product of its internal weakness (domestic production versus domestic spending on consumption and investment, January 2000 = 100). *Sources: Eurostat; Matthew Klein's calculations*

earned: household surpluses worth roughly 4 percent of GDP were off-set by corporate and government deficits each worth about 2.5 percent of GDP. By 2004, Germany's current account balance had swung into a surplus worth about 5 percent of GDP thanks to the combination of the corporate sector's substantial cuts to wages and capital investment, a modest increase in the household saving rate, and excessively tight fiscal policy.

Export competitiveness had little to do with Germany's surplus: Germany's share of world exports was the same in 2004 as in 1998, and Germany's share of intra-European trade rose by less than one percent-age point in the 2000s. Czechia, the Netherlands, and Poland all boosted their share of the European market by comparable amounts despite being far smaller economies. Moreover, the real value of German exports grew far more slowly in this period than when Germany had a current ac-count deficit. From 1994 through 2000, German goods export volumes grew about 9 percent each year on average. From 2001 through 2004, goods exports grew just 4 percent each year.

The trade surplus can be explained by an even greater slowdown in the growth rate of the volume of German goods imports. Germans spent fewer euros on imported goods and services in 2004 than in 2000 de-

spite the impact of inflation and rising oil prices. Surpluses and net financial outflows were the inevitable results. The surpluses of the early 2000s
persisted after Germany began to recover because of policy choices that
constrained domestic spending and redistributed income to the rich.[24]

Agenda 2010 and the Hartz Reforms

Back in 1998, Schröder had said that he would not deserve a second
term if there were still more than 3.5 million unemployed Germans by
the time of the next general election in 2002. In the spirit of the time, his
government's signature economic policy had been a sweeping program
of tax cuts with the hope of encouraging additional work and investment. The top personal income tax rate fell from 53 percent to 42 percent, and the average effective corporate profit tax rate dropped from
about 52 percent to about 39 percent. Perhaps most significant was the
elimination of the capital gains tax on shares of companies held by other
companies for at least a year. (Corporate divestments had previously
been taxed at 53 percent.) While middle-class Germans also saw their
taxes fall, these measures mainly benefited the rich.

Worse, they were insufficient to improve the attractiveness of Germany as an investment destination or to stimulate domestic spending.
By the end of 2001 there were more than 3.8 million unemployed—and
their ranks were rising. The bursting of the tech bubble, tight policy from
the ECB, and stringent budget rules were the obvious explanations, but
the Red-Green coalition was in no position to do anything about them.
Something else would have to be done to get the jobless numbers down
before the next federal elections in 2002.[25]

A scandal at the federal agency charged with placing the unemployed into jobs provided the pretext for Schröder, in February 2002, to
appoint a commission of experts to come up with suggestions for policies to boost employment. Peter Hartz—Volkswagen's longtime head of
human resources and an old friend of Schröder's—was picked to lead
the commission. Thanks to his previous job as minister president of the
state of Lower Saxony, Schröder had been on the board of Volkswagen
in 1993 when Hartz had successfully negotiated with the IG Metall labor

union to preserve thirty thousand jobs in exchange for shortening the workweek from five days to four. That trade—more employment for less pay—had been commonplace throughout the 1990s. It would become institutionalized in what would eventually become known as the Hartz Reforms.

The Hartz Commission delivered its report in August 2002. It was filled with recommendations for making the existing system of benefits more efficient, such as combining welfare payments to the indigent with unemployment insurance, and for improving the government's job placement service. The commission also recommended reducing regulations on the kinds of jobs people could take, including temporary work and freelancing contracts. Most significant, however, was the report's attack on the German welfare state in a manner that Roman Herzog would have found familiar. Hartz and his colleagues argued that many Germans chose to remain unemployed—or retire early—because the payments they received from the government were better than what they could get working one of the many available (low-paid) jobs. Hartz's proposed solution was to both cut the level of benefits and shorten the length of time they lasted. The unemployment rate would fall because the jobless would be forced to work. The dramatic expansion of the welfare state to the East after reunification had been too expensive and would soon be reversed.[26]

On September 22, shortly after the report came out, Germany experienced its closest federal election in modern history. Several newspapers incorrectly reported the CDU/CSU as the winners before the final margin had been calculated the next morning. Broad dissatisfaction with the economy had been offset by Schröder's personal charisma, his effective response to the devastating five-hundred-year floods that hit eastern Germany over the summer, and the Red-Green government's firm opposition to the unpopular Iraq War.

Moreover, the center-right bloc was not a viable alternative for opponents of the Hartz program. The SPD lost votes in the West, including to its Green coalition partners, but gained ground in the East at the expense of the PDS. Thanks to Germany's hybrid system of direct elections and proportional representation, the Red-Green government was returned to office with a razor-thin majority in the Bundestag while the center-right bloc boosted its share of seats by six percentage points. (The PDS lost all but two of their parliamentarians.)[27]

Despite the shrunken mandate, Schröder felt he had to go forward with his reform program, which he called "Agenda 2010." He made his case in a speech to the Bundestag on March 14, 2003. Delivered on the eve of the Iraq War, the speech linked the need for domestic reform with the urgency of preventing conflict in the Middle East. To maintain an independent foreign policy, Schröder insisted, Germany needed to "become increasingly flexible" and "undergo internal transformation." Although he occasionally sounded like a traditional social democrat in his criticism of "the law of the jungle" and "market forces that pay no respect to social aspects," his program and rhetoric were almost identical to what Roman Herzog had called for six years earlier. The welfare state needed "restructuring." "Individual responsibility" would trump collective provision, and "nobody will be allowed to live off the community." "Modernization" was essential.

Agenda 2010 had many parts, including significant changes to the health care system and the introduction of new kinds of labor contracts, but the most significant was the idea that social benefits should be cut so that tax burdens could be lowered. As Schröder said to his colleagues, the cost of paying these benefits is "already today overburdening the younger generation" while "the people working in factories and offices expect us to reduce the burden of taxes and levies." Under what became known as Hartz IV, unemployment insurance would stop after twelve months for Germans under the age of fifty-five. (Previously it had lasted for thirty-two months.) Meanwhile, Germans who rejected a job offer for paying too little would lose their welfare. Retirement ages would rise.[28]

This was deeply unpopular. Almost immediately after his speech in March, the SPD faced an internal revolt led by none other than a young Andrea Nahles, who would become party leader in 2018. Mass protests began in the summer of 2004 after the legislation passed Germany's upper house but were insufficient to prevent the new law from kicking in on January 1, 2005. Despite vocal opposition from the affected minority, most Germans supported the changes. The problem for the Red-Green coalition was that this majority naturally affiliated with the center right.

By contrast, East Germans who had flocked to the SPD in 2002 felt they had been betrayed. Sky-high unemployment rates made them worried that they would face the brunt of the cuts. The SPD base in the old West German industrial heartland also rebelled. Hartz IV meant that the loss of a job would almost immediately lead to a sharp cut in income, which frightened Germans with decent jobs in cyclical industries. Oskar Lafontaine, who had been Schröder's finance minister in 1998, quit the SPD to run as the leader of a new western German left-wing party (WASG) in an alliance with the eastern PDS.[29]

On May 22, 2005, the SPD lost its grip on the state government of North Rhine–Westphalia, which it had ruled continuously since 1966. Losing the state's votes in Germany's upper house meant that the Red-Green coalition would have a difficult time passing meaningful legislation before the next scheduled federal election at the end of 2006. Schröder responded by engineering an early general election for September 2005. The SPD attempted to rally its base by calling for a new surtax on high-income Germans and what would have been Germany's first minimum wage. The WASG/PDS alliance, also known as Die Linke (The Left), vowed to raise inheritance taxes, boost welfare spending, and repeal Hartz IV, which they called "legally decreed poverty." Meanwhile, in one of history's little ironies, Peter Hartz was forced to leave Volkswagen in disgrace after lurid sex and bribery scandals became public in July.[30]

Both the center-left and center-right blocs lost votes to Die Linke, which won 9 percent of Bundestag seats. Nearly a quarter of voters in the former East Germany supported Die Linke in 2005, up from roughly 15 percent in 2002. Even more striking, Die Linke won 5 percent of voters in the former West Germany (excluding Berlin). In 2002, just 1 percent of westerners had voted for PDS. Thanks in part to the popularity of local hero Lafontaine, Die Linke pulled in more than 18 percent of the vote in Saarland, which had once been the center of Germany's coal and steel industry before those industries had moved abroad. In 2002, PDS had won less than 2 percent of the vote in Saarland. Even in the prosperous and conservative southern states of Baden-Württemberg and Bavaria, Die Linke won more than 3 percent of the vote.

The hard left's strong showing created a political impasse. Neither the Red-Green coalition nor the center-right bloc could command and a majority in the Bundestag. In theory, Die Linke could have joined a new Red-Red-Green coalition that could have taken credit for the subsequent recovery, but there was too much animosity on both sides to make that work. Schröder would have to go. The question was who would replace him as chancellor. At first, the center right tried to convince the Greens to join them in a larger grouping, which would have relegated the SPD to the opposition alongside Die Linke.

After a few years, Germany's leftists might have gotten over their differences. The Greens, however, were not interested in joining a center-right government. The only remaining option (besides new elections, which nobody wanted) was a grand coalition between the CDU/CSU and the SPD. Even though the left-wing parties had won the most votes and the most Bundestag seats, the result was a government led by Chancellor Angela Merkel of the CDU. While they did not embark on further cuts to the German benefits system, the grand coalition ensured the survival of Agenda 2010 and Hartz IV.[31]

The impact of Hartz IV itself is often overstated. Germany's meager wage growth and underinvestment were consequences not of welfare cuts, but of choices made in the 1990s by German elites. Some Germans who had previously received welfare outside of the traditional social security system benefited from the changes. Nevertheless, the policies of the Red-Green coalition reinforced the weakness in Germany's domestic spending and the concomitant rise in the country's current account surplus. According to economist Christian Odendahl, Hartz IV "moved the system from one that protected living standards indefinitely to temporary protection of living standards followed by much lower income with strict conditions attached."[32]

The most straightforward effect of the law has been a steady rise in the poverty rate, particularly for Germans who have jobs. In 2005, when the data begin, only 5 percent of German workers were at risk of poverty. By 2015 that proportion had doubled to 10 percent. This was driven by a shift to low-paying part-time work. Since the mid-1990s, more than all the net increase in German employment has come from self-employed and part-time workers. Full-time employment fell for a decade and remains lower than it was in 1995. Nearly 30 percent of all jobs in Germany

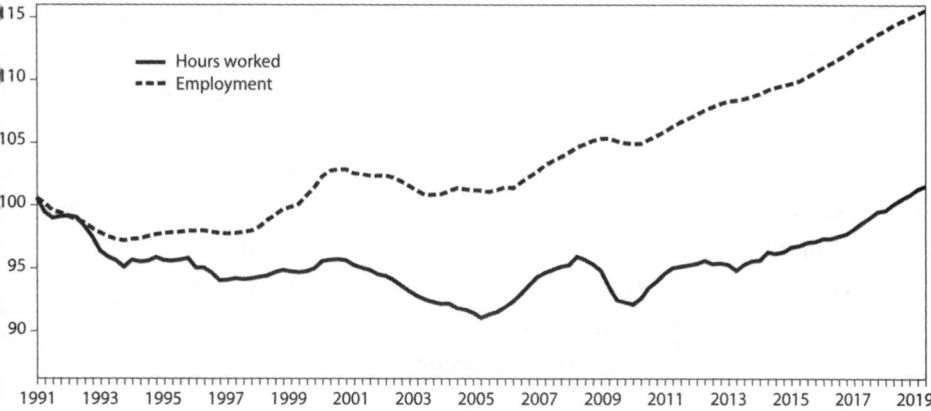

Fig. 5.3 Germany's employment "miracle" (people working versus hours worked, January 1991 = 100). *Sources: Destatis; Matthew Klein's calculations*

today are part-time, roughly double the proportion in the early 1990s. Most of those additional workers would otherwise have taken early retirement. In the 1990s, fewer than 40 percent of Germans aged fifty-five to sixty-four had jobs. That proportion steadily rose after 2003 and is now above 70 percent.

When forced, Germans were able to find work. But the jobs paid so badly that workers were often worse off than when they were on the dole. The share of Germans claiming they could not meet an unexpected expense jumped from 25 percent in 2005 to 41 percent just one year later, once Hartz IV had come into effect. As of 2017, more than 30 percent of Germans felt incapable of meeting an unexpected expense. On the eve of the 2008 financial crisis, the share of Germans experiencing "severe material deprivation" was significantly higher than the share in Austria, France, the Netherlands, and Spain. Employment increased, but well-being did not.[33]

Marcel Fratzscher, the president of the German Institute for Economic Research, believes that the impact of Agenda 2010 was bigger than any specific policy. Instead, it was a psychological "turning point for the German economy and society . . . reflected in the actions of employers, employer associations, and labor unions." From this perspective, the most important moment in Schröder's March 14 speech was when he warned unions against "dogmatic inflexibility" and "self-righteousness" in their labor contracts.[34]

This exhortation was not accompanied by any legislation, but workers and bosses took the hint. In the 1990s, modest wage increases were paid to fewer and fewer workers. In the 2000s, German companies increased employment because workers accepted real wage cuts. Hourly pay and benefits fell nearly 5 percent between 2001 and 2007 after subtracting the impact of inflation. After accounting for the impact of taxes, social benefits, and inflation, the average German household's income was slightly lower by 2013 than it had been in 1999.[35]

Verteilungskampf (the Distribution Struggle) and Germany's Excess Saving

Rich Germans had a better experience between reunification and the global financial crisis. This was a consequence of choices by businesses and the government that cumulatively had the effect of redistributing purchasing power from those most likely to spend it on goods and services to those most likely to accumulate financial assets.

First, the German elite's relentless focus on international competitiveness enabled a massive shift in the balance between workers and the owners of capital. In the mid-1990s, about 25 percent of the net value added by nonfinancial businesses went to shareholders, creditors, and property owners while the rest went to workers. The proportions began to shift in the late 1990s. By 2007, the capital share had increased to 36 percent. The labor share had commensurately declined by about 12 percentage points. That same year, a study by the Bundesbank drily noted that "the industrial sector, which is, on the whole, subject to especially powerful international competitive pressure, has seen its returns on fixed assets increase noticeably since the mid-1990s." About two-thirds of the total increase in Germany's national income between 2000 and 2007 came from the rapid growth of capital income, rather than from rising employee compensation.

According to the Bundesbank, two factors were especially important. First, "wage moderation and the reduction in non-core payments readjusted the remuneration structure of labor." Second, companies had

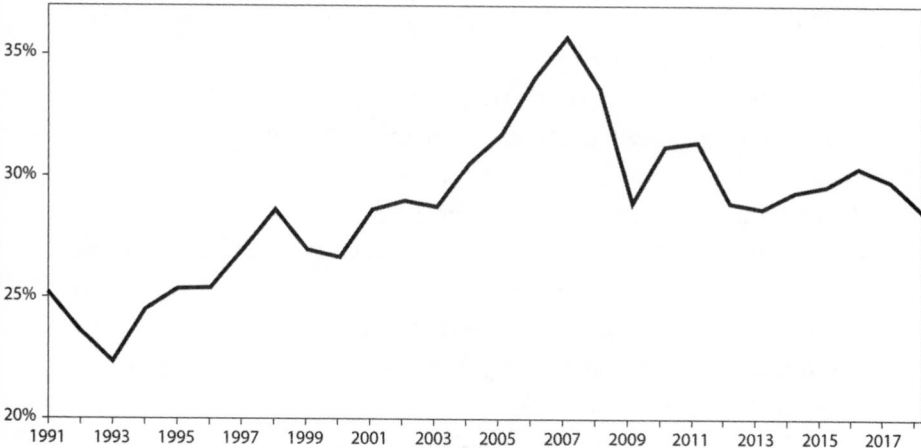

Fig. 5.4 Germany's class war (net operating surplus of German nonfinancial corporations as a share of net value added). *Sources: Destatis; Matthew Klein's calculations*

shifted "production activities requiring a low-skilled workforce to foreign countries with a more favorable (wage) cost structure." In other words, German companies had boosted their profitability at the expense of German employees by slashing pay and capital investment at home, by outsourcing work to low-paid contractors, and by moving operations abroad.

Since workers are also customers, economywide wage cuts usually fail to increase profits. Germany companies got away with it because they could avoid Germany's moribund domestic market by selling to foreigners. From 1991 to 1999, the German corporate sector had an average current account deficit worth about 2 percent of GDP. Corporations needed external finance to cover the difference between their investment needs and their cash flow from operations. Since the early 2000s, however, German businesses have been perennial savers and consistently generate a surplus worth more than 2 percent of GDP. The combination of sustained income from exports and lower domestic spending mechanically led to a higher national saving rate and a higher current account surplus.[36]

In theory, the shift from labor income to capital income would have made little difference to people who both work and own assets. In practice, however, wealth—and therefore capital income—in Germany is extremely concentrated. On average, Germans are richer than almost anyone else in Europe. The average German is about 50 percent richer than the average Italian and twice as wealthy as the average Spaniard. The distribution of wealth is so unequal in Germany, however, that the median German household is far poorer than the median Spanish household and only about as wealthy as the median Greek or Polish household. According to a comprehensive survey by the European Central Bank, Germans on lower incomes have less net wealth, in absolute terms, than low-income Estonians and Hungarians. Many Germans either have no assets at all or owe debts greater than the assets they do own.

The skewed distribution of wealth is exacerbated by the types of assets held by the richest Germans. Only 10 percent of German households directly own shares in listed companies, and only 13 percent own mutual funds. (There is likely significant overlap in those two groups.) Most important, 90 percent of all businesses in Germany—accounting for more than half of all corporate cash flow—are family-owned businesses held by just 10 percent of German households. These businesses are passed from generation to generation because they are mostly exempt from inheritance tax as long as jobs are preserved for seven years after the handover.[37]

The perverse result is that the effective tax rate on German inheritances of more than €10 million is about 1 percent, while the effective tax rate for inheritances of €100,000 to €200,000 is roughly 14 percent. A legal change in 2016 modestly tweaked the exemptions, but the basic inequity remains.

Wealth inequality was always high in Germany but became more extreme starting in the mid-1990s. To some extent this was a natural consequence of increasing income inequality, since wealth is accumulated out of income. Policy choices also played a role, however. Prussia began taxing net wealth in the 1890s, and Germany as a whole started doing so in the 1920s. In 1995, however, Germany's constitutional court outlawed the practice. The tax was officially abolished in 1997. Aside from the immediate impact of increasing the wealth of the few Germans who had been exposed to the tax, the change also raised the effective rate of return on saving. That encouraged the highest-income Germans to spend less so that they could accumulate more. According to one estimate, the impact of the tax change raised Germany's household saving rate by several percentage points relative to what it otherwise might have been.

The constitutional court ruling was based on the reasonable concern that the net wealth tax was unfair because it treated residential property differently from other types of assets. Here too, policy favors the wealthy minority. Unlike many other countries, Germany's property taxes are not based on market values. Instead, they are based on assessments dating back to either 1964 (in the former West Germany) or 1935 (in the former East Germany). The result is that German property tax payments are far lower than in other countries, such as the United States.

This is regressive, because only 44 percent of German households own their main residence. That is one of the lowest shares in the rich world. Moreover, German homeowners are far richer than the majority of Germans who rent. According to the Bundesbank, the median homeowner with a mortgage has more than fourteen times as much net wealth as the median renter. Most German homeowners do so without a mortgage, however. The median net wealth of these households is more than twenty-six times as high as that of the median renter. Part of the explanation is that a third of all German homeowners own multiple residential properties that they rent out to others. Homeowners are also far more likely to own one of Germany's many family businesses. A recent study found that, unlike in other countries, rising rents in Germany systematically transfer income from people on low incomes to people with high incomes.[38]

Inequality also increased among workers. Some of this was due to the ongoing weakening of unions. Union membership, which had dropped by a third from 1991 to 2000, fell by another 25 percent from 2000 to 2010. This has gone hand in hand with a collapse in the share of German workers covered by collective bargaining: whereas more than 80 percent of German workers had been covered by collective bargaining in the mid-1990s, fewer than 45 percent of German workers are covered by a collective bargaining agreement today. Economists estimate that "Germany's wages in 2008 would have been higher if union coverage had remained the same as in 1995 throughout the entire wage distribu-

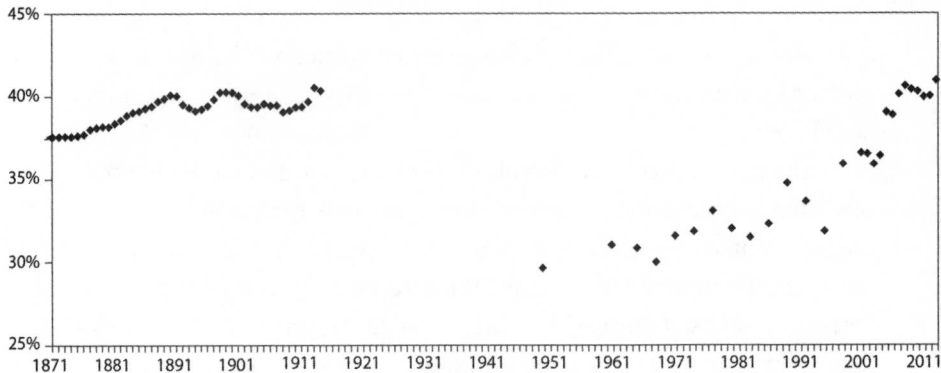

Fig. 5.5 *Verteilungskampf* (share of German national income going to the top
10 percent). *Source: Charlotte Bartels via the World Inequality Database*

tion, but the difference is particularly large at the lower end of the wage
distribution."

Inequality even rose within the ranks of the unionized thanks to
the replacement of sectorwide collective bargaining with bespoke agreements negotiated by individual "works councils." Real wages in the upper
portion of the distribution grew while incomes for workers in the bottom
half fell. The combined result, according to one study, is that "income
concentration at the top decile in Germany today is even greater than it
was during the industrialization period of 1871–1913."[39]

This concentration of income was substantial enough to depress
German household spending. The Bundesbank estimated in 2007 that
more than a quarter of the total increase in the personal saving rate
since 2000 could be explained just by changes in the income distribution. As the bank put it, "The distribution of income has shifted in favor
of sections of the population that tend to save more." Poor Germans, like
poor people everywhere, save none of their income because they need
every euro to sustain their modest living standards. Rich Germans, like
rich people elsewhere, have much higher saving rates, with some saving
more than 40 percent of their income. The shift noted by the Bundesbank was attributable mainly to changes in market wages but was exacerbated by the Red-Green government's policies of lower taxes and lower
welfare spending.

The Bundesbank identified two other explanations for the "exceptional" and "very unusual" weakness in real household consumption since 2000, both of which can be traced to the preferences of Germany's business elites. First, workers' income stagnation since the 1990s—itself a consequence of the "decisive countermeasures" taken by German companies in response to "competition from emerging economies and transition countries"—reasonably convinced regular Germans that they would need to save more today to guarantee their living standards in the future. Second, the saving rate rose as "households have become more acutely aware of the strains on the public social security systems." Germans were compensating for the prospect of cuts to their government pension benefits. What the Bundesbank euphemistically referred to as "permanent corrections to current pension entitlements" would be economically equivalent to a large reduction in the typical household's net worth. The rational response to this "(anticipated) wealth loss" was to save more "at the expense of current consumption."[40]

How Germany's Domestic Weakness
Contributed to the Euro Crisis

Germany's transformation would not have been possible without the trade and financial links connecting the country to the rest of the world. Had Germany been a closed economy, its moribund business investment, tight government budgets, and falling wages would have forced down domestic spending and limited the rise in corporate profits. Production and income would not have grown faster than spending. That was Keynes's insight with the "paradox of thrift." National saving would have been unchanged, there would have been no trade surplus, and there would have been no impact on other countries.

Germany, however, was not a closed economy. More than a quarter of the value generated by German workers and capital was sent abroad before 2008, mostly to Germany's European neighbors. German businesses were able to avoid the stagnation in their home market by selling to customers in other countries. Profits rose dramatically as costs (wages) held steady and export revenues rose in line with global growth. German underspending generated surplus income that was used to accumulate foreign financial assets, which in turn supported foreign demand for German exports and boosted corporate profitability. Germany's increasingly unequal distribution of income effectively transferred purchasing power from German workers to consumers in the rest of the world. The July 2019 Country Report on Germany published by the IMF's European Department found an almost perfect relation between changes in the current account balance and changes in the share of income going to the wealthiest households.[41]

This process depended on the willingness of others to absorb German financial outflows by spending far more than they earned and borrowing the difference. Deficits elsewhere were the necessary counterpart to Germany's surplus. Before the financial crisis, this meant that rich Germans and the companies they controlled would finance spending by their European neighbors by accumulating trillions of euros of foreign financial assets.

From the beginning of 2002 until the start of the crisis at the end of 2008, German residents collectively spent about €702 billion less than they earned. This cumulative current account surplus was matched by an equivalent net financial account outflow. Over that period, German residents bought a bit more than €2.7 trillion assets abroad while foreigners bought just €2.0 trillion worth of German assets. Direct investment in companies and factories accounted for just 15 percent of these total cross-border flows and only 22 percent of Germany's overall surplus.

Germany's precrisis current account surplus—and the corresponding deficit in the rest of the world—was recycled abroad by Germany's banks. Of the country's cumulative €2.7 trillion in financial outflows, a little more than €1.6 trillion can be attributed to banks in Germany buying bonds and making loans abroad. Those banks raised just under €900 billion from foreigners between January 2002 and September 2008, for a net outflow from German savers of €739 billion. In other words, the banks alone were responsible for more than 100 percent of the net financial outflows from Germany. Massive lending abroad was the only way the banks could reconcile weak German demand for credit and heightened German saving.

While German households and businesses also bought foreign assets, they raised enough money from foreigners to limit the total net financial outflow to just €400 billion over the same period. Of that surplus, just €150 billion can be explained by German nonfinancial companies investing in productive capacity outside Germany. The German government, meanwhile, sold some of its foreign assets and borrowed about €370 billion by selling bonds to savers in the rest of the world. Those inflows more than offset the net outflows from the domestic private sector.[42]

German bank credit often traveled abroad through local banks in other countries rather than through loans made directly to foreign borrowers. At the start of 2002, German banks had about €490 billion in loans outstanding to foreign nonbanks and about €500 billion in loans to foreign banks. At the peak in October 2008, credit to the foreign nonfinancial sector had grown to €860 billion (an increase of about €370 billion), while credit to banks outside Germany had ballooned to more than €1.3 trillion (for an increase of roughly €850 billion). Total lending to foreigners had more than doubled in less than six years, with 70 percent of that growth consisting of loans made to foreign banks.

Germany's big internationally focused banks such as Deutsche, Dresdner, and Commerzbank were not the main contributors to this bubble: the big banks accounted for just 31 percent of the total growth in German bank lending abroad between the start of 2002 and October 2008. Germany's state-owned Landesbanken played a much larger role, especially after they lost access to government guarantees on their debt in 2005. Those subsidies had suppressed their funding costs and made it worthwhile for them to lend to Germany's small and medium-sized family-owned industrial companies. Without state support, however, loans to safe borrowers at low interest rates were no longer worth the trouble. Despite being woefully unprepared to invest outside their home markets, the Landesbanken therefore decided to search for opportunities abroad. Between January 2005 and October 2008, fully 46 percent of the total growth in German bank lending to foreigners can be explained by the engorgement of the Landesbanken.[43]

Although German banks were major participants in America's mortgage boom, that activity was funded mostly by dollars sourced from the United States rather than by German savers. It did not show up as a net flow in the balance of payments. By contrast, Germans directly financed the current account deficits of their European neighbors through their banks. Essentially all the growth in German banks' net foreign lending was denominated in euros, most of which can be explained by a boom in German bank lending to just three countries: Ireland, Italy, and Spain. German banks were far from alone in this—the Dutch, French, and Swiss were also significant—but German banks were consistently the largest lenders to what would become Europe's crisis countries, especially Spain.[44]

The counterparts to these lending booms were borrowing booms elsewhere, especially in countries with faster inflation where interest rates were nonetheless converging to German levels. Spanish banks, for example, went from owing about €300 billion to the rest of the world in 2002 to owing about €800 billion by the middle of 2008. Other Spanish businesses and Spanish households also racked up foreign debts. These Spaniards went from owing about €160 billion to the rest of the world at the start of 2002 to owing €650 billion by the middle of 2008. In the span of six years, more than €1 trillion flowed into Spanish private-sector credit from the rest of the world, which in practice mostly meant from other members of the euro area. (The Spanish government's debts to foreigners did not rise during the boom and fell dramatically relative to Spanish GDP.)

This foreign borrowing was not matched by any comparable acquisition of claims on the rest of the world: Spanish residents managed to accumulate only €380 billion of liquid foreign assets from the start of 2002 through the middle of 2008. The result was that Spaniards' net obligations to the rest of the world ballooned from roughly €250 billion in 2002 to about €900 billion by the eve of the crisis.[45]

These debts financed spending by Spaniards far in excess of Spanish incomes. Spanish consumption and investment together grew about 30 percent more than Spanish output between the start of 2001 and the end of 2007. The growing difference between Spain's domestic demand and its domestic production had to be covered by imports, which caused Spain's trade deficit to widen from roughly 2 percent of GDP to 6 percent. Competitiveness was not the issue: Spanish export volumes grew at a respectable pace in lockstep with Spanish GDP throughout the 2000s, and Spain's share of intra-European trade held steady throughout the period. The problem was that Spanish import volumes grew more than twice as much.[46]

Spain was far from unique. In Italy, gross external debt almost doubled from €1 trillion to €1.9 trillion. In Portugal, external debt doubled from roughly €160 billion to €340 billion. In Greece, debts to foreigners more than tripled from about €100 billion in 2001 to about €330 billion by the middle of 2008. The most extreme case was Ireland. Irish residents, particularly Ireland's absurdly oversized banks, quadrupled their debts to foreigners from roughly €450 billion to €1.8 trillion. External debt also quadrupled in Slovenia and more than quadrupled in the Baltic countries over the same period, albeit from much smaller starting points. Added together, the euro area's crisis countries took out almost €4 trillion in additional foreign debt between 2001 and 2008. Over that same period, their collective current account balance went from a deficit of less than 2 percent of GDP to a deficit of more than 7 percent.[47]

Rarely, if ever, has any society been able to borrow so much in such a short time and use the money productively. While the debt binge funded some worthwhile projects, such as Spain's high-speed rail network and Greece's improvements to the Athenian subway system, much of the debt was wasted on boondoggles such as Spain's aptly named Don Quijote Airport, which opened in 2009 and had been built to accommodate ten million passengers per year despite being more than two hours from Madrid—or any other desirable Spanish destination. The Irish countryside was blighted by golf courses that were quickly abandoned.[48]

The surge in imports and the binge of wasteful investments were the almost inevitable consequences of the financial inflows coming into the crisis countries from the surplus countries, particularly Germany. The spending booms had nothing to do with cultural traits, the weather, or differences between Catholics and Protestants. As Germany's own experience in the 1870s demonstrates, windfalls of cheap money produce the same responses everywhere. Soaring real estate valuations and rising stock prices made people feel richer and encouraged them to spend more out of current income. At the same time, banks flush with funding from abroad needed to increase their lending—and did so by lowering standards. Some governments, such as in Greece, also took advantage of the opportunity to borrow cheaply, but this was incidental to the larger private debt booms. German residents were not solely to blame for the choices that drove Europe's precrisis imbalances, but German under-consumption and underinvestment were the most important underlying factors.

Given their membership in the euro area, the crisis countries could not raise interest rates during the boom. They also could not manage the subsequent downturns through currency depreciation and central bank bond-buying. Lacking the standard tools for managing business cycles put them in a precarious situation. Some think that Spain and the others could have mitigated the impact of the crisis by raising taxes and cutting government spending before 2008. From this perspective, fiscal surpluses would have offset private deficits to generate an overall current account balance and offset the changes in private behavior. Even if that could work without simply encouraging additional household and corporate borrowing, the economists Philippe Martin and Thomas Philippon estimated such a strategy "requires a reduction in [government] debt which we think is unrealistic."[49]

Since 2008, German banks have retrenched, cutting nearly €800 billion in their portfolio of foreign loans. More than half of this decline can be attributed to the Landesbanken, which have cut their lending to foreigners to just €274 billion—the same level as in 2001. This did not affect Germany's surplus for three reasons. First, about €600 billion of Germany's banking assets were effectively shifted to the public sector's balance sheet through the European Central Bank's Target2 system and through loans made by the German government to borrowers in the rest of the currency bloc.

Second, German households and nonbank businesses switched from using banks to invest abroad to using bond funds, life insurers, and pensions. Their underlying saving and spending patterns did not change. Finally, savers in the rest of the world stopped buying German assets. The German government and Bundesbank bought back nearly €350 billion in debt from foreign savers while issuing almost no new supply to domestic savers, while German banks shrank their foreign liabilities more than €520 billion.[50]

The consensus German view was that the crisis had been caused by the profligacy of borrowers in neighboring countries. The recklessness

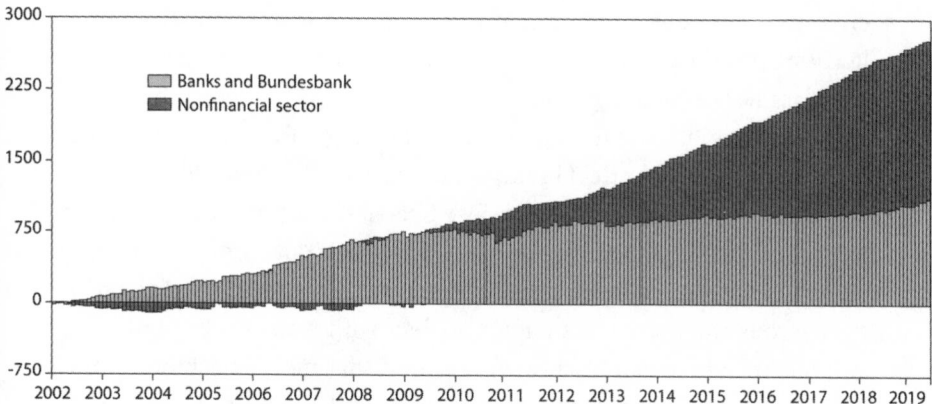

Fig. 5.6 How Germans invest abroad (cumulative net financial outflows by sector, EUR billions). *Sources: Deutsche Bundesbank; Matthew Klein's calculations*

of German lenders was not considered significant, nor were the structural inequities of the German economy that ultimately produced its excess savings and necessarily forced dissaving elsewhere. This blinkered perspective naturally led the German establishment to recommend that its neighbors become more like Germany. The government's approach has been characterized by what the German newsmagazine *Der Spiegel* calls "pedagogical imperialism." The rest of Europe was supposed to follow Germany's example as defined by the Hartz IV welfare cuts and, most significantly, its newfound constitutional commitment to fiscal restraint.[51]

The *Schuldenbremse:* Germany's Fiscal Straitjacket

From 1969 through 2010, Article 115 of Germany's Basic Law had said that the government's borrowing should be limited by its investment spending, although there were allowances for additional borrowing in the event of economic "disturbances." On the eve of the crisis, German politicians agreed on a fateful change to this provision. They replaced the old golden rule with a new constitutional limit on borrowing at the federal, state, and municipal levels known as the *Schuldenbremse*—literally, the "debt brake." It was not a farsighted compromise but a monumental error that has squeezed German infrastructure investment and needlessly sapped the private sector's purchasing power. Yet Germany's political class has become convinced that it discovered the secret to macroeconomic stability and has insisted on exporting it to the rest of Europe.

The origin of the debt brake can be traced to the unwieldy compromise between two historically opposed parties that produced the grand coalition at the end of 2005. The CDU/CSU-SPD government lacked an electoral mandate to do much of anything, but even worse, it felt trapped. A generous welfare state, an aging society with a stagnant population, and minimal productivity growth ensured that more and more of the budget was being devoted to pensions, unemployment benefits, health care, and debt service. By the early 2000s, the social security system and interest payments alone were consuming half of the federal budget. Another 25 percent of the budget went to long-term jobless benefits and the salaries of federal bureaucrats.

Wolfgang Streeck, the director of the Max Planck Institute for the Study of Societies, summarized the situation as one where the "long-term build-up of financial commitments and legal obligations" had "curtailed the degrees of freedom of public policy." In the absence of "opportunities for statecraft to make a difference," Germany's elected officials opted instead for "stagecraft" to maintain the "façade of free political choice." Streeck traced the problems to reunification, which had produced "an endemic, or chronic, shortfall of government revenue" and rising demands on the social security system. The federal government had been forced to cover the widening difference between worker contributions and mandated benefit payments out of general tax revenues and, more important, the budget deficit. The result was a seemingly inexorable increase in the government's debts from just under 40 percent of GDP in the 1980s to nearly 70 percent by the mid-2000s.

Streeck did not recommend any solutions to the problems he identified, but the emergent consensus was that spending would have to be cut and new rules put in place to permanently alter the trajectory of public debt. Conveniently, this appealed to the richer Germans in the prosperous southwest who formed the core of the country's center right. They were tired of paying for Eastern reconstruction and saw fiscal retrenchment as an opportunity to limit further transfers.[52]

Shortly after taking office at the end of 2005, SPD finance minister Peer Steinbrück led the charge to develop a permanent solution. He identified several problems with the old golden rule, including the absence of enforcement mechanisms to ensure compliance and a failure to account for the implicit debts created by unfunded commitments in the social security system. Worst of all, according to an official paper later published by Germany's finance ministry, was that "the existing rule reacts asymmetrically over the business cycle." Flexibility to respond to downturns was not balanced with an imperative to run surpluses and repay debt "in times of cyclical upswing or boom." Even though Germany had not experienced much of a cyclical upswing or boom in nearly twenty years, this "asymmetry" was considered "a major design flaw" in the old Article 115.

The resulting debt brake requires all the elements of the German government—"the Federation, Länder, local authorities and social security funds, including their off-budget entities"—to balance their combined budget each year, on average. This was much more stringent than the old rule because it made no exceptions for infrastructure investment and did not let the government use revenues from asset sales to pay for additional spending.

Some flexibility was provided to respond to cyclical conditions, but not much: "Under the debt brake, the only fiscal policy option generally available for stabilizing the economy is to allow automatic stabilizers to operate in both directions." Even this flexibility is limited, since the German government cannot expand its existing automatic stabilizers without violating the debt rule. There is also an allowance for larger budget deficits "to cover natural disasters and exceptional emergencies," but this is only available after a special vote in the Bundestag and needs to be paired with a "binding amortization plan" for repaying the extra debt.

Had the debt brake been in effect earlier, German fiscal policy would have been markedly tighter. The IMF thinks that the German government's budget deficit from 1993 to 2010 was consistently about 2–3 percent of national output after accounting for the state of the business cycle. Imposing the debt brake would therefore have required some combination of higher taxes and lower spending worth several percentage points of GDP every single year. Germany's finance ministry estimated in 2009 that the government would have borrowed just €55 billion from 2000 through 2008 if it had been bound by the debt brake. In reality, spending exceeded tax receipts by about €240 billion over that period. Tellingly, the finance ministry's analysis did not attempt to explain how constraining the government's borrowing would have affected German households and businesses, much less the rest of the world.[53]

Even before the debt brake came into effect, Germany's ideological and constitutional commitment to fiscal rectitude caused lasting harm to ordinary Germans. In addition to imposing the welfare cuts described earlier, Germany's federal, state, and local governments tightened their budgets by slashing spending on infrastructure investment and maintenance. Since 1998, government capital spending has not even been enough to maintain existing infrastructure. Spending net of depreciation has consistently been negative.[54]

The reason, according to Marcel Fratzscher, is that "the debt brake has changed incentives for governments in a fundamental way." During downturns, tax revenue falls and mandatory spending on welfare programs rises. Although the debt brake is supposed to provide some flexibility to budgets to weather these cycles, the reality is that governments, especially at the local level, "are forced to cut public investment projects" in order to sustain spending on everything from teachers' salaries to jobless benefits. Making matters worse, years of slow growth "encouraged many local and state governments to cut back on staff and the expertise necessary for implementing public investment projects."[55]

The result is that Germany's municipalities alone have an investment backlog of about €160 billion. About half of the roads and bridges in Germany need repair. The Leverkusen Bridge, which crosses the Rhine between Cologne and Düsseldorf, was closed to trucks in 2012 because it was no longer deemed safe for heavy vehicles. Trucks were forced to reroute through other highways and villages, slowing traffic, creating congestion for commuters, and increasing air pollution.

Economists estimate that these costs have been worth multiples of the amount of money it would have cost to repair the bridge. Delaying necessary maintenance caused the Leverkusen Bridge to degrade so much that it needed to be rebuilt. The new bridge will not open until 2020. The A40 Bridge, which crosses the Rhine near Duisburg, has repeatedly been shut to truckers for safety concerns. These are but some of the thousands of bridges that need urgent maintenance or will have to be totally rebuilt.[56]

Germany also has notoriously slow Internet speeds. Fewer than 3 percent of Germans have access to broadband at speeds of at least 100 megabits per second, and only 1 percent of Germans have fiber subscriptions—comparable to Italy and far worse than Portugal, Spain, and Eastern Europe. Germany also ranks poorly in terms of mobile broadband access, about equivalent to Turkey and far below Poland or Spain.[57]

On January 13, 2015, the German finance ministry triumphantly announced that years of spending restraint and onerous taxation finally meant that "no new borrowing was required" in all of 2014. This was the prize that Finance Minister Wolfgang Schäuble had long sought: the *schwarze Null,* or black zero. The budget had been balanced and no debt would be added to Germany's €2.2 trillion in outstanding obligations. Since then, the budget has moved further and further into surplus even as German infrastructure continues to deteriorate. The surplus now stands at 2 percent of GDP. Policy has been progressively tighter than required even by the restrictive debt brake. Between 2011 and 2015, the German government borrowed €142 billion less than allowed under its rules and continued to squeeze the private sector by underinvesting and overtaxing.[58]

German officials say that they are trying to save as much as possible now to prepare for the future of rapid aging and outright population decline. This is a reasonable premise, but it does not justify current policy. The German government is squeezing infrastructure investment, education spending, and the private sector's disposable income for the sake of repaying debt with an average real interest rate far below zero. That would make sense only if the expected return on investment in the German economy were deeply negative.[59]

The likelier explanation for the government's course is that ideology is overwhelming logic. Schäuble's obsession with the black zero was such that staffers in the finance ministry dressed in black and posed in a big circle to wish him farewell when he retired after the 2017 federal elections. While people everywhere have suffered for this, ordinary Germans have arguably fared among the worst. This may help explain the dwindling electoral appeal of Germany's traditional establishment parties, particularly the SPD.[60]

Despite the evident problems with Germany's economic model, Merkel's government and much of the German public believe that it has been essential to the country's ability to weather the financial crisis without suffering the fate of its European neighbors. In May 2010, the Europeans, led by Germany, committed to resolve the euro crisis with "fiscal consolidation" and concluded that the Stability and Growth Pact had been insufficient to guarantee "compliance." By 2012, the entire euro area had agreed to accept the Treaty on Stability, Coordination, and Governance in the Economic and Monetary Union, also known as the Fiscal Compact. The treaty effectively imposed Germany's debt brake on the rest of Europe. Governments across the bloc are now supposed to run balanced budgets—or surpluses—in almost all circumstances. They are required to seek the approval of the rest of Europe "on their public debt issuance plans." Failure to comply leads to sanctions.[61]

From a certain perspective, the treaties have done their job. The aggregate budget deficit of the euro area is now less than 1 percent of GDP and approaching zero. The deficit is narrower now than it was when Europe's economy was booming on the eve of the crisis, which means that fiscal policy is extremely tight relative to business conditions. Many countries within the bloc now have sizable budget surpluses, including Germany, Greece, Ireland, Lithuania, Luxembourg, Malta, the Netherlands, and Slovenia. The consolidated gross public debt of the euro area has dropped by 7 percentage points relative to GDP and is at its lowest level since 2010. In Germany, public indebtedness has plunged more than 21 percentage points and is lower than at any point since 2002. When forced, Germany's neighbors were able to copy its purported successes. Unfortunately for them and the rest of the world, this required adopting Germany's pathologies: depressed consumption, government austerity, job insecurity, underinvestment, and rising inequality.[62]

Europe Becomes Like Germany

In the years before the crisis, residents of the euro area spent about as much as they earned. The aggregate current account balance of the currency bloc was roughly zero because large internal divergences between member countries more or less canceled out: surpluses in Germany and the Netherlands were offset by deficits in Spain and Greece. By extension, the combined government deficit and private sector surplus of the euro area also canceled each other out. Europeans were neither contributing to nor detracting from overall global demand.

The private debt crisis that began in 2008 forced large changes in household and business spending patterns across the continent. Even the Netherlands, which missed the euro crisis, had to deal with the toxic combination of high household debt and a deflating housing bubble. The result is that the euro area's private sector surplus has consistently been about 5 percentage points of GDP higher than it was before 2008. At first, the shift in private behavior was matched by an offsetting increase in the aggregate fiscal deficit. Governments borrowed and spent when households and businesses would not (or could not). That kept Europe's overall current account in balance for the first few years after the crisis.

The ECB's failure to support euro area governments when they came under speculative attack, the ensuing sovereign crisis, and the widespread embrace of fiscal austerity changed all this starting around 2011–12. Government budget deficits were forced to close, and the rest of the world has been forced to make up the difference. Even though external demand was not especially strong, it grew much more than consumption and investment within Europe. Trade and current account surpluses have been the inevitable result: Germany's experience in the 2000s writ large.[63]

This was driven by changes in the European crisis countries, most of which now have trade and current account surpluses. Like Germany in the 2000s, the shift in their external position can largely be explained by severe contractions in domestic spending rather than by any improvements in export performance. This came at an enormous human cost. Between 2008 and 2016, the combined current account balance of the crisis countries shifted from a deficit worth about 6.5 percent of GDP to a surplus worth 2 percent of GDP. Over the same period, real domestic spending on consumption and investment plunged by about 11 percent in Spain, by 9 percent in Italy and Portugal, by 14 percent in Cyprus, and by 13 percent in Slovenia. The most extreme case has been Greece, where domestic consumption and investment have shrunk by a third. (Ireland probably had a similar experience, but the postcrisis Irish data are nearly unusable thanks to the profit-shifting activities of multinationals.)

Domestic spending has grown somewhat since then, which has reduced the crisis countries' combined current account surpluses commensurately. It is important, however, not to overstate the magnitude of the recent changes. As of 2019, real consumption and investment in Italy remains 8 percent lower than it was in 2008, while domestic demand is still about 5 percent below its precrisis level in Slovenia and Spain. Cyprus and Portugal have done somewhat better but are still poorer than they were a decade ago. Greece remains in depression.[64]

The deficit countries collectively shifted toward surplus, but for a variety of reasons, spending in Europe's existing surplus countries— most notably, Germany and the Netherlands—did not increase relative to production. There was no rebalancing within Europe. Instead, the rest of the world, mainly emerging markets in Africa, the Middle East, India, Indonesia, and Latin America, as well as the United Kingdom and United States, ended up being forced to absorb the resulting financial outflows through rising trade deficits and rising debt. The Europeans' decision to force the crisis countries to adjust by squeezing domestic spending has pushed the euro area as a whole into a massive external surplus relative to the rest of the world, currently worth about 4 percent of the bloc's GDP.

Unsurprisingly, the European countries that adopted Germany's economic policies also experienced rising inequality and a decline in purchasing power for their ordinary citizens. Value-added tax rates rose by several percentage points, while corporate income taxes and wealth taxes fell. As the economist Zsolt Darvas notes, "Wealthy Italians and Spanish lost very little (perhaps even increased their income) while lower earning Italians and Spaniards have lost a great deal." Rising income inequality in the surplus countries was caused in part by the desire to increase competitiveness through lower wages. After a massive credit boom and bust, the deficit countries were eventually forced to copy that approach, to the detriment of their citizens.[65]

As of this writing, Europe remains committed to relying on for-

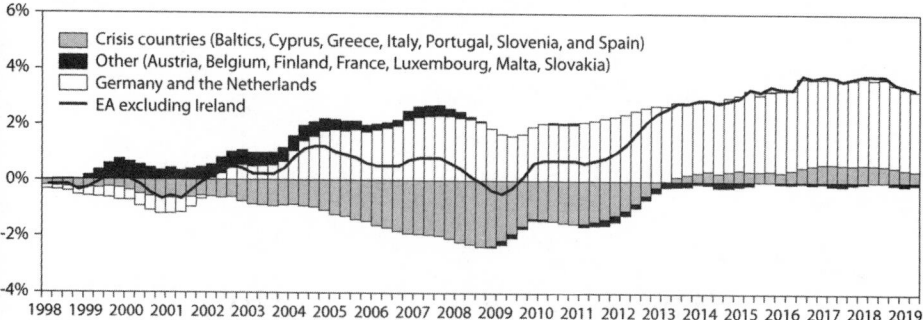

Fig. 5.7 The birth of the euroglut (contributions to the current account balance of the euro area excluding Ireland). *Sources: Eurostat; Matthew Klein's calculations*

eign spending to bail it out of its misguided fetishes of competitiveness and balanced budgets. Even as the German private sector has tentatively begun to rebalance toward a higher labor share and better wages, the government remains committed to its budget surplus. (Its protestations that it is boosting public investment should not be taken too seriously, given the continued depreciation of existing infrastructure.) The rest of the euro area, which either suffered as victims of the euro crisis or watched nervously from the sidelines, has determined to avoid repeating the experience by pushing fiscal policy even tighter than required. Governments would rather keep domestic demand permanently suppressed than risk ending up like Greece.[66]

While this might make sense for small open economies, such as Portugal, it cannot be a sustainable strategy for the euro area as a whole. The world's second-largest economy is simply too big to attempt to foist the consequences of its internal distortions on others without creating even larger global imbalances. Once again, the United States will have to reprise its role as the ultimate source of global demand.

The American Exception
The Exorbitant Burden and the Persistent Deficit

For decades, the United States has been the world's indispensable spender. Countries whose residents save too much and spend too little have consistently been accommodated by Americans who borrow to spend more than they earn. This has been true for so long that it is easy to forget how surprising it is.

In many ways, the American experience of the past several decades has much in common with that of Germany. Both countries saw sharply rising inequality among workers and a shift in the distribution of income from labor to capital. Both saw domestic business investment and employment crater after the tech bust. Where German companies sought to employ cheap labor in Central and Eastern Europe, American companies moved jobs to Mexico and China. Germany had the Schröder tax cuts and Hartz IV, while the United States had Clinton-era welfare reforms and the Bush tax cuts. Since the crisis, Germany has had the *Schuldenbremse* while America has had the Tea Party, the debt ceiling, and sequestration. Yet Germany became the world's largest surplus country while the United States remains the world's largest deficit country. How could two societies with such similar domestic environments have had such different economic relations with the rest of the world?

The answer can be traced to specific features of the U.S. financial system. Its flexibility, its size, and its concern for the rights of foreign

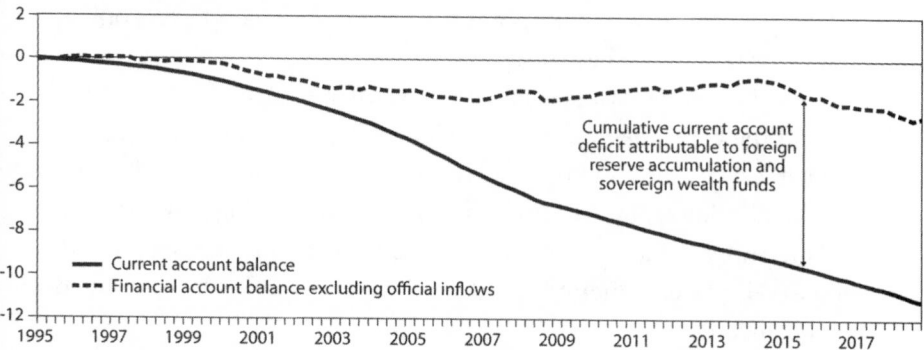

Fig. 6.1 The exorbitant burden (cumulative transactions since January 1995, USD trillions). *Sources: Bureau of Economic Analysis; Brad Setser; Matthew Klein's calculations*

investors make it a uniquely attractive venue for anyone in the world trying to save more than they earn. Moreover, the United States is the issuer of the world's premier safe asset. American sovereign debt is plentiful, easy to trade, and free of default risk. The U.S. economy is large, diversified, and open. By extension, the dollar can be cheaply converted to any other currency and is always accepted as payment by the world's producers of essential manufactures and commodities. These qualities make America the great repository for the world's excess savings, as they do to a lesser extent to countries, like the United Kingdom, that share these qualities.

Since the late 1990s, these excess savings have primarily entered the United States when foreign governments and related entities buy financial assets issued or guaranteed by the U.S. government. They acquire these reserves at the expense of domestic spending—a transfer of wealth in the reserve-buying countries from consumers to the owners of export industries. Their purchases were motivated not by a desire to earn high returns, but by the desire to avoid risk, no matter how low the yield. These uneconomic capital flows were as large as America's entire current account deficit between the end of 2001 and the end of 2014. Even if some of those inflows were partly offset by additional financial outflows from the United States, the net effect, by definition, was a combination of higher U.S. investment, higher U.S. consumption, and lower

U.S output. (Since 2014, Europeans have been the biggest buyers of U.S. assets, for reasons we have discussed.)[1]

Profit-seeking savers would not have enabled Americans to spend beyond their incomes, because the United States was not an especially profitable investment opportunity relative to the rest of the world. Indiscriminate inflows, however, inflated American purchasing power relative to American production and forced the current account deficit to widen. Imports displaced American productive capacity, and debt substituted for lost income.

Foreigners were throwing cheap money at Americans, and the U.S. financial system responded by creating new assets to accommodate this demand. Continuous inflows from abroad suppressed U.S. borrowing costs, lowered lending standards, inflated asset prices, and kept the U.S. dollar elevated even as the current account deficit ballooned. Had the United States been trying to attract foreign money to sustain its spending habits, real interest rates would have gone up and the currency would probably have gone down. Instead, America's natural tendency toward surpluses was overwhelmed by financial inflows from the rest of the world.

The Mystery of America's Missing Surplus

A core argument of this book is that the distribution of purchasing power within a society affects its economic relations with the rest of the world. People who cannot afford to buy what they produce must rely on foreign demand for their output. Without sufficient foreign or domestic demand, they will have no choice but to produce less. When a large enough chunk of a country's income shifts from entities that spend most of what they earn on consumption to entities that spend less than they earn—the rich and the companies they control—that country is therefore likely to experience a shift toward a larger current account surplus or a smaller current account deficit.

We have shown how this should work: developments in China and Germany since 1989 caused those countries to save too much and spend too little. Their experiences are instructive because together they cover much of what has happened in the other major surplus countries such as Japan, the Netherlands, and Singapore. The strange fact that needs explaining is that the United States has persistently run current account deficits despite sharing many of the characteristics of the stereotypical surplus country. Before we answer this question, it is important to understand why America should have been running current account surpluses for much of the past few decades.

Start by looking at the household sector. Inequality in the United States has skyrocketed since the late 1970s. After accounting for taxes and government transfers, the share of U.S. national income going to those in the top tenth of the distribution rose from 30 percent to 40 percent of the total. The ultra-high earners within the top 1 percent drove most of that increase. Their gains came at the expense of those lower down. Americans in the bottom half of the distribution have experienced essentially no income growth since the late 1970s after accounting for taxes, inflation, and cash benefits from the government.

These shifts in the income distribution have had predictable effects on the wealth distribution: the share of U.S. wealth held by the richest 1 percent of the population has soared from 22 percent to 42 percent, with almost all of that increase attributable to the richest 0.1 percent. The concentration of wealth has corresponded to an extreme concentration of capital income among the elite: about 70 percent of all earnings generated from owning assets now go to the richest 1 percent of Americans, up from 35 percent in the late 1970s.

As in Germany, policy exacerbated these shifts. Dramatic reductions in top tax rates gave high earners a strong motive to push for more pay, while changes to the regulatory treatment of stock buybacks and leveraged buyouts enabled executives and financiers to earn outsized incomes. The effective tax rate on capital gains fell by more than 10 percentage points between the mid-1990s and the mid-2000s. Regressive payroll taxes effectively replaced taxes on corporate profits between the early 1950s and the end of the 1980s. Welfare benefits were cut in the 1990s in a manner similar to what would happen with Hartz IV. Like their counterparts in Germany, American workers were made progressively more insecure as jobs were relocated abroad and private-sector unionization rates collapsed.

Because the highest earners save about 40 percent of their income while most other households save closer to zero, these shifts ought to have caused America's aggregate household saving rate to rise. Instead, the household saving rate fell from about 10 percent of disposable income in the late 1970s to 5 percent by the late 1990s, mainly because the vast majority of Americans ended up saving even less. (This is the puzzle that needs explaining.) By the eve of the financial crisis, the average U.S. household's saving rate had dropped to barely 3 percent because most Americans had negative saving rates: they were borrowing and spending more on goods, services, and interest payments than they were earning in income. Since the financial crisis, the overall household saving rate has reverted to about 6–7 percent, similar to where it was in the mid-1990s.[2]

American companies had a similar experience to their counterparts in Germany in the 1990s and 2000s. Encouraged by the financial markets, businesses in both countries were overoptimistic about the potential profitability of new investments during the tech boom. Their mistakes forced them to spend the subsequent decade retrenching and shifting their investment spending from their home market to countries where wages were much lower. In Germany, this process led to a large and sustained current account surplus. (Germany's investment bust was somewhat deeper and more protracted than America's, likely due to unfavorably high interest rates, an appreciating currency, and a weaker domestic market.)

After roughly two decades in which American business investment stayed essentially flat net of depreciation and inflation, real capital spending by U.S. companies grew by 20 percent each year between 1994 and 2000. Manufacturing capacity for durable goods—industrial machinery, motor vehicles, airplanes, and computers—expanded at an annual average rate of 10 percent between the start of 1995 and the end of 2000. From 1967 through 1994, the average yearly growth rate was just 3 percent.

Companies and their investors eventually paid the price for this "irrational exuberance," as Federal Reserve chairman Alan Greenspan memorably described it in 1996, with a wave of corporate bankruptcies and a roughly 40 percent decline in U.S. share prices. Net business investment fell by more than half between 2000 and 2003. Over the same period, the American business sector's current account balance swung from −5 percent of U.S. output to a surplus worth more than 1 percent of GDP. Scarred by the experience, U.S. companies chose to invest less, focus on cost control wherever possible, and hoard profits. Durable goods manufacturing capacity has grown just 1 percent each year, on average, since 2000. Overall U.S. manufacturing capacity has grown just 10 percent in total since the bubble burst almost two decades ago.[3]

As in Germany, the change in corporate priorities manifested itself as a shift in the split between workers and investors. Employee compensation as a share of net corporate value added steadily fell by 9 percentage points between 2001 and 2007. At the same time, the share paid to investors as interest, dividends, buybacks, or retained earnings rose by 6 percentage points. (The rest was captured by the government in the form of higher taxes on profits as fewer companies lost money.) Between the end of 2000 and the middle of 2006, just 37 percent of the total increase in corporate net value went to workers—slightly less than the share of the increase that went to creditors and shareholders. This was broadly comparable to what happened in Germany over the same period.

American companies have been even more restrained since the financial crisis. After subtracting inflation and depreciation, business investment spending in 2017 was 2 percent lower than in 2000. Investment jumped in 2018 thanks in part to the one-off incentives of tax cuts, but that was only enough to raise the average annual growth from 2000 to 2018 to just under 1 percent. With the notable exception of the shale producers and a few technology start-ups, most U.S. companies have been generating far more cash flow than they need to pay for their research, development, and investment spending.

This surplus allowed American nonfinancial businesses to pay nearly 18 percent of the net value they generated to creditors and shareholders in 2010–14. Investors did better in that period than at any point since the 1920s. From the start of 2008 through the end of 2014, investors were paid 34 percent of the total increase in corporate net value added, which was similar to what happened in 2001–6. While there has been some rebalancing toward workers more recently, as in Germany, workers are still much worse off than before the 2000s.[4]

Is Fiscal Policy to Blame?

There is a widespread and bipartisan consensus that Americans are to blame for their current account deficit because the U.S. government spends too much and taxes too little. Robert Skidelsky, the noted biographer of John Maynard Keynes, complained in 2005 that "the United States has relied on other countries to adjust their economies to profligate American spending." His suggestion was that the U.S. government "reduce domestic consumption" with some combination of tax increases and spending cuts. George P. Shultz and Martin Feldstein, two former officials from the Ronald Reagan administration, echoed Skidelsky's view in 2017. According to them, "Federal deficit spending, a massive and continuing act of dissaving, is the culprit" for America's trade imbalances. Their solution is to "control that spending." Just a few months later, Jason Furman, a former chairman of the Council of Economic Advisers under President Barack Obama, argued in 2018 that "to prevent the trade deficit from growing, the United States should increase national savings" by "cutting the federal budget deficit." Furman suggests that Americans should "stop blaming others and start examining ourselves." Joseph Stiglitz, a left-wing Nobel-winning economist, has also chimed in, claiming that "America has been saving too little" and that the best way to rebalance U.S. trade is to "increase national savings" by cutting consumption spending.[5]

While there is much to criticize about U.S. policies, these critiques are misguided. The spending and saving decisions of any individual sector rarely explain a country's overall current account balance, as counterintuitive as this may at first seem. What matters is the combined effect of the spending and saving decisions of households, businesses, and the government and the systemic distortions that drive the overall combined effect.

In Japan, for example, households have steadily cut their saving rate since the early 1990s as workers turned into retirees because of aging. For the past decade, the Japanese personal saving rate has been essentially zero. At the same time, the Japanese government has had large and persistent budget deficits since the early 1990s, averaging about 6 percent of GDP. Yet the country consistently has massive current account

surpluses. By definition, national savings far exceed national investment. In Japan's case, this is because corporate margins are high and
because Japanese companies are extremely reluctant to invest domestically. The corporate surplus is large enough to outweigh the deficits of
the government and households. The combined system generates high
savings and current account surplus even when individual sectors appear "profligate."[6]

Similarly, America's current account balance would not have been
meaningfully different even if the U.S. government had tried to suppress
consumption through tighter fiscal policy. The reason is that the combined budget balance of the various layers of the U.S. government almost perfectly mirrors the behavior of the American private sector. Tax
hikes and government budget cuts deprive households and businesses
of income. Consumption and investment fall, but not by as much as the
drop in earnings. The result is that the private sector saves less and the
national saving rate stays the same. By contrast, lower taxes and higher
government spending increase the income of the private sector. While
some of that extra income is spent on consumption and investment,
some of it is used to buy financial assets. At least in the United States,
fiscal policy mostly affects the distribution of saving among different
sectors of the economy rather than the overall amount of saving.

In fact, there have been many instances when the total current account deficit widened during a period of fiscal discipline or contracted
during periods of large budget deficits. Changes in the U.S. government's
budget balance rarely line up with changes in America's overall current
account balance. The private sector's behavior is at least as important.

The belief that changes in fiscal policy explain changes in the current account balance originated in the 1980s. Yet almost the entire U.S.
experience since then suggests that the current account is not driven by
the fiscal deficit.

From the beginning of 1983 to the end of 1985, the United States
went from a balanced current account to a deficit worth 3 percent of
GDP. Over this same period, the collective budget deficit of America's
federal, state, and local governments shrank from about 8 percent of
GDP to 6.5 percent as the economy recovered from the recession of the
early 1980s. This fiscal tightening was more than offset by U.S. house-

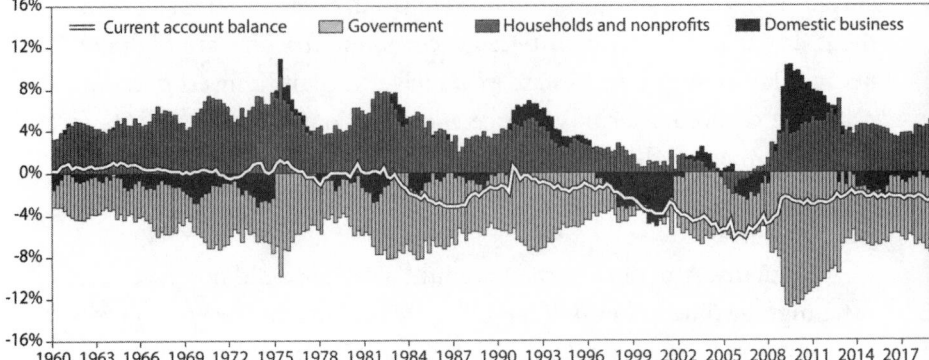

Fig. 6.2 U.S. fiscal policy does not drive the current account balance
(contributions to aggregate balance as a share of GDP). *Sources:*
Bureau of Economic Analysis; Matthew Klein's calculations

holds and businesses, which saw their combined surplus plunge from
roughly 8 percent of GDP to just 3.5 percent.

By 1987, the fiscal deficit had shrunk to 5 percent of GDP thanks to
continued economic growth and tax increases, yet this was fully offset
by the ongoing decline in the private sector's surplus below 2 percent
of GDP. By 1992, the United States was back in recession and the fiscal
deficit was back to 7.5 percent of GDP. Yet the current account deficit
was less than 1 percent of GDP because America's private sector had returned to a substantial surplus of nearly 7 percent of GDP. By the middle
of 1996, the U.S. current account deficit had grown slightly to 1.5 percent
of GDP even though the fiscal deficit had shrunk to just 4 percent of
GDP—the smallest it had been since the 1970s. By definition, the difference can be explained by the private sector, which saw its surplus collapse again to just 2.5 percent of GDP.

America's current account deficit expanded throughout the second
half of the 1990s, reaching 4 percent of GDP by 2000. Americans were
collectively spending more than they earned than at any point since the
nineteenth century. This occurred while the combined U.S. government
budget moved into balance for the first time since the 1950s. Fiscal policy had tightened dramatically, but this was more than offset by American households and businesses, which had transformed their combined

surplus into a deficit worth 4 percent of GDP. This dissaving was driven mainly by the U.S. corporate sector, which had gone on an investment binge despite declining profitability. American households were also spending more relative to their incomes in the 1990s.

By the middle of 2003, the U.S. current account deficit was roughly 4.5 percent of GDP—slightly wider than in 2000, but not by much. The mix between the private sector and the government had radically shifted, however. While the government surplus had transformed into a deficit worth 7 percent of GDP, this was mostly offset by the private sector, which moved from a 4 percent deficit to a surplus worth about 2.5 percent of GDP.

The 7 percentage point change in the government's fiscal position had almost no effect on America's balance of payments because it was almost totally offset by changes in private behavior, particularly that of the corporate sector, which had slashed investment spending even as margins improved. America's current account deficit kept growing wider from then until 2006, peaking at just over 6 percent of the U.S. economy. Yet this occurred at the same time as the combined government budget deficit shrank to just 3.5 percent of GDP because the private sector switched from a 2.5 percent surplus to a 2.5 percent deficit. Households and businesses contributed about equally to this shift. Just as in the late 1990s, fiscal rectitude was more than offset by foreign money.

The financial crisis featured the same basic pattern, but in reverse. Between mid-2006 and mid-2009, the U.S. government's combined budget deficit exploded by almost 10 percentage points of GDP. This was more than offset by American households and businesses, which experienced a swing in their saving position worth 13 percentage points of GDP. The combined effect was a dramatic shrinkage in the U.S. current account balance below 3 percent of GDP. America's total spending relative to its income has not changed much since then: the current account deficit has held remarkably steady between 2 percent and 3 percent of GDP.

What has changed is the mix between public and private spending. Before the tax cuts passed at the end of 2017, the U.S. government budget deficit had shrunk to about 5.5 percent of GDP while the private sector's surplus had dropped down to 3 percent. This was driven mainly by sharp cuts in government investment spending net of inflation and depreciation, which fell by 62 percent between the peak in 2008 and the trough in 2014. Despite a modest recovery since then, real investment spending is still lower than at any point since the early 1980s. While some of the drawdown can be attributed to a reduction in military expenditures, which has since begun to reverse, most of it can be explained by cutbacks in infrastructure investment and maintenance at the state and local levels. After the passage of the tax cuts, the overall government budget deficit has widened to about 7 percent of GDP. The impact on the current account balance has so far been negligible, however, because the domestic private surplus rose commensurately to 4.5 percent of GDP.[7]

The choices of American households, businesses, and the government are not enough to understand why the United States has persistently run current account deficits across a range of economic conditions. Whenever one sector cuts spending, another steps in to take its place. It is more helpful to think of the current account balance as the independent variable, with U.S. households, businesses, and the government adjusting their behavior in response to the financial inflows from abroad. The specific mix between private and public borrowing, or between corporate capital spending and home building, is largely a function of U.S. domestic conditions and policy. But the aggregate result is determined outside America's borders.

This is why, despite sharing so many characteristics with Germany, the United States has consistently run current account deficits. The key difference between America and Germany is the robust foreign appetite for U.S. assets, without which no sustained current account deficit would be possible. That appetite, in turn, can be explained by the special role that American sovereign debt and related obligations have come to play in the international financial system.

The easiest way to understand today's system is to look at how it evolved. Somewhat surprisingly, the international monetary system has retained many core features over the past two centuries. The essential change that explains the dollar's preponderance—and therefore America's persistent current account deficit—is the collapse of the gold standard during the Great Depression. Despite repeated efforts over the subsequent ninety years, no one has generated a suitable replacement. The next best alternative has been a regime centered on the dollar as the world's reserve asset. So, what are reserve assets, and why do they exist?

Understanding Reserve Assets

Money is what people use to pay their debts. Although many kinds of money can coexist at the same time, not all forms are accepted at all points in time. There is a hierarchy of what creditors will accept. When creditors are optimistic, they accept forms of payment lower down the hierarchy. Creditors are more discriminating about how they are paid when they are nervous: paper money takes priority over stock portfolios. Reserve assets are at the top of the money hierarchy because their money-ness is unquestionable. Their value derives from a combination of government authority and public consensus. People hold reserve assets so that they can be confident that their money will retain its usefulness when it is most needed.

For centuries, gold was the ultimate reserve asset. Gold is difficult to destroy, its supply changes little from year to year, and its value does not depend on anyone's creditworthiness. Banks used to issue notes to the public that could be redeemed for fixed amounts of the precious metal. At first, banks made money by charging depositors to store gold on their behalf. Later, as it became clear that redemption notes could act as money, banks profited by issuing more notes than the value of the gold they held in reserve and using the additional notes to make interest-bearing loans. This worked as long as most people were content to hold banknotes instead of gold.[8]

Problems arose when immediately redeemable notes were used to back longer-term loans and too many holders of the notes tried to redeem them for gold at the same time. Banks might simply refuse to exchange gold for notes by "suspending convertibility." At other times, banks tried to placate noteholders by offering only some of the gold that was promised. Either way, banks failed to honor their obligations. Noteholders suddenly realized that their money was something not quite as good as they had thought. Believing themselves poorer, they cut their spending and sold assets to get hold of money higher up the hierarchy.

When enough banks were hit at the same time, the result was a financial crisis.[9]

Central banks emerged in response to these crises. They could lend gold to private banks in exchange for claims on other assets held by the banks. Unreasonably panicked noteholders could convert their paper to gold and the crisis would eventually stop. The point was to protect banks that were technically solvent but for whom the maturity mismatch between assets and liabilities made it impossible for them to redeem liabilities on demand. Only genuinely insolvent banks would blow up, at least in theory. These lenders of last resort came to print their own notes, backed by gold, because they were easier to transport and could be printed at will. Banks eventually deposited their gold with the central bank and came to hold these central banknotes as their main reserve asset. Gold still underpinned the whole system, but the credibility of gold pegs had been shifted from private lenders to national governments.

By the nineteenth century, this process had transformed the obligations of certain central banks, especially the Bank of England, into reserve assets almost as good as gold. Similarly, claims on the most dependable British banks were also considered roughly equivalent to gold—even when held outside the British Empire. The gold standard had effectively become a paper standard.

On the eve of World War I, the Bank of England held only 3.4 percent of the world's gold reserves, and fewer than 5 percent of its notes were backed by gold. Yet many of the world's governments felt comfortable holding British pounds as reserve assets to cover imports and foreign debts. Outside of the four biggest economies—France, Germany, the United Kingdom, and the United States—currencies issued by other governments accounted for about a third of all reserve assets. (The rest was gold bullion.) Beyond continental Europe, where the French franc and German reichsmark were more prevalent, and Canada, which held its reserves in U.S. dollars, the pound sterling was by far the dominant reserve currency. Almost all of Japan's holdings of reserve assets in 1913, for example, took the form of financial claims issued by the U.K. government and banks, rather than gold or other foreign currencies.[10]

During the war, all the major powers except the United States suspended the convertibility of paper currency into physical gold. Governments were printing money to pay for their war efforts and would quickly have run out of gold had they let noteholders exchange paper for metal. At the Genoa Conference in 1922 the powers agreed to restore something resembling the prewar gold standard. The goal was to stop inflation and return to normalcy.

In the classical gold standard, each country's domestic credit supply was supposed to be constrained by the amount of gold held by its governments and its banks. Private lenders could create paper claims without limit but were discouraged from doing so because those claims could ultimately be exchanged for the finite supply of gold. This constraint was weak, as demonstrated by the Bank of England's limited gold coverage in 1913, but it was real. The corollary was that gold inflows were supposed to encourage additional lending and spending, raising prices and production in whichever country was receiving more bullion.

The combination was supposed to make persistent global imbalances impossible. Surplus countries would receive gold, which boosted the local credit supply and inflated wages and prices. That would lead to higher spending, including on imports, even as exports became more expensive. Deficit countries would be forced to deflate the prices of their exports and cut spending on imports as their credit supply tightened. Eventually, the changes in trade flows would cause gold flows to reverse, ending the booms in the surplus countries and the busts in the deficit countries. The adjustments would not be painless, but they would be symmetrical.

The restored gold standard failed in the 1920s because France and the United States gamed what would otherwise have been a fairly flexible system by preventing their domestic economies from responding to gold inflows in the usual ways. France had reset the gold value of the franc much lower than it had been before the war, which suppressed spending on imports and lowered the price of French exports. While the United States did not change the gold value of the dollar, its exchange rate had effectively depreciated relative to the Europeans because it had experienced far less inflation during the war years and had also been more successful in reversing the inflation after the war. (That, in turn, was a consequence of America's superior productive capacity relative to its domestic needs during and after the war.) As with France, this boosted

U.S. export earnings while discouraging spending on imports. Americans were also earning substantial interest from loans to their wartime allies, as well as their postwar loans to Germany. Both France and the United States, in other words, were running massive current account surpluses. The necessary consequence was that France and the United States were receiving large inflows of gold from the rest of the world.

These gold inflows should have boosted spending power in France and the United States while making French and American exports more expensive in world markets. The imbalances should have self-corrected and eventually caused the gold inflows to reverse. However, the Bank of France and the U.S. Federal Reserve "sterilized" their gold imports to keep domestic inflation under control and to remain internationally competitive. Rather than expanding money and credit, gold entering France and the United States effectively disappeared from the global financial system. This decision dramatically increased French and U.S. holdings of reserve assets, distorted the world economy, and eventually destroyed the monetary regime agreed at Genoa. There would be no symmetrical adjustments by creditors. In the 1920s, the deficit countries chose to honor their international commitments to gold at the expense of domestic economic conditions.

By the time the Great Depression hit, however, this choice was no longer tenable. The first country to succumb to the temptation to leave the gold standard was the United Kingdom, which abandoned its peg in September 1931. The Scandinavian countries and Japan followed later that year. Ironically, the Federal Reserve's fear of losing America's gold hoard caused it to tighten credit conditions and exacerbate bank failures until the U.S. government broke the dollar's link to gold in 1933. France waited the longest, finally depreciating the franc in 1936 after years of domestic weakness and diminishing trade competitiveness. Germany technically kept its peg to gold until its defeat by the Allies, but this came at the cost of draconian controls on moving money out of the country, including the death penalty for people who paid foreign debts in hard currency. Cut off from the international financial system, the Nazi regime resorted to barter trade to get what it needed by selling advanced manufactures for raw materials, often from the Soviet Union, its ostensible ideological adversary. By the end of the decade, the last vestiges of both the prewar gold standard and the interwar gold-exchange standard had ended.[11]

Bretton Woods, the Rise of the Dollar, and the Birth of "Exorbitant Privilege"

Less than a month after the landings at Normandy, 720 delegates representing forty-four Allied countries met in Bretton Woods, New Hampshire, to discuss what international trade and finance would look like after the war. Everyone agreed that the gold-exchange standard of the 1920s had been a failure and that the monetary anarchy of the 1930s had exacerbated the breakdown in trade and the rise of militarism. A new order was needed to promote international cooperation and economic stability. The question was what this new order would look like.

John Maynard Keynes had forcefully argued against the punitive reparations imposed on Germany in 1919, had warned Winston Churchill against returning to gold at an overvalued exchange rate in 1925, and had written what remains one of the best analyses of economic cycles and the Great Depression. He represented the British position at Bretton Woods, which was to prevent the imbalances of the 1920s from returning and to ensure that adjustment costs would be borne by both surplus and deficit countries.

Keynes was acutely aware of how the British economy had been undermined in the 1920s by its decision to maintain an overvalued exchange rate. (That decision, in turn, had been motivated by Britain's desire to preserve the value of sterling assets accumulated by residents of India and the Commonwealth before and during the war.) While Britain maintained an overall current account surplus, its trade deficit had ballooned thanks to a collapse in exports and the displacement of domestic industry by imports. Keynes understood in a way few others did that persistent deficits were as likely to be caused by problems abroad as by problems at home.

His proposal was for all trade finance to be settled through a single "international clearing bank" that would use its own settlement unit, the "bancor." Each country would have its own account, earning bancor from selling exports and paying for imports using accumulated bancor balances. Countries could run overdrafts up to a certain amount but would have to devalue their domestic exchange rate against the bancor if overdrafts were too large. Crucially, his proposal penalized countries that held too many bancor as severely as those that had bancor deficits. Overdraft limits were effectively symmetrical, so any excess bancor balances would be confiscated and put in a reserve fund. Alternatively, surplus countries would have to appreciate their currency against bancor. The goal was to promote balanced trade and facilitate cooperative exchange rate adjustments.

The United States vetoed this plan. American negotiators wanted the rest of the world to use the dollar as the currency of international trade and finance in a system of fixed exchange rates. The United States also insisted—foolishly, in retrospect—that there would be no mechanism to distribute the burden of adjustment across surplus and deficit countries. Countries unable to finance their current account deficits would simply have to cut their domestic spending and force up the national saving rate, whether this occurred through depreciation, government budget tightening, rising unemployment, or some other mechanism. Surplus countries, on the other hand, would face no pressure to adjust by spending more. An "international monetary fund" would offer temporary emergency loans to countries under pressure to defend their peg to the dollar. Countries could devalue against the dollar, but only by limited amounts unless given explicit IMF approval.

At the time, this seemed like a good deal for the United States, because the United States did not want to be penalized for its large surpluses or sacrifice its position as the world's largest creditor. But Americans also believed that their domestic spending had been inflated by the war effort and would fall after the war had ended. Furthermore, Americans (correctly) expected that their abundant productive capacity would be needed to offset the destruction in Europe and Asia. Large U.S. trade surpluses, and the corresponding financial outflows needed to rebuild a world torn apart by two world wars, would be good for the global economy, not an undesirable imbalance to be penalized.

America's proposed system encouraged central banks in the rest of the world to hold U.S. government obligations as reserve assets. This was the natural outcome of replacing the gold standard with a dollar stan-

dard. As in the gold standard, central banks had to manage the link between the value of their paper currency and the reserve asset. At the same
time, central banks needed to be able to provide emergency loans to
private-sector banks in times of crisis. For the U.S. Federal Reserve, this
was easy, since the reserve asset was the U.S. dollar. It could create as
many as needed without worrying about the exchange rate. In the rest
of the world, this tension between international and domestic priorities
could be resolved only by accumulating stockpiles of dollar-denominated
assets that could be drawn on as needed.

This, too, seemed like a good deal at the time for the United States.
It had created a captive market for its debts that would suppress borrowing costs, freeing up resources to cut taxes and spend more on things
people wanted. It also meant that the U.S. government had far greater
license to inflate domestic spending than foreign governments. By definition, there was no exchange rate peg to defend in a dollar standard.
Valéry Giscard d'Estaing, French finance minister under President Charles
de Gaulle, eventually labeled this America's "exorbitant privilege."

The Europeans grudgingly accepted this arrangement because they
had protection against U.S. abuse of the system: dollars could be exchanged for gold at a fixed rate of $35 per ounce. As long as the United
States retained the confidence of its allies, the postwar monetary system
would endure. If those allies believed that the United States was taking
advantage of them by devaluing its currency, however, they could preserve the value of their reserves by converting their dollars into gold.[12]

"Our Currency, but Your Problem"

Robert Triffin was a Belgian monetary economist who began teaching at
Harvard University in 1939 and became an American citizen three years
later. By the late 1950s, he had come to believe the Bretton Woods regime was inherently unstable because of a built-in tendency for dollar
obligations to grow faster than the gold supply. There was no limit to
how many U.S. dollars foreigners could hold, but there was a finite (and
shrinking) amount of gold in the depository in Fort Knox, Kentucky.
The U.S. government was like a bank under the old gold standard, one
issuing growing amounts of notes in excess of its declining reserves, prof-

iting from the difference, but always vulnerable to a run. As he put it in his testimony to Congress in October 1959, "We have been lending long— and even given funds away—while borrowing short and losing gold."[13]

Throughout the 1950s, Americans spent less than they earned: excluding foreign aid, the average current account surplus in those years was worth about 1 percent of gross domestic product. This also meant, by definition, that Americans bought more assets abroad than foreigners bought in the United States. The problem was that the current account inflows were significantly smaller than the financial account outflows. The balance of payments balanced only because Americans were funding some of their foreign investments by selling claims against their finite supply of reserve assets. The dollar was overvalued, but instead of letting the currency depreciate, Americans were transferring claims on gold abroad to maintain an unreasonable peg. Toward the end of the 1950s, foreigners began exercising their rights to convert dollar reserves into physical gold: U.S. gold reserves fell by about 15 percent between the end of 1957 and the end of 1959. At first, U.K. residents were the most aggressive at redeeming dollars for metal in those years, later to be replaced by the French.

Triffin feared that the growing mismatch between actual U.S. gold holdings and foreign claims on American gold would itself undermine the credibility of the dollar and, by further accelerating the conversion of dollars into gold in a self-reinforcing process, would precipitate a crisis. Foreign central banks would try to swap their dollars into gold all at once, and while some would succeed, most would fail. The notes issued by the world's bank would be called into question, money and credit would collapse, and the global economy would be plunged into deflation and depression. The U.S. government could try to limit foreign holdings of dollars to defend the gold peg, but this would "deprive the rest of the world of the major source, by far, from which the international liquidity requirements of an expanding world economy are being met." Triffin's "dilemma" was the choice between an unsustainable model of global finance or perpetually strangled credit.[14]

Things got worse once John F. Kennedy emerged as a serious presidential contender. He had campaigned on greater social spending, tax cuts, and military rearmament—a combination thought to risk inflation.

American gold reserves fell by another 9 percent in 1960. The United Kingdom, Switzerland, the Netherlands, France, and Belgium were the main recipients. More worryingly, the price of gold bullion traded in London spiked to nearly $40 an ounce in October 1960, far above the official exchange rate of $35. Although the spike subsided after concerted intervention by the Federal Reserve and the Bank of England, it was a warning of what could happen.[15]

In response, the Federal Reserve Bank of New York began sending representatives to the Bank for International Settlements in Basel to convince the Europeans to keep their reserves in dollars. The United States and seven European allies formed the London Gold Pool to fix the international price of gold at $35 an ounce. The International Monetary Fund was given new powers to lend gold to the United States in case of emergency. The Federal Reserve established swap lines with foreign central banks to lend and borrow currencies. The U.S. Treasury issued so-called Roosa bonds denominated in foreign currencies, such as deutschmarks, to discourage Europeans from calling in gold (the name came from Treasury official Robert Roosa). Congress passed an "interest equalization tax" to discourage Americans from investing abroad. Foreign aid recipients were told to spend their dollars on American exports.[16]

To the surprise of many, including Triffin, these measures helped preserve Bretton Woods for another decade. But they were not enough. All told, the United States lost nearly ten thousand metric tons of gold reserves—just over half of its total holdings—between the end of 1957 and March 1968. France and the United Kingdom together got about half, with most of the rest going to other countries in Western Europe such as Austria, Belgium, the Netherlands, Spain, and Switzerland.[17]

Outflows of this magnitude made it impossible for the Gold Pool to keep the market price of gold pegged at $35 an ounce. By March 1968, the cartel was forced to shut down and the United States declared that it would only allow central banks the right to exchange dollars for gold at the statutory price of $35. The result was a two-tiered market: central bankers could theoretically trade gold for dollars at $35 an ounce while the rest of the world was trading the metal at more than $43 an ounce by 1969. The gold price fell back to $35 by the end of that year, however, thanks in part to the recession of 1969–70.

By the middle of 1971, things had changed yet again. The London price of gold had crossed $40 by May, and the Bundesbank decided to let the deutschmark float against the dollar. By August, continued threats to American gold holdings, rising unemployment, and the sharp deterioration in the U.S. trade balance convinced President Richard Nixon to end the convertibility of dollars into gold. The Bretton Woods regime had finally ended.[18]

The Bretton Woods system could have lasted much longer if foreign holders of U.S. dollars had declined to convert their holdings into gold. The world's bank would have kept growing its balance sheet, accumulating more and more long-term claims on the rest of the world while selling more and more short-term reserve assets. The problem was inflation: the dollar kept losing value against goods and services—including the goods and services employed to mine gold. Consumer prices in the United States rose about 40 percent between the beginning of 1958 and the end of 1970 while the official price of the yellow metal remained unchanged. This hit the margins of gold producers and discouraged supply from expanding sufficiently.[19]

More important, the system of fixed exchange rates exported U.S. inflation to the rest of the world. As Treasury secretary John Connally had put it when talking to his European counterparts, the dollar was "our currency, but your problem." Charles de Gaulle complained that Americans could fight expensive wars against communists in Southeast Asia and against poverty at home without having to raise taxes or cut spending on imports. German leaders were more circumspect but nonetheless blamed American profligacy for accelerating price increases in the late 1960s. Both had responded rationally by replacing dollars with gold until they brought down the system.

Some economists later argued that if U.S. policymakers had done a better job keeping inflation under control, perhaps by tolerating significantly higher domestic unemployment, the Europeans might never have felt compelled to break Bretton Woods. If it had, the world might have gradually embraced a global dollar standard to replace the gold standard, with the Federal Reserve setting monetary policy for the entire planet. Instead, the world entered what felt at the time like a period of monetary anarchy. Exchange rates swung wildly in the 1970s and

1980s. Europeans—especially the French—hated this so much that they deliberately tried to re-create a fixed exchange rate system for themselves, eventually establishing the euro as a Gaullist rebuke to the Americans and their economists who pushed for floating currencies.

Yet for all their complaints about exorbitant privilege and imported inflation, the Europeans were more than willing to exacerbate the flaws in the system as they benefited from American spending. Europeans sold their exports to the booming American market, and they depended on American military spending to protect them from the Soviets. European welfare states might not have been affordable without strong external demand and depressed defense budgets. America's inability to sustain the dollar's peg to gold was caused by the same forces that helped Europe prosper. The solution then was to break the link to gold. This, however, did not solve the underlying problem. Foreign demand for U.S. assets only grew after 1971, increasingly distorting both the global and American economies.[20]

Excess Savings, Mercantilist Manipulation, and Bretton Woods II

The world eventually adjusted to the new regime. While countries such as New Zealand and Sweden have prospered with their own free-floating currencies and independent monetary policies, most nations rejected this approach. Some tried to stabilize their domestic inflation rates by pegging their currencies to countries with monetary credibility, such as Germany (if they were in Europe) or the United States (if they were anywhere else). Others decided to manage their currencies against the dollar or the deutschmark in the hopes of encouraging foreign investment and the development of export markets. Most international trade in manufactured goods is now denominated in dollars for the sake of convenience, even though most transactions do not directly involve the United States. The surprising popularity of exchange rate pegs after the 1980s has led some scholars to talk about the emergence of Bretton Woods II.[21]

At first, these fixed and quasi-fixed exchange rate regimes were sustained by nothing more than verbal commitments and the confidence of traders. Governments with pegged currencies did not own nearly enough hard currency—dollars, deutschmarks, and yen—to defend their currencies if their pegs were ever questioned. Accumulating those reserves was expensive: money spent buying safe assets is money that could have been spent on roads and hospitals. This created a systematic mismatch between the supply of reserve assets and the amount of money linked to those assets, just like under the gold standard before World War I. That mismatch was not a problem as long as underlying economic conditions supported the pegs.

If, however, underlying conditions changed, the absence of adequate reserves meant that governments would have to choose between defending their commitments by imposing extreme hardship on their citizens, resetting their exchange rates at new, achievable levels, or scrapping their pegs entirely. Governments rarely had much of a choice. Economies and financial markets are social phenomena where beliefs affect reality. In most cases, the mere possibility of devaluation would prompt locals and foreign investors to move their money out of the country. Their actions would push up interest rates, thereby increasing the cost of maintaining the peg until it became impossible to sustain. The hedge fund manager George Soros, who made some of his greatest trades betting on the collapse of fragile exchange rate regimes, describes this self-reinforcing process as "reflexivity."[22]

Devaluations are often beneficial for countries where households, businesses, and the government borrowed in their own currency, because breaking the exchange rate peg allows the local central bank to lower interest rates and ease credit conditions. The classic example is the United Kingdom, which was forced out of the European Exchange Rate Mechanism in 1992 by the mismatch between its recessionary domestic conditions and Germany's temporary reunification boom. (George Soros played what was in retrospect a constructive role by betting that the peg to the deutschmark could not be maintained, which increased the cost the British government had to pay to defend its currency regime.) Freed from the strictures of the peg to the deutschmark to deploy looser monetary policy, the United Kingdom began recovering almost immediately.

By contrast, countries with extensive debts in foreign currency usually find devaluations to be extraordinarily painful, mainly because the depreciated currency raises the value of those debts relative to economic activity. Many countries in Latin America borrowed in dollars in the 1970s only to find themselves forced to repay their debts at unfavorable exchange rates in the 1980s. With the notable exception of Taiwan, which bought $70 billion in foreign exchange reserves in the 1980s—equivalent to a year's worth of economic output—most countries outside Latin America did not think that they had much to learn from the experience. Taiwan, of course, was unusual in that the government knew that it could never access emergency loans from the IMF if it ever ran into trouble.[23]

The Asian Financial Crisis of 1997–98 changed everything. For years, Indonesia, South Korea, Malaysia, the Philippines, and Thailand had attracted substantial financial inflows from savers in North America, Europe, and Japan. All were growing rapidly—Korea's living standards had already converged to those in New Zealand and Spain, while Malaysia was at Central European levels of development—and all had maintained stable exchange rates against the U.S. dollar in the 1990s. For a variety of reasons, things began to reverse in the first half of 1997. This was a surprise to many, especially the IMF. As Timothy Lane, then the chief of the Policy Review Division at the IMF, wrote in a retrospective analysis, the Asian crisis countries "had fiscal surpluses, high private saving rates, and low inflation." To Lane and his colleagues, "their exchange rates did not seem out of line."[24]

The problem was that banks and businesses in the afflicted countries had borrowed extensively in foreign currencies to bid up the prices of domestic assets. Worse, the debt was often short-term. As long as money kept flowing in, exchange rates held steady, the stock and real estate markets kept rising, and the situation appeared sustainable. Relatively small changes in sentiment, however, could—and did—lead to a self-reinforcing cascade of falling asset prices, currency depreciation, and rising real interest rates. The mistake was not that these countries had borrowed from abroad to finance their development but that they had structured their obligations in ways that were prone to collapse.[25]

Indonesia was hit the hardest. Its currency, the rupiah, lost 80 percent of its value between January 1997 and July 1998. Real output per person fell by more than 14 percent between 1997 and 1999. The chaos was so traumatizing that it led to the collapse of the Suharto regime, which had ruled Indonesia since 1967, and to the independence of East Timor, which had been occupied since 1975. Indonesia's economy was also slow to recover: average living standards did not return to their previous peak until the mid-2000s. Thailand and Malaysia did only marginally better at first, with real living standards falling by 12 percent and 10 percent, respectively, but had somewhat quicker recoveries. Korea and the Philippines fared relatively better, with the shallowest downturns and the fastest returns to growth.

Emergency loans from the IMF and other international lenders—as well as a substantial loosening of monetary policy by the Federal Reserve—helped end the crisis, but this aid did not come cheaply: governments had to follow outsiders' recommendations if they wanted help. Many of these recommendations, while perhaps individually justifiable, often appeared to be targeted swipes at the governments requesting aid. Moreover, they often failed to address the immediate problem at hand. One of the more notorious examples was the IMF's demand that the Indonesian government end its monopoly on cloves used in the manufacture of cigarettes. The monopoly was a source of profits for Suharto and his friends at the expense of ordinary Indonesian farmers, and should have been abolished, but it had little to do with the crisis afflicting the financial system and economy.[26]

Other recommendations were downright counterproductive. Government spending cuts and tax increases did not restore investor confidence, but they did crimp domestic spending. Raising interest rates was supposed to help rebuild credibility and staunch outflows, but the resulting contractions in economic activity simply made locals in the crisis countries increasingly desperate to get their money out. The IMF later admitted that its "programs were initially less successful than hoped" because consumption and investment fell much more than they had anticipated, thanks in large part to their policy recommendations. That in turn led to substantial current account adjustments, driven mainly by sharp drops in imports as businesses and households in the afflicted countries cut back on spending.[27]

The experience was so painful, and so humiliating, that a generation of policymakers vowed never to repeat it. That meant acquiring foreign reserves on an unprecedented scale to avoid ever having to approach the IMF again. On the eve of the Asian crisis, governments across the world owned about $970 billion in dollar-denominated reserve assets, and a large chunk of those reserves were owned by European governments and Japan. By the middle of 2008, however, the sum had grown to $5.2 trillion, with most of that held by governments of poor countries. The trauma of the global financial crisis encouraged even further accumulation: as of the beginning of 2019, foreign governments owned roughly $8 trillion in dollar-denominated assets.[28]

The necessary tradeoff has been a reduction in domestic spending in countries that accumulated reserves. Central banks and sovereign wealth funds bought foreign financial assets with purchasing power that otherwise would have been used to buy additional imports. Governments increased their wealth at the expense of ordinary households, who spent less on goods and services. The understandable desire for self-insurance has therefore led to a chronic shortfall of demand—and large trade surpluses—across much of East Asia. Regardless of intent, the combination of large and persistent trade surpluses, sustained state-sponsored purchases of foreign financial assets, and managed exchange rates has been economically equivalent to mercantilism through currency manipulation. Instead of tariffs or quotas to discourage imports, governments simply hold down the value of their currencies, suppress interest rates, and otherwise subsidize exporters, gaining export market share while keeping out foreign goods.[29]

The single most consequential practitioner of self-insurance (or currency manipulation) has been the Chinese government, which has accumulated more reserves than any other country in history. By the eve of the Asian crisis, China's State Administration for Foreign Exchange (SAFE), the entity charged with managing the reserves of the People's Bank of China, owned about $100 billion of reserve assets. At the time, it was a poor country at roughly the same level of development as Honduras. China's capital account was mostly closed: foreigners had difficulty bringing money in, and locals had even greater difficulty getting money out. Many within the government had planned to loosen those controls gradually and liberalize the Chinese financial system, with the eventual goal of letting the yuan float freely against other currencies.

Events in Indonesia changed everything. China's leaders were horrified as they watched a seemingly stable authoritarian regime collapse because the private sector had run into debt trouble. They determined never to let the same thing happen to them. The easiest solution was to maintain China's exchange rate peg and prevent the yuan from appreciating to where it would have been under a floating regime. The cheap yuan transferred income from consumers and workers to the government and the owners of export-oriented companies. That transfer discouraged domestic spending relative to domestic production and therefore minimized China's reliance on foreign financing.

Maintaining the peg was a challenge, however, because foreign savers were eager to invest in China. Capital controls kept some foreign money out, but more than enough was still coming in. Left unchecked, these flows would have pushed up China's exchange rate and increased Chinese spending on goods and services. The Chinese government could have offset some of those foreign inflows by loosening its outbound capital controls and allowing Chinese savers to buy foreign assets. Liberalization, however, would have threatened the government's control of the economy and financial system.

Beijing therefore chose to buy trillions of dollars of foreign exchange reserves to sustain its currency peg. Between 1996 and the eve of the global financial crisis, SAFE spent $1.8 trillion accumulating foreign reserves, roughly two-thirds of which were invested in the United States. After the global financial crisis, the Chinese government spent another $2 trillion accumulating even more foreign assets to prevent its currency from appreciating further.[30]

Outside of East Asia, the major buyers of reserve assets have been commodity exporters, mainly the oil and gas producers of the Arabian Peninsula, Norway, and Russia. China's rapid industrialization was a windfall for them. After being range-bound between $20 and $30 per barrel from 1999 through 2003, the international benchmark oil price steadily rose to $75 per barrel by 2006 and then to more than $130 per barrel by the summer of 2008. While the biggest beneficiaries spent some of their windfall, they were generally prudent enough to save much of it in foreign assets as a hedge for a future with lower prices, lower oil sales, or both.

The combined current account surplus of the energy exporters therefore rose from about $90 billion in 2002 to more than $600 billion by 2008. International oil prices temporarily dropped during the financial crisis but managed to hover around $110 per barrel from the start of 2011 through the middle of 2014. That provided another windfall for the energy producers, much of which was saved rather than spent: their combined current account surplus averaged more than $500 billion per year. While their surplus has since shrunk as oil prices have dropped, this has mainly led to even larger surpluses in the demand-deficient oil-importing countries of Europe and East Asia.[31]

These unsolicited state-sponsored inflows explain why America's current account deficit expanded at the same time that the dollar appreciated and real interest rates fell. In the late 1990s, when the U.S. current account deficit was just 1.5 percent of national output, the real, inflation-adjusted yield on a long-term Treasury bond was about 4 percent. If Americans had been trying to attract foreign financing, they would have had to pay for it by offering foreign investors higher returns. That, in turn, would have meant higher yields and lower asset prices. Yet real interest rates steadily dropped to less than 2 percent by 2005 as the current account deficit widened to 6 percent of GDP. When the deficit was expanding, the dollar was about 15 percent more valuable relative to a broad basket of other currencies, on average, than it was in the mid-1990s when America's net financing from abroad was much smaller.[32]

The Safe Asset Shortage

Foreign central banks and other reserve managers spent about $4.1 trillion buying dollar-denominated assets between the start of 1998 and the middle of 2008. This was in addition to Americans' own purchases of dollar assets during this period, as well as those of private savers in rich countries that were not stockpiling reserves. Reserve managers did not finance any unmet needs. Rather, they distorted the U.S. economy and sowed the seeds of the financial crisis.

Reserve managers created two linked problems for the United States. First, the extra demand for dollar assets had to be matched by additional supply; Americans had to create more than $4 trillion in safe financial obligations. Second, governments accumulated their dollar reserves by suppressing domestic spending relative to domestic production. That exacerbated the global glut, particularly of manufactured goods. Someone had to absorb this excess production to prevent a global depression. The preeminence of the U.S. dollar meant that Americans were the ones who absorbed the bulk of both the excess capital inflows and the excess manufactured goods from the rest of the world. The consequences were the housing debt bubble and a displaced manufacturing base. Rather than an exorbitant privilege, the dollar's international status imposed an exorbitant *burden*.

The United States had no good response to the challenge posed by foreign reserve accumulation. Recycling the inflows, as in the 1950s, by buying an equivalent amount of foreign—in practice, European—assets would have been theoretically possible, but highly impractical and likely unprofitable. Taxes or regulations to discourage or prevent foreign purchases of U.S. assets might have helped but would have been fundamentally opposed by the intellectual consensus of the time. Moreover, any form of capital controls would have looked hypocritical in light of American advice to other countries in the 1990s. Even if capital controls had diverted inflows from the United States to Europe, they would not have addressed the underlying problem of excessive saving and insufficient demand. Similarly, trade protections against imports would, at best, have shifted the problem elsewhere rather than addressed the fundamental imbalances in the global economy. More likely, trade protections would have backfired by reducing foreign income available to buy American products.

In retrospect, the best response would have been for the federal government to borrow as much as necessary to accommodate the excess inflows and to spend the money supporting demand for U.S. manufactured goods, investing in infrastructure, reversing the policies that had led to the concentration of income, and reducing poverty. Domestic spending would still have outstripped domestic production, but the overall composition of economic activity would have been less distorted. American manufacturing would not have been unduly displaced by imports, there would likely have been no housing bubble, and the increase in U.S. debt would have been borne by the entity (the federal government) best able to bear the burden.

That is not what happened. From the start of 1998 through the middle of 2008, federal government debt available for purchase rose by just $1.3 trillion, while foreign investors bought a little more than $1.4 trillion. (Not all foreign buyers of Treasury debt were reserve managers, but many were.) In other words, savers outside the United States bought all of the additional Treasury bonds issued in the ten years before the crisis—and more. Yet this was not nearly enough to satiate foreign appetite for safe U.S. assets to hold as reserves.

Reserve managers next turned to debt issued by the mortgage companies Fannie Mae and Freddie Mac. Although Fannie and Freddie were technically private businesses, they had been created by the state and were among the biggest of the government-sponsored enterprises, or GSEs, which provided the imprimatur of safety. (The perception proved justified, since the U.S. government ended up refusing to impose losses on GSE bondholders in 2008 partly to preserve diplomatic relations with China and others.)

According to the Federal Reserve, the value of "U.S. government agency securities" outstanding grew by more than $5 trillion between the start of 1998 and the middle of 2008. Most of that extra debt was issued by Fannie and Freddie. Foreign investors, including reserve managers, bought about $1.5 trillion of it. (American banks, insurers, pension funds, and bond funds bought the rest.) The remaining $1.2 trillion or so of foreign reserve demand went to bank deposits and occasionally more exotic assets.

These statistics understate the pressures on the American financial system in the 2000s. As the irrational exuberance of the late 1990s turned into the investment bust of the early 2000s, many Americans and Europeans tried to spend less, buy fewer risky assets, and save more. The total supply of U.S. corporate debt issued by nonfinancial companies grew by just $200 billion between the start of 2002 and the end of 2007, and most of that debt was issued at the end of the period. At the same time, pension funds and life insurers the world over needed to buy more fixed income to offset the growth of their long-term liabilities.

Even without Asian and Middle Eastern reserve managers hoovering up every new U.S. Treasury bond and much of the debt issued by Fannie and Freddie, there would have been a fundamental shortage of

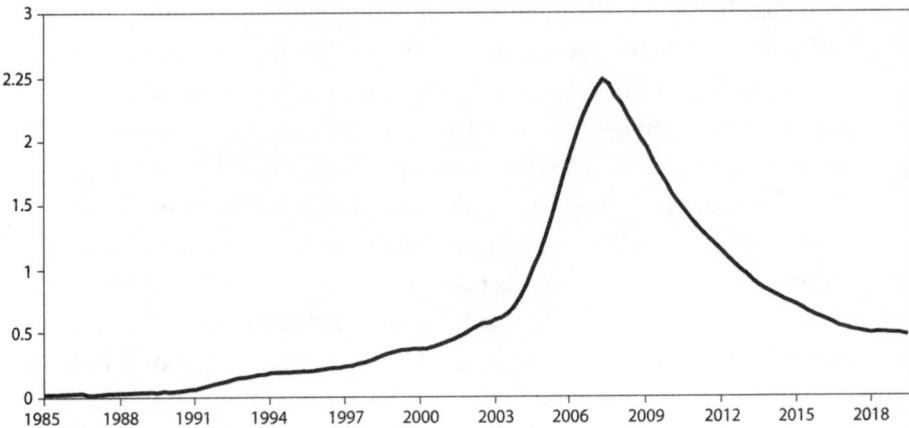

Fig. 6.3. "When the ducks are quacking, feed them" (value of residential mortgages held in private-label conduits, USD trillions). *Source: Federal Reserve Board*

safe assets relative to demand. The heightened demand for U.S. fixed income needed to be matched with a massive increase in American borrowing, but neither the American government nor its businesses were willing to participate.

The world's savers wanted to buy trillions of dollars of low-risk bonds that did not exist. American and European investment bankers responded with a burst of creativity. As the old Wall Street saying goes, "When the ducks are quacking, feed them." Between the start of 2001 and the middle of 2007, the world's financiers produced about $2.5 trillion of private-label U.S. mortgage-backed securities (MBS), most of which were based on residential mortgage loans that did not conform to normal underwriting standards. During the peak years of the bubble, half of all new U.S. residential mortgage borrowing was being funded by private-label MBS. Investment bankers also created about $650 billion of structured finance products derived from MBS. The value of these assets has since shrunk by $2.8 trillion. Investor revulsion has forced down the volume of new issuance back to where it was in the late 1990s.

The American experiment with private-label MBS was not supposed to be a risky business. Residential mortgages have long been considered one of the safest private investments available, and for good reason. Unlike credit card debt or other unsecured personal loans, mortgage borrowers have a strong incentive to stay current on their payments because default and foreclosure would force them to find a new place to live. Moreover, mortgage creditors typically get an extra cushion of protection because most mortgages are worth significantly less than the value of the underlying homes. Under most circumstances, creditors can recover their principal even after evicting a delinquent borrower and selling the collateral.

There was also nothing dangerous or unprecedented about selling bonds backed by portfolios of mortgages. After all, a diversified mix of loans is safer than any individual loan. European banks have been issuing covered bonds—bank debts tied to specific real estate loans—since the 1700s. Freddie Mac started issuing mortgage-backed securities in 1971. By 1985, total MBS issuance guaranteed by Fannie, Freddie, and Ginnie Mae (a government-sponsored enterprise fully owned by the U.S. government) had reached more than $100 billion a year. By the early 1990s, more than $1 trillion in American residential mortgages had been packaged into agency mortgage bonds. By 1993, more than 40 percent of all U.S. residential mortgages were held in agency MBS, while traditional banks held just 33 percent of all residential mortgages on their balance sheets.[33]

More Credit Supply Leads to Lower Credit Standards

The combination of voracious demand for low-risk U.S. fixed income and the federal government's failure to issue enough debt to meet that demand therefore produced a massive expansion in the supply of American mortgage credit. The problem was that most people who could afford a mortgage already had one.

The bankers' solution was to lower standards to the point that practically anyone who wanted a mortgage was given a loan regardless of the ability to repay. Mortgage originators were able to create the trillions of dollars of loans that investors wanted to buy by making sacrifices those investors would later regret. Credit histories were ignored. Documents were falsified, assuming anyone even bothered to ask for them. Because the financial system had to increase the supply of assets one way or another to satisfy demand, the result was that the biggest increases in debt were driven by the people with the worst credit scores and the lowest incomes to buy homes in the poorest neighborhoods. Unsurprisingly, these borrowers were also responsible for the overwhelming majority of the eventual losses on U.S. mortgages.

Lowering standards was not enough for originators to hit their production targets. To generate enough debt to satisfy investor demand, originators also had to abandon the old wisdom about how much to lend against the value of a house. In the past, a borrower with reasonable credit might have bought a $200,000 house with a $40,000 down payment and $160,000 in debt. A down payment of that size would have provided lenders with a 20 percent cushion against changes in the value of the house. Larger loans, loans to borrowers with dodgier credit histories, and loans to borrowers with volatile incomes would have required higher down payments in addition to higher interest rates.

During the bubble, however, down payment requirements collapsed across all categories. By the peak in 2006, the typical private-label mortgage had a down payment worth just 3 percent of a home's appraised value. Originators sometimes offered additional liens to cover the down payment or increased the total mortgage to be worth even more than the home's appraised value. Borrowers might have to pay higher interest rates on a subprime or an Alt-A mortgage, but they could get the mortgage and generate the debt needed to satisfy investor demand.

This was often unethical, and in some cases may have been illegal, but it was also the logical response to the enormous pressures on the U.S. financial system coming from outside. In any functioning market, high demand relative to supply leads to some combination of higher prices and additional production. Think of the oil shocks of the 1970s, which eventually led to deepwater exploration in the North Sea, the Gulf of Mexico, Alaska, and elsewhere, or how the rise of the technology industry in the San Francisco Bay Area since the 1990s has led to soaring housing prices. The main difference between financial assets and physical assets such as oil and housing is that it is much easier to create additional financial assets. Part of the reason, sadly, is that there will always be participants in the system willing to engage in unethical and fraudulent behavior to meet the needs of their customers. That is why every financial bubble in history has been accompanied by an enormous increase in financial fraud that became apparent only when the bubble collapsed.

More important for our purposes, expanding the pool of borrowers and increasing how much they could borrow created a substantial increase in U.S. household purchasing power. While the construction sector absorbed some of this additional credit by building new homes—often in places where they would later be abandoned—most of the extra spending power was used to bid up house prices. Given who was borrowing the money, the most rapid increases in house prices occurred in the zip codes that had the worst credit scores and highest poverty rates before the bubble began. Rising house prices gave lenders the confidence to keep originating more loans to questionable borrowers. There was little point worrying about default risk as long as the collateral continued to appreciate in value. The decline in lending standards and down payment requirements reinforced each other by pushing up house prices and encouraging lenders to expand credit even further.

Americans also responded to the credit boom by spending more. This took the form of both higher consumption and higher investment. (In America, the distinction between saving less and investing more is often nothing more than semantics. Installing a hot tub in the bathroom is considered investment, while paying for a high-quality education is labeled consumption.) Rising home values meant that people who sold their homes could generate capital gains to pay for vacations or new cars. Those who did not sell nevertheless appeared wealthier and therefore felt less pressure to save out of their incomes. Inflating asset prices were doing their saving for them.

Compounding all this were the changes in lending standards that made it easier for homeowners to take out additional debt on the same home. Many who had been steadily paying down their mortgages chose to become more indebted so that they could spend more. All that spending boosted local economies, which became self-reinforcing as it made borrowers appear more creditworthy than they otherwise would have been and encouraged even more speculation on rising house prices. Unfortunately, self-reinforcing processes on the way up become even more self-reinforcing on the way down.

In 2005, Federal Reserve chairman Alan Greenspan and Fed staff economist James Kennedy published a study tracking these transactions and estimating how much additional purchasing power American households were "extracting" from their homes. (Kennedy continued to update their model through the end of 2008.) The amounts involved were massive. During the 1990s, Americans had boosted their disposable income by about 2–3 percent each year by tapping the wealth in their homes. This mostly came from capital gains when homes were sold, rather than from additional borrowing.

Between the start of 2004 and the middle of 2006, however, home equity withdrawals boosted Americans' disposable income by 10 percent—about $1 trillion in each year. Over the course of the entire bubble, from the start of 2002 through the end of 2007, Americans extracted $4.7 trillion in wealth from their homes. The corresponding debt boom explains why Americans' housing wealth rose by less than $2 trillion at a time when U.S. home values increased by roughly $7 trillion. It also explains why so many Americans had a negative saving rate during the 2000s: from their perspective, rising home prices were effectively saving for them, freeing up cash from their meager wages to buy more goods and services.

Eventually, however, lenders ran out of ways to expand the credit supply. Despite the best efforts of the investment bankers and the mortgage originators, the limit had been reached. Minimum down payment requirements had dropped to almost nothing. Everyone who wanted a mortgage already had one.

At that point, the entire process naturally went into reverse. Home prices had been rising because the purchasing power available to buy housing had been rising far faster than the supply of homes. Once credit growth slowed down, prices stopped going up. That was a problem for the people who had gotten mortgages they knew they could not afford in the hope that they would be bailed out by rising home prices. These speculators were forced to sell, or default, which put downward pressure on prices. That quickly became a problem for the many Americans who

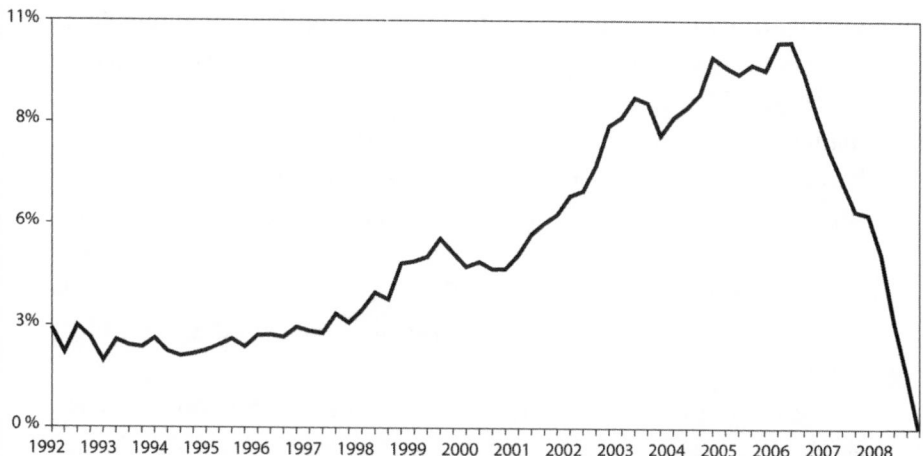

Fig. 6.4 When American houses became ATMs (home equity withdrawal relative to disposal income). *Source: James Kennedy's update of the mortgage system presented in "Estimates of Home Mortgage Originations, Repayments, and Debt on One-to-Four-Family Residences," Alan Greenspan and James Kennedy, Federal Reserve Board FEDS Working Paper No. 2005-41*

had depended on steadily rising home values to boost their spending at a time when real incomes were flat or falling.

By the middle of 2008, Americans had stopped taking money out of their homes altogether. Debt repayment was now the priority. Their spending cuts on everything from restaurants to haircuts reduced the incomes of their neighbors, which led to job losses, more defaults, and more home inventory hitting the market, which pushed down prices even further. Investors in "safe" assets belatedly realized that they were exposed to catastrophic losses. Originators and bankers responded to the collapse in demand for their product by tightening lending standards. The shrinking credit supply reinforced the decline in home values, and the spending cuts, and the job losses, and the defaults, which reinforced the tightening standards. The process that had built paper wealth and boosted consumption on the way up now threatened economic collapse on the way down.[34]

Despite the explosion of mortgage debt, America did not experience an economic boom. It was not Greece or Ireland or Spain. As in

Germany, sharply higher inequality, anemic corporate capital spending, and relatively tight fiscal policy all dampened U.S. domestic demand. Private fixed investment spending net of depreciation and inflation remained below the 2000 peak until 2014. There was no consumption boom, either. Real household consumption spending per person grew slightly slower in 2000–2006 than it did in 1947–2000. Private sector employment fell by 3 percent between 2000 and 2003 and never grew enough afterward to keep pace with the expanding population. Inflation was so moribund that the Federal Reserve was worried about falling prices.

America's current account and trade deficits nevertheless expanded as domestic production grew even less than domestic demand. This was most acute in manufacturing. According to the Federal Reserve, U.S. manufacturing production rose just 10 percent between the peak in the middle of 2000 and the middle of 2006, when the current account deficit peaked. However, that figure is distorted by estimates of productivity improvements in semiconductors. Exclude that sector, which employed fewer than 4 percent of all American manufacturing workers in 2000, and the picture looks very different: output fell about 6 percent between 2000 and 2003, after which it barely recovered to the previous peak by the end of 2006.

While most categories, including motor vehicles and parts, machinery, fabricated metal products, packaged foods, plastics, and furniture were all flat, others experienced severe declines. Despite surviving the emergence of sweatshops in the 1990s, American textile and apparel output shrank by roughly 30 percent between 2000 and 2006. (The main growth areas were aerospace, chemicals, and concrete.)

American *demand* for manufactured goods did grow between 2000 and 2006. Essentially all of that growth, however, was satisfied by foreign production rather than domestic capacity. American workers reaped none of the benefits, although American companies that owned factories elsewhere did much better. This would not have been a problem for Americans if U.S. manufacturers had been able to offset those losses by selling more abroad as exports. Unfortunately, while export revenues did rise, they did not grow nearly enough.

Competition from abroad was not, by itself, the problem. American manufacturers had done relatively well in the 1990s because they were competing with imports at a time of strong domestic and foreign demand. A strong global market had also supported American manufacturing employment in the 1990s despite massive improvements in labor-saving technology. In the 2000s, however, demand was depressed in large parts of the world, including the United States. The result was that foreign imports displaced American productive output at the expense of American jobs and incomes. Making matters worse, U.S. manufacturers were starved of the profits they needed to commit to investments in research and development, which helps explain why productivity growth has been so weak since 2006.[35]

More than 80 percent of the decline in private-sector employment between 2000 and 2003 can be directly attributed to the manufacturing sector. Losses were concentrated in the places and sectors most exposed to competition from manufacturers in countries where workers are paid far less than they are worth, most notably China. There was nothing inherently wrong with American manufacturers opening operations in China. The problem was that workers in China and elsewhere were unable to consume additional imports from the United States, which broke the link between rising trade and rising living standards.[36]

In theory, the hit to manufacturing could have been offset by gains elsewhere in the economy. Yet despite the inflation of the health care, government, construction, finance, and education sectors—which accounted for most of the jobs created in the years before the financial crisis—the age-adjusted share of Americans with a job never surpassed the peak reached in 2000. The drop was particularly severe for those without college degrees. The collapse of the housing bubble eventually revealed the full extent of the damage wrought by deindustrialization.[37]

Government disability payments helped displaced workers make ends meet but could not replace the lost income. This magnified the impact of imports to everyone who lived in affected communities, regardless of whether they worked in retail, restaurants, or higher-paid industries such as accountants and lawyers. For those parts of America, it was a catastrophe. Men without jobs were unable to find women to marry or to have children with. Men without jobs and families were driven to drinking, drugs, and—especially—suicide. Local governments

Fig. 6.5 International value of the U.S. dollar (real trade-weighted index, January 1988 = 100). *Sources: Federal Reserve Board; Matthew Klein's calculations*

struggled to provide services as tax revenue dried up and demands on the welfare system grew. Even though crime rates plunged nationally in the past two decades, crime rates in the places most exposed to low-cost import competition slightly increased.[38]

The problem was the rest of the world's voracious demand for dollar-denominated assets. In addition to inflating the mortgage debt bubble, overabundant foreign financing also savaged America's terms of trade as trillions of dollars of uneconomic asset purchases distorted the U.S. exchange rate. Between the start of 1997—the eve of the Asian Financial Crisis—and the beginning of 2002, the dollar appreciated by more than 20 percent against the currencies of its trading partners. While the dollar declined from then until 2008, it consistently remained far above its 1988–96 average. To the misfortune of American workers, the overvaluation of the dollar meant that American consumers would prefer to buy goods made abroad at the expense of domestic manu-facturing.[39]

The rest of the world's unwillingness to spend—which in turn was attributable to the class wars in the major surplus economies and the desire for self-insurance after the Asian crisis—was the underlying cause of both America's debt bubble and America's deindustrialization. Foreign financial inflows forced Americans to absorb their glut of manufacturing capacity at the expense of U.S. jobs and incomes. This necessarily required foreign savers to mitigate the impact of job losses on American spending by buying dollar-denominated assets, which pushed down interest rates, expanded credit, and facilitated a surge in household borrowing.

A careful study published in 2017 by the Federal Reserve Bank of New York explicitly linked these forces. The researchers compared different parts of the United States based on how exposed they were to cheap manufactured imports. It turns out that the places most vulnerable to foreign competition were also the places where households took out the most debt, both in absolute terms and relative to incomes. As they summarized it, "The displacement of domestic production by imports fueled demand for credit" to substitute for lost wages.[40]

The Exorbitant Burden since 2008

The financial crisis should have led to a rebalancing of global saving and spending, with the United States shifting from a deficit country to a surplus country through a mix of falling imports and rising exports. Domestic production would have increased faster than domestic demand, debts would have been repaid, and other countries would have borne the burden of sustaining global spending. The redistribution of global demand could even have accommodated a reversal of the rising inequities within the United States.

That is not what happened. While America's current account deficit has consistently been smaller than in 1998–2008, it has nevertheless persisted at about 2–3 percent each year. As before, this cannot be explained by excessive spending in the United States. American domestic demand has been exceptionally weak since the financial crisis. Personal consumption spending per person is more than 12 percent lower than it would have been if it had continued to follow the long-term pre-1998 trend. Business investment net of inflation and depreciation is finally higher than the peak reached in 2000, but spending on home building

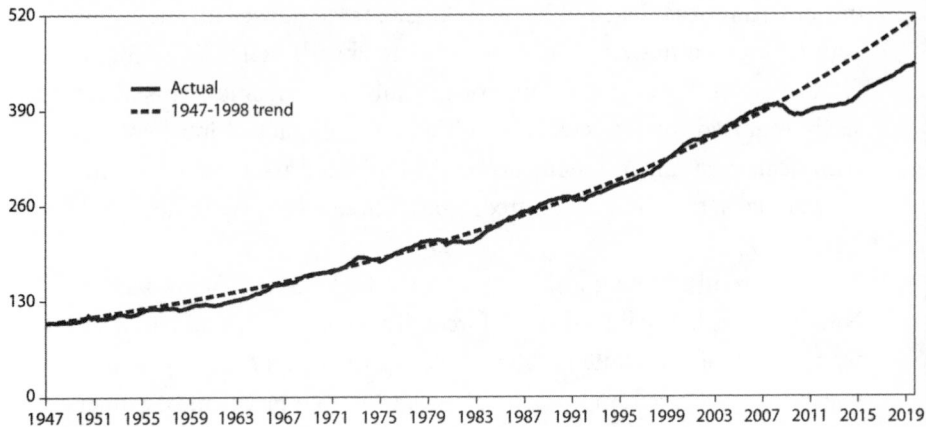

Fig. 6.6 The great slump (real household consumption spending per person, January 1947 = 100). *Sources: Bureau of Economic Analysis; Matthew Klein's calculations*

is still at levels associated with the recession of the early 1990s. Government investment spending is less than half what it was in the mid-2000s. The share of working-age Americans with a job remains roughly where it was in 2007 and significantly below where it was in 2000.

The impact on American producers has been even worse than in the 2000s: as of the end of 2018, manufacturing output and manufacturing capacity were both lower than at the previous peak in 2008. Manufacturing employment was still down about 10 percent from its levels in 2006. America's trade deficit in manufactured goods (excluding refined petroleum products) was now worth more than 4 percent of GDP—its highest level since the nineteenth century. Worryingly, this deterioration in America's manufacturing trade position is mostly attributable to stagnant exports of advanced capital goods combined with soaring imports of competing products from abroad. The overall current account deficit has been kept in check by the transformation of the U.S. oil industry and by rising exports of American software (some of which is measured as foreign direct investment income for tax reasons).[41]

The persistence of the American current account deficit can only be explained by excessive saving abroad and the U.S. role in absorbing these excess savings. Calls for Americans to behave more prudently miss the point: it is not *Americans* who have decided to borrow too much. As

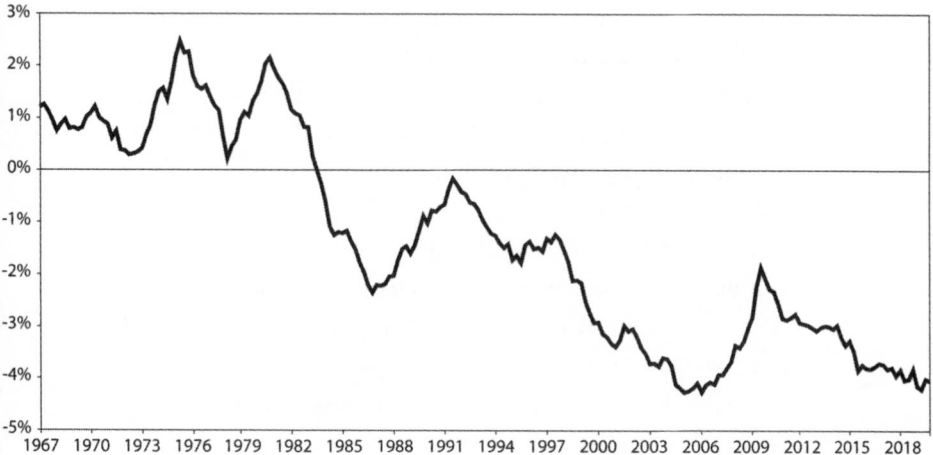

Fig. 6.7 The U.S. manufacturing trade deficit is near its all-time high (net trade in goods excluding food, feed, beverages, and energy products as a share of GDP). *Sources: Bureau of Economic Analysis; Matthew Klein's calculations*

long as there are Americans who want to borrow—and in every country, there are always people who are willing to borrow under the appropriate conditions—the U.S. financial sector will find them and lower interest rates and lending standards until loan targets are met. The financial system will continue to force adjustments in the real economy until savings decline. Either borrowing will rise or income will fall.

For example:

- Net inflows into the U.S. can cause the dollar to become more expensive than it otherwise would be. Currency appreciation increases household purchasing power at the expense of export revenues and incomes, which means less saving through a combination of higher consumption and lower production.
- Cheap imports can displace existing workers and raise U.S. unemployment. Unemployed workers have a negative saving rate because they still consume even if they have no income, which means that rising joblessness mechanically lowers the national saving rate.

- Lower employment leads to additional government borrowing to fund larger fiscal transfers, most of which would have caused consumption to rise and savings to decline.
- To reduce unemployment, the Fed might try to encourage additional borrowing through lower interest rates and looser credit conditions.
- The combination of foreign inflows and the Fed's monetary response can boost the prices of real estate, stocks, and other American assets to levels above where they otherwise would have been, even setting off asset bubbles. Higher asset prices make people feel richer and cause them to spend more out of their current income.

All of these mechanisms cause some combination of falling income (rising unemployment) and rising debt. Insufficient spending on goods and services by foreigners, in other words, necessarily translates into excessive purchases of American financial assets, thanks to the dollar's unfortunate status as the premier international reserve asset, which then results in an increase in American debt.

Until 2014, excessive foreign saving was led by foreign reserve managers. Between the start of 2009 and the middle of 2014, Americans consistently bought more assets abroad than private investors bought in the United States. Had there been no change in these private-sector flows and had there been no foreign government purchases of U.S. assets, America's cumulative current account surplus would have been worth about $1 trillion, or about 1.2 percent of GDP each year. Reserve managers, however, more than offset those private flows by purchasing U.S. dollar assets at an annual rate equivalent to about 3.6 percent of American GDP.

After the middle of 2014, however, reserve managers were no longer the main funders of the U.S. current account deficit. In some cases, such as China, reserves fell to offset outbound investment from rich households and businesses. The overall effect on China's external position was minimal, and all that was changing was which set of elites was allowed to invest abroad.

More seriously, China's credit tightening and investment slowdown coincided with collapsing prices of oil and other commodities. Many exporting countries chose to run down their reserves to mitigate the hit to purchasing power and prevent a collapse in imports. As oil prices rebounded, however, many producers began rebuilding their stash of savings.

At the same time, the decline in the oil price reduced spending on imported energy in the rest of the world. Asian governments other than China—particularly Japan, South Korea, Singapore, Taiwan, and Thailand—responded by accumulating additional foreign exchange reserves, by directing their government-backed pensions and life insurance funds to increase their investment abroad, or both. According to data compiled by Brad Setser of the Council on Foreign Relations, cumulative state-sponsored purchases of U.S. financial assets have been roughly zero since the start of 2014.[42]

The decline in official reserve accumulation was offset by a new source of demand for U.S. financial assets: Europeans. Members of the euro area had committed to suppressing domestic demand to satisfy their ideological objective of balanced government budgets without excessive taxation of the rich. Government spending on pensions, welfare, and infrastructure investment went down, while taxes on consumption and labor income went up.

Dwindling deficits crushed the supply of government bonds available for private savers to buy, but the European private sector still wanted to save. After all, the economy was still weak, and they were still dealing with the consequences of the private debt accumulated during the bubble years. Making matters worse was the European Central Bank's asset purchase program, which ended up buying trillions of euros' worth of European government and corporate bonds. An estimate by the ECB concluded that just 15 percent of the German government's bonds were held by private investors at the beginning of 2018, because the rest had been hoovered up by central banks.

European savers have responded to these pressures by buying about €1.5 trillion in foreign bonds from the middle of 2014 through the end of 2018. (In the aggregate, non-Europeans sold euro-denominated bonds to the ECB.) The net flow of bond buying from the euro area has been about equivalent in magnitude to the total U.S. current account deficit over that period. European savers did not exclusively buy U.S. bonds, of course, but they have bought about $800 billion worth since the middle of 2014. They did so because they knew that the United States would accommodate buying on that scale.

Crucially, unlike the pre-2008 transatlantic financial flows, these purchases were unreciprocated. That contributed to the roughly 20 percent increase in the real value of the dollar between the middle of 2014 and the beginning of 2016. As of the middle of 2019, U.S. exports of capital goods and motor vehicles have fallen, while imports are up by nearly 20 percent. Americans have therefore had to bear the burden of the Europeans' unwillingness to spend on their own domestic needs. Despite their ongoing complaints about American policy, European leaders have done nothing to change this situation. It is as if the 1960s have returned.[43]

Keynes's Revenge

The conventional wisdom is that it is good to be an issuer of a reserve currency, but that is a misconception grounded in psychology rather than economics. Unless the reserve issuer overwhelmingly dominates the world economy, there will always be conflicts between its domestic needs and the global demand for reserve assets. For more than six decades, the United States has satiated savers in the rest of the world at the expense of its own workers. Rather than an exorbitant privilege, as the French wrongly described it, the dollar's primacy has been an exorbitant burden.

John Maynard Keynes would have understood this. The United Kingdom was less than 10 percent of the world economy after World War I, yet it had committed to maintaining an unreasonably strong exchange rate in the 1920s to protect the value of sterling assets purchased by savers in India and the Commonwealth. That decision—which Keynes vigorously opposed as an economic adviser to the U.K. government—came at the expense of British industry. British exports were about 25 percent lower throughout the 1920s than they were in 1913, while artificially cheap imports displaced domestic production. British workers endured nearly a decade of extremely high unemployment. Issuing one of the world's major reserve currencies was no privilege for them.

But things changed in the period from 1930 to 1932, when the British public voted to place domestic concerns above international responsibilities. The United Kingdom abandoned its international commitments, devalued its currency against gold, lowered domestic interest rates, and imposed tariffs, after which the country quickly closed the gap in living standards that had emerged in the 1920s between it and the rest of the rich world.[44]

Before then, the British government had deliberately imposed pain on its own citizens to maintain the status of the pound sterling. It was a policy choice that could be, and was, reversed. Similarly, the U.S. government made a choice to tie the international financial system to the dollar after the end of World War II. At first, issuing the reserve currency was not a burden. It may even have made sense at a time when American production made up nearly half of global output.

Those early postwar years, however, were an anomaly. By 1971, the choice made at Bretton Woods had become untenable, so the Nixon administration broke the link to gold. Starting in the 1990s, however, savers in the rest of the world decided that the dollar was the international reserve asset, regardless of any formal commitments. The resulting financial inflows were accommodated by the U.S. political and financial system—with disastrous consequences for Americans.

When foreign savers buy U.S. assets, America's current account deficit rises through some combination of lower income from deindustrialization and higher spending on imports. Unless there are trillions of dollars of worthwhile investments in the United States waiting for funding—and there are not—the higher spending must take the form of wasteful investment or additional consumption. And unless the U.S. government fully offsets the purchases from foreign central banks by commensurately increasing its debt issuance, the American private sector will have to absorb additional foreign financial inflows by selling assets, issuing equity, or borrowing. There is no other plausible outcome.

The deeper problem is that institutional distortions in the surplus countries have led to chronic shortfalls in spending. The inevitable consequences are a glut of productive capacity, excess saving, and excessive demand for American financial assets. A functioning trading system needs a symmetrical mechanism to constrain these distortions. Before World War I, the constraint was the gold standard: deficit countries losing gold would be forced to cut their spending, while surplus countries receiving gold inflows would get a boost to domestic demand. The world went off gold to fight the war, however, and lost the discipline it had imposed. Keynes tried, but failed, to create a substitute: a new stateless currency—the bancor—that would serve as the global reserve asset. He recognized that no country should have to bear the cost of the world's imbalances alone. Keynes lost the argument at Bretton Woods, but his analysis remains sound.

It is time to try again. The alternatives are voluntary commitments by the surplus countries to adjust their domestic imbalances or unilateral and potentially destructive responses by the deficit countries, particularly the United States.

Conclusion

To End the Trade Wars, End the Class Wars

T rade war is often presented as a conflict between countries. It is not: it is a conflict mainly between bankers and owners of financial assets on one side and ordinary households on the other—between the very rich and everyone else. Rising inequality has produced gluts of manufactured goods, job loss, and rising indebtedness. It is an economic and financial perversion of what global integration was supposed to achieve. For decades, the United States has been the largest single victim of this perversion. Absorbing the rest of the world's excess output and savings—at the cost of deindustrialization and financial crises—has been America's *exorbitant burden.*

But Americans are not the only victims. All the peoples of the world suffer from this arrangement, because the U.S. financial system and consumer market function as a safety valve for exploitation elsewhere. America's openness to international trade and finance means that the rich in Europe, China, and the other major surplus economies can squeeze their workers and retirees in the confidence that they can always sell their wares, earn their profits, and park their savings in safe assets.

If the United States were not such an open economy, surplus countries would be forced either to divert their excess production to other countries, none of which have ever been as willing as the United States to absorb it, or to watch unwanted inventory pile up until factories were closed and workers were fired. The costs of rising income inequality in one country would be internalized, and there would be limited impact on others. Instead, by preventing political and industrial elites in the surplus countries from facing the consequences of their actions, the open system has enabled destructive behavior in the rest of the world.

From a certain perspective, the United States—and the United Kingdom, Canada, and Australia, all of which play a similar role in the global economy—therefore resembles the imperial colonies of Europe of the late nineteenth century. Back then, subject peoples were forced to buy Europe's excess production in exchange for taking on unneeded debt. Remarkably, a similar situation exists today. Instead of violence, however, the modern regime depends on the English-speaking countries' political commitment to open markets. This is a choice, but in democracies, the people have the option to change their mind.

We may already be starting to see this. In the 2016 election, all of the major U.S. presidential candidates disavowed the Trans-Pacific Partnership (TPP). Bernie Sanders warned that it would "make it easier for corporations to throw American workers out on the street" and would "reward some of the biggest human-rights violators in the world." Hillary Clinton was concerned the agreement failed to address the problem of currency manipulation and gave too much protection to pharmaceutical patents. Larry Summers, the former U.S. Treasury secretary who was a confidant of both Barack Obama and Clinton, was not explicitly opposed to the TPP, but he also thought it was a waste of time compared to reforming the IMF or boosting the funding of the United Nations. To Summers, "more globalization" was unnecessary, and politicians should instead focus on making "sure the globalization we have works for all our citizens."[1]

One of Donald Trump's first actions as president was to pull the United States out of TPP. The Transatlantic Trade and Investment Partnership—the other major trade deal negotiated by the Obama administration—also seems dead as of this writing. In the years since taking office, Trump has imposed punitive tariffs on everything from Korean washing machines to Canadian steel to almost all of America's imports from China. The net effect has been to double the amount of customs revenue collected between the end of 2017 and the middle of 2019. Trump's threats could expand the tariff base even more by going after auto imports from Europe. While some of these actions are unpopular, many leading Democrats, including many of those running for president in 2020, support the tariffs imposed on Chinese goods.[2]

As we have shown in this book, however, addressing trade imbalances through tariffs is likely to be ineffective at best and harmful under certain conditions. That is why it matters that capital controls are becoming increasingly popular, especially in the other English-speaking economies. New Zealand recently banned all nonresidents from buying residential property. Australia limits foreign buyers to new homes, which has helped stimulate construction, and it taxes foreign purchases, although the rates vary by state. Some local governments in Canada have begun taxing foreign purchasers of housing. The United States could go even further. On July 31, 2019, two U.S. senators—one a Democrat, one a Republican—introduced a bill that would direct the Federal Reserve to force the current account deficit to shrink to zero by discouraging foreign investment with a "market access charge."[3]

The surprise is that Americans have tolerated the open system for as long as they have. When that system was first constructed, the U.S. economy was about equal in size to the entire rest of the world. Today, however, the United States makes up less than a quarter of global output. Compared to seventy years ago, the rest of world is now three times bigger relative to the United States, which means that America has far less capacity to absorb the rest of the world's savings imbalances. If the U.S. share of the global economy continues to shrink, the burden imposed on Americans will continue to rise until, as a matter just of arithmetic, the system will break down. Yet no one in the American political mainstream has felt comfortable challenging this system until recently.

This apparent surprise can be explained by America's own class wars. After all, plenty of Americans have prospered producing financial assets to accommodate the rest of the world's excess savings. The world's preference for American markets and the U.S. dollar inflates the incomes of the financiers who control access to these markets—as well as their domestic political clout. For decades, the U.S. Treasury's approach to international finance was driven largely by what made sense for the major American commercial and investment banks and the owners of financial capital. The interests of everyone else in the economy were largely ignored, if not outright opposed by counterproductive commitments to maintain a strong dollar. This was always justified on the grounds that deregulating capital and increasing its mobility would lead to the best possible investment outcomes.

The resulting increases in wealth, they explained, would inevitably trickle down to all Americans—never mind that international capital flows are far more likely to be driven by speculation, investment fads, capital flight, and reserve accumulation (often for mercantilist purposes) than by sober investment decisions about the best long-term uses of capital. Many American companies adapted to the massive financial inflows coming into the United States by relocating their production to countries where workers are underpaid and then selling goods back to U.S. consumers at higher margins.

The influence of the bankers was amplified by U.S. officials who were willing to sacrifice domestic industry for geopolitical reasons during the Cold War. The U.S. government repeatedly negotiated trade agreements that Commerce Department officials privately argued were disadvantageous to American businesses and workers because of the supposed strategic benefits. More recently, the dollar's role in the global payments system has given the Treasury immense power to impose financial sanctions on targets anywhere in the world. But as Paul Volcker—who, among other things, was the Treasury's undersecretary for international affairs in 1969–74—put it in a recent interview, "The top dog pays the price."[4]

The world's rich were able to benefit at the expense of the world's workers and retirees because the interests of American financiers were complementary to the interests of Chinese and German industrialists. Both complemented the interests of the wealthiest throughout the world, even from the poorest countries. The modern surplus countries do not need colonies to absorb their excess production because they can work with bankers, their willing collaborators in the deficit countries.

The perverse result is that deepening globalization and rising inequality have reinforced each other. Businesses across the world use international competition as an excuse to push for lower wages, weaker environmental and safety regulations, preferential tax regimes, and regressive transfers. Squeezing ordinary households has, apparently, been much easier than increasing productivity, investing in infrastructure, and improving health and education. This is unsustainable, however, because depressing wages must lead to some combination of lower consumption, which reduces total spending in the global economy, and higher indebtedness, which is ultimately self-limiting and self-defeating. It is not just a coincidence that throughout modern history, high levels of income inequality have coincided with soaring levels of debt.

Over the past several decades, demand for goods and services has therefore become the world's scarcest and most valuable resource, with the United States playing the role of swing producer. Companies everywhere fight for larger shares of a global market even as they collaborate to suppress the size of their domestic markets. This is the very definition of "beggar thy neighbor." Because "competitiveness" has become a euphemism for pushing wages down, either directly or through currency depreciation and weaker social safety nets, the fetish of competitiveness has generated a global spending shortage. Trade wars are an almost inevitable consequence of globalization as it has been practiced. Peoples who fundamentally share common interests are being set against each other because the ultrarich have been successfully waging a class war against everyone else.

Current trade negotiations address none of these questions, which is why they will accomplish little. It makes no difference how many American airplanes or tons of American soybeans China promises to buy or indeed how much the American bilateral deficit with China is reduced. It does not even matter how many U.S. companies that had earlier relocated to China return to the United States. As long as ordinary Chinese retain so little of what they produce, which necessarily depresses their spending on goods and services, China must run a trade surplus and it must export huge amounts of savings. The same is true of Germany, Japan, the Netherlands, South Korea, Taiwan, Switzerland, Singapore, and the other major surplus economies. Unless the deficit countries force those foreign capital flows elsewhere, they must inevitably absorb the rest of the world's excess savings and excess production.

There is no question that an American withdrawal from global trade—the gradual closure of the world's largest consumer market and largest capital market—would impose significant costs at first on the rest of the world and eventually on the United States itself. If the United States retreats from its traditional role without agreeing on a new set of rules with the rest of the world, global trade will become unstable and increasingly contentious as countries try to shift the burden of adjustment elsewhere. Instead of the historically anomalous period of peaceful globalization in the second half of the twentieth century, the world would resemble the anarchy—and potentially the violence—that characterized trade from the 1600s through the first half of the twentieth century. That would be a tragedy.

What Should America Do?

The United States, like Germany, is racked by extreme inequality and degraded infrastructure. Unlike Germany, however, it has a large current account deficit. That means Americans cannot address all their problems simultaneously within the context of the open system. Reducing inequality and repairing infrastructure would lead to higher consumption and higher investment. While U.S. output would likely rise as well, some of the increase in spending would likely be absorbed by foreign producers, which means that the U.S. current account deficit would increase.

Unless policies in the rest of the world change, the United States cannot unilaterally reduce inequality, raise living standards, and stabilize or reduce its current account deficit at the same time without restricting foreign investment. The same is true for any other country with a current account deficit and open capital markets, such as the United Kingdom or France. The question is how to manage those competing priorities.

In the short term, America's first objective should be to shift the burden of absorbing unwanted financial inflows from the U.S. private sector to the federal government. American households and companies should not be pushed to borrow more than they can afford out of misguided concerns about the budget deficit or the level of government spending. As we have shown, the fact that the United States must absorb a permanent financial account surplus means that the only way to prevent rising American unemployment is with some combination of higher private borrowing and higher government borrowing. That is why, in the near term, U.S. Treasury debt should be issued as needed to accommodate the desires of foreign savers. Lower payroll taxes, larger standard deductions on income taxes, and a better social safety net, particularly for health expenses, would all help generate the necessary budget deficits while simultaneously ameliorating the unequal distribution of income.

It would be even better if the federal government absorbed foreign financial flows by directly or indirectly increasing investment in much-needed American infrastructure, particularly public transit and green energy. Many years of fiscal austerity and neglect have generated a large backlog of worthwhile projects. Moreover, infrastructure investment in the United States would almost certainly generate increases in debt-servicing capacity that substantially exceeded the additional debt-servicing cost, so it would not even result in a higher overall debt burden: debt would rise, but GDP would rise by more.

Federal spending could also help sustain demand for American manufactures even if the domestic market remained swamped by gluts from abroad. Increasing defense procurement is the easiest approach, but other measures could be more effective and should be considered. The goal should not be preventing foreigners from selling to Americans, but to maintaining the existence of a domestic industrial base despite the distortions caused by underspending in the rest of the world.

At the same time, the United States should also find a way to accommodate the legitimate desires of certain governments to protect themselves from crises without having those governments accumulate emergency savings denominated in dollars. Making it easier for foreigners to borrow dollars from the Federal Reserve would help. In 2008, the Fed offered almost unlimited credit to America's major allies—including Korea and Mexico—under relatively generous conditions. In 2013, the Fed established standing arrangements with central banks in Canada, the euro area, the United Kingdom, Japan, and Switzerland, although these facilities could theoretically be terminated at any time. Shifting to a permanent institutional structure and expanding to a wider field of eligible borrowers should help reduce foreign reserve demand for U.S. assets.[5]

These measures, however, are mainly short-term stopgaps. They are not enough to resolve the underlying problems in the global economy. The United States would still remain the world's dumping ground for the world's excess savings and the surplus production that comes with it. The open global trading system will remain under threat as long as elites in the major surplus economies remain committed to a system that continuously squeezes the purchasing power of their workers and retirees.

If we want to end the trade wars before they further damage the global economy and undermine international peace, we must therefore address the twin problems of income inequality and the world's unhealthy dependence on the U.S. financial system. The United States must take the lead in reforming a broken system of global trade and, above all, of global capital flows. The deficit countries must find a way to *force* the elites in the surplus countries to internalize the costs of their behavior, and they must do so in the face of substantial opposition from their own elites. There are enormous benefits to a world of open trade, but there are also costs, and these costs must be addressed if we wish to retain the benefits.

What Should the Surplus Countries Do?

The global spending shortage comes from the surplus countries. Although German policymakers often insist that Germany's surpluses are the reward for superior production techniques, this is total nonsense. The reward a country receives for superior productivity is higher imports through improving terms of trade. Persistent surpluses are almost always the consequence of highly unbalanced distributions of income in favor of businesses and the rich. The United States and the other deficit countries can try to deflect those surpluses, but even if they succeed, the problems we have described would remain unresolved. The peoples of Asia and Europe deserve better.

The latest data suggest that China has either the second-largest or third-largest current account surplus in dollar terms. The danger is that this surplus could grow rapidly as domestic investment declines in the years ahead. Without an offsetting increase in household spending, the result would be a return of the glut that plagued the world in the 2000s. Fortunately, the Chinese government has many tools at its disposal to prevent this by shifting income from elites to ordinary workers and retirees—should it choose to do so.

First, the *hukou* system should be reformed and eventually eliminated so that all Chinese can gain access to the government benefits they pay for with taxes regardless of where in the country they currently live. Second, the government should expand the quality of its safety net and guarantee reasonable income security in retirement, including health care. Third, the government should make it easier for workers to organize and negotiate better pay and labor conditions. Fourth, state-owned enterprises should pay higher dividends. Ideally, those dividends would be distributed directly to Chinese households through a dedicated social wealth fund. Fifth, the government should continue its efforts to improve air and water quality through tighter environmental regulations. Sixth, the government should reform its tax system by lowering the burden on the poor and middle-income consumers while raising taxes on the highest earners. Last, the government should continue to prop up the value of the yuan, including by selling foreign exchange reserves, if necessary, which would help shift purchasing power from the owners of exporting companies to regular Chinese consumers.

None of these proposals is new. All except the last were listed in the reforms proposed officially during the Third Plenum of October 2013, and even the last was supported by the former governor of the central bank. But these reforms have been ferociously opposed by China's powerful vested interests who stand to lose from a policy of rebalancing. As long as China is able to postpone its rebalancing—which it can do as long as it can dump its excess savings in the United States—it will continue to be tempting for China to avoid the necessary adjustments.

The euro area is now the world's biggest source of global imbalances. Before 2008, households and businesses in the crisis countries of Spain, Greece, Italy, Ireland, and others offset the stagnation in Germany by borrowing heavily and spending more than they earned in income. This drove growth for the economic bloc as a whole but proved unsustainable. The financial crisis forced those households and businesses to cut spending and focus on debt repayment.

Their governments initially stepped in by borrowing and spending to cushion the impact. More recently, however, those governments have been forced to retrench. The results have been higher taxes, more unemployment, higher poverty, worse infrastructure, and lower overall living standards. The combined effect has been to drive interest rates on sovereign debt below zero for almost all countries on even the longest maturities. The euro area's twin goals should therefore be reducing the overall private surplus and expanding the aggregate budget deficit.

Europe's large private surplus is ultimately a function of the rise in inequality. That means it can be reversed through straightforward policies that shift income from the ultrarich and the businesses they control to ordinary European households. The obvious contenders are higher taxes on high earners, lower social security taxes, lower value-added taxes, stronger social safety nets, and higher minimum wages. Germany in particular should reform its inheritance tax regime to discourage the concentration of corporate wealth in a handful of family-owned businesses and update its property tax system to account for changes in home values.

Fixing Europe's fiscal position requires more creativity. Ideally, each country would cut taxes and boost spending as appropriate to its own domestic needs. Germany, for example, could shift from a budget surplus worth 2 percent of GDP to a 4 percent deficit by lowering its high taxes, by improving income security for its workers, and by finally making necessary investments in roads, bridges, high-speed rail, broadband, and green energy. The Netherlands, meanwhile, could help its struggling households get out from their massive housing debt burdens by lowering income and value-added taxes and by loosening its onerous bankruptcy laws.[6]

Those policies would be good for people in Germany and the Netherlands, but they would not be nearly enough to affect Europe's overall balance, which has shifted so much since 2012 because of changes in the crisis countries. Based purely on economic conditions, the biggest budget deficits should be in the euro area countries least able to sustain them: Greece, Italy, and Spain. This is a problem.

The most practical solution is to federalize European fiscal policy as much as possible. National governments would spend less, tax less, and borrow less, thereby allowing them to honor their treaty commitments without turning the euro area into a permanent menace for the rest of the world. The European Investment Bank could become the main funding source for infrastructure projects across the bloc and could coordinate projects across national borders. Common deposit insurance and bank resolution would ensure that savings at banks in Greece and Portugal are always as good as savings at banks in Germany and the Netherlands. Finally, a new central euro area treasury would take over core spending functions such as unemployment reinsurance and retirement security, backstop the EIB, issue debt that would be as desirable for international investors as U.S. Treasury bonds, and levy common taxes. Ideally, those new taxes would crack down on corporate profit shifting within the currency bloc and target the net wealth of the richest residents of the euro area.

If China and Europe follow the general prescriptions outlined above, living standards would rise across the world and indebtedness would fall. Rising consumption would encourage businesses to invest in additional productive capacity to meet demand. Transferring income to ordinary households would therefore result in both more consumption and more investment. Redistribution, in this case, would lead to higher output. The open system would be preserved, and the current conflicts over trade would disappear as each country's internal class conflicts were peacefully resolved. This is our preferred outcome. The alternatives are far worse. At the very least, they would involve a refusal by the United States to continue accommodating global imbalances by absorbing them.

What we are suggesting may seem difficult, but it has been done before. At Bretton Woods, the Allies created a new system of rules for the global economy and international finance. At home, governments strengthened their social democracy by guaranteeing basic living standards and improving the security of workers and retirees. Leaders responded to the challenges of the time and learned from the experiences of the past. Their solutions were imperfect—that is why we are where we are—but they were based on the values of egalitarianism, global cooperation, and peace. The peoples of the world deserve a comparable response to the challenges of today.

Notes

Abbreviations

BEA	Bureau of Economic Analysis
BIS	Bank for International Settlements
CFR	Council on Foreign Relations
ECB	European Central Bank
FRB	Federal Reserve Board
GGDC	Groningen Growth and Development Centre
IMF	International Monetary Fund
IRS	Internal Revenue Service
NBER	National Bureau of Economic Research
NSD	Norwegian Centre for Research Data
OECD	Organisation for Economic Co-Operation and Development
UNCTAD	United Nations Conference on Trade and Development

Introduction

1. David Autor et al., "Importing Political Polarization? The Electoral Conse-quences of Rising Trade Exposure," December 2017, NBER Working Paper No. 22637; Bob Davis and Jon Hilsenrath, "How the China Shock, Deep and Swift, Spurred the Rise of Trump," *Wall Street Journal,* August 11, 2016; David Autor et al., "A Note on the Effect of Rising Trade Exposure on the 2016 Presidential Election," MIT Working Paper, rev. March 2, 2017.

2. Senate Democrats, "Schumer Statement on New Tariffs on Chinese Imports," Press Release, June 15, 2018, https://www.democrats.senate.gov/newsroom/press-releases /schumer-statement-on-new-tariffs-on-chinese-imports.

3. Brad W. Setser, "The Continuing Chinese Drag on the Global Economy," CFR (blog), July 18, 2019, https://www.cfr.org/blog/continuing-chinese-drag-global-economy.

4. Eurostat, "GDP and Main Components (Output, Expenditure and Income)," https://appsso.eurostat.ec.europa.eu/nui/show.do?dataset=bop_c6_q&lang=en.

5. IMF, "World Economic Outlook Database," April 2019, https://www.imf.org/external/pubs/ft/weo/2019/01/weodata/index.aspx.

6. "Verkauft doch eure Inseln, ihr Pleite-Griechen . . . und die Akropolis gleich mit!," *Bild*, October 27, 2010; Stefan Wagstyl, "Greeks Find Support for German Reparations Claims—in Germany," *Financial Times*, March 17, 2015; Mehreen Khan and Paul McLean, "Dijsselbloem under Fire after Saying Eurozone Countries Wasted Money on 'Alcohol and Women,'" *Financial Times*, March 21, 2017.

7. John A. Hobson, *Imperialism: A Study* (New York: James Pott, 1902). See also Thomas Hauner, Branko Milanovic, and Suresh Naidu, "Inequality, Foreign Investment, and Imperialism," Stone Center Working Paper 2017, for a modern quantitative analysis of Hobson's thesis.

8. Kenneth Austin, "Communist China's Capitalism: The Highest Stage of Capitalist Imperialism," *World Economics*, January–March 2011, 79–94.

ONE From Adam Smith to Tim Cook

1. Adam Smith, *An Inquiry into the Nature and Causes of the Wealth of Nations*, 2 vols., ed. Edwin Cannan (London: Methuen, 1904), vol. 1, bk. 1, chap. 1, available at https://oll.libertyfund.org/.

2. R. H. Coase, "The Nature of the Firm," *Economica* 4, no. 16 (November 1937): 386–405.

3. Smith, *Wealth of Nations*, vol. 1, bk. 4, chap. 2.

4. David Ricardo, *On the Principles of Political Economy and Taxation*, 3rd ed. (London: John Murray, 1821), chaps. 7, 27, available at https://oll.libertyfund.org/.

5. Ricardo, *Principles*, chap. 7.

6. Cameron Hewitt, "Brits on the Douro: A Brief History of Port," *Rick Steves' Europe*, https://www.ricksteves.com/watch-read-listen/read/articles/the-history-of-port.

7. Ricardo, *Principles*, chap. 7.

8. "President's Address to Both Houses of Congress," *Annals of Congress*, 1st Cong., 2d sess., January 8, 1790.

9. "Alexander Hamilton's Final Version of the Report on the Subject of Manufactures [5 December 1791]," Founders Online, https://founders.archives.gov/documents/Hamilton/01-10-02-0001-0007.

10. Douglas A. Irwin, "The Aftermath of Hamilton's 'Report on Manufactures,'" NBER Working Paper No. 9943, August 2003; Act to Regulate the Duties on Imports and Tonnage, 14th Cong., 1st sess., Ch. 107, 3 Stat. 310 [Tariff of 1816 (Dallas Tariff)].

11. Friedrich List, *Outlines of American Political Economy, in a Series of Letters . . . to Charles J. Ingersoll . . .* (Philadelphia, Samuel Parker, 1827), available at https://oll.libertyfund.org/.

12. Friedrich List, *The National System of Political Economy*, trans. Sampson S. Lloyd (London: Longmans, Green, 1909), available at https://oll.libertyfund.org/.

13. Paul Bairoch and Richard Kozul-Wright, "Globalization Myths: Some Historical Reflections on Integration, Industrialization, and Growth in the World Economy," UNCTAD Discussion Paper No. 113, March 1996.

14. Adam Tooze, *The Deluge: The Great War, America, and the Remaking of the Global Order, 1916–1931* (New York: Penguin, 2014); John H. Williams, "The Foreign Trade Balance of the United States since the Armistice," *American Economic Review* 11, no. 1, suppl. (March 1921): 22–39.

15. Harold James and Kevin O'Rourke, "Italy and the First Age of Globalization, 1861–1940," paper presented at the conference "Italy and the World Economy, 1861–2011," Rome, October 12–15, 2011; Barry Eichengreen and Douglas A. Irwin, "The Slide to Protectionism in the Great Depression: Who Succumbed and Why?," *Journal of Economic History* 70, no. 4 (December 2010): 871–97.

16. BIS, Annual Report, 2017, "Understanding Globalization," https://www.bis.org/publ/arpdf/ar2017e6.htm; BEA, "National Income and Product Accounts," table 4.1, https://apps.bea.gov/iTable/.

17. Benn Steil, *The Battle of Bretton Woods: John Maynard Keynes, Harry Dexter White, and the Making of a New World Order* (Princeton, N.J.: Princeton University Press, 2013); "Resolution VII: International Economic Problems" and "Closing Address by Henry Morgenthau, Jr. [July 22, 1944]," in *Proceedings and Documents of the United Nations Monetary and Financial Conference, Bretton Woods, New Hampshire, July 1–22, 1944*, ed. U.S. State Department (Washington, D.C.: U.S. Government Printing Office, 1944), available at https://fraser.stlouisfed.org.

18. Benn Steil, *The Marshall Plan: Dawn of the Cold War* (New York: Simon and Schuster, 2018); Robert E. Baldwin, "The Changing Nature of U.S. Trade Policy since World War II," in *The Structure and Evolution of Recent U.S. Trade Policy*, ed. Robert E. Baldwin and Anne O. Krueger (Chicago: University of Chicago Press, 1984).

19. Marc Levinson, *The Box: How the Shipping Container Made the World Smaller and the World Economy Bigger*, 2nd ed. (Princeton, N.J.: Princeton University Press, 2016).

20. Based on Google Maps directions; Canada Border Services Agency, "Border Wait Times," http://www.cbsa-asfc.gc.ca/bwt-taf/menu-eng.html; U.S. Customs and Border Protection, "CPB Border Wait Times," https://apps.cbp.gov/bwt/mobile.asp?action=n&pn=3800; and Statistics Canada, "Canada's Merchandise Trade with the U.S. by State," June 19, 2017, https://www.statcan.gc.ca/pub/13-605-x/2017001/article/14841-eng.htm.

21. Based on manufacturing value added by country according to the World Bank, https://data.worldbank.org/indicator/NV.IND.MANF.CD; Richard Baldwin, "Global Supply Chains: Why They Emerged, Why They Matter, and Where They Are Going," in *Global Value Chains in a Changing World*, ed. Deborah K. Elms and Patrick Low (Washington, D.C.: Brookings Institution Press for the World Trade Organization, 2013); Robert C. Johnson and Guillermo Noguera, "Accounting for Intermediates: Production Sharing and Trade in Value Added," *Journal of International Economics* 86, no. 2 (May

2011): 224–36; Marcel P. Timmer, Bart Los, Robert Stehrer, and Gaaitzen J. de Vries, "An Anatomy of the Global Trade Slowdown Based on the WIOD 2016 Release," GGDC Research Memorandum 162, December 2016.

22. International trade data from BEA, https://www.bea.gov; OECD, "Trade in Value Added: United States," December 2018, https://www.oecd.org/industry/ind/TIVA -2018-United-States.pdf; Jude Webber, Shawn Donnan, and John Paul Rathbone, "Nafta: First Shots in a Trade War," *Financial Times,* January 30, 2017; Kristin Dziczek et al., "NAFTA Briefing: Trade Benefits to the Automotive Industry and Potential Conse- quences of Withdrawal from the Agreement," Center for Automotive Research, 2017.

23. Based on balance of payments data from Eurostat, https://appsso.eurostat.ec .europa.eu/nui/show.do?dataset=bop_c6_q&lang=en, and IMF, European Department, "German-Central European Supply Chain-Cluster Report: Staff Report, First Back- ground Note, Second Background Note, Third Background Note," Country Report No. 13/263, August 20, 2013.

24. See, e.g., Kenneth L. Kraemer, Greg Linden, and Jason Dedrick, "Capturing Value in Global Networks: Apple's iPad and iPhone," Working Paper, July 2011; UNC- TAD statistics, http://unctadstat.unctad.org/CountryProfile/GeneralProfile/en-GB/156 /index.html; OECD, "Trade in Value Added: China," December 2018, https://www.oecd .org/industry/ind/TIVA-2018-China.pdf; OECD, "Trade in Value Added: Korea," De- cember 2018, https://www.oecd.org/industry/ind/TIVA-2018-Korea.pdf; Ruey-Wan Liou et al., "Unveiling the Value-Added of Cross-Strait Trade: The Global Value Chains Ap- proach," Working Paper.

25. The best reference is OECD, tables on trade in value added, https://stats.oecd .org/Index.aspx?DataSetCode=TIVA_2018_C1.

26. Based on BEA, "International Transactions," table 1.3, https://www.bea.gov /iTable/index_ita.cfm.

27. Revenue Act of 1962, Pub. L. 87-834, October 16, 1962, 76 Stat. 960. See also Keith Engel, "Tax Neutrality to the Left, International Competitiveness to the Right, Stuck in the Middle with Subpart F," *Texas Law Review* 79, no. 6 (May 2001).

28. IRS, "26 CFR Parts 1, 301, and 602," https://www.irs.gov/pub/irs-regs/td8697 .txt; Cynthia Ram Sweitzer, "Analyzing Subpart F in Light of Check-the-Box," *Akron Tax Journal* 20 (March 2005), article 1; IRS, Treasury Notice 98-11, https://www.irs.gov/pub /irs-drop/n-98-11.pdf; IRS, LB&I International Practice Service Concept Unit on Sub- part F, https://www.irs.gov/pub/int_practice_units/DPLCUV_2_01.PDF; FactSet, data for companies in the S&P 500 stock index, http://www.factset.com.

29. Thomas R. Tørsløv, Ludvig S. Wier, and Gabriel Zucman, "The Missing Profits of Nations," NBER Working Paper No. 24701, June 2018.

30. David Barboza, "How China Built 'iPhone City' with Billions in Perks for Apple's Partner," *New York Times,* December 29, 2016; Brad W. Setser, "Apple's Exports Aren't Missing: They Are in Ireland," CFR (blog), October 30, 2017, https://www.cfr.org /blog/apples-exports-arent-missing-they-are-ireland; BEA, "International Services," https:// apps.bea.gov/iTable/index_ita.cfm; Central Statistics Office of Ireland, "International

Trade in Services 2017," https://www.cso.ie/en/releasesandpublications/er/its/international tradeinservices2017/.

31. Calculations based on Apple consolidated financial statements, https://www.apple.com/newsroom/pdfs/fy17-q4/Q4FY17ConsolidatedFinancialStatements.pdf.

32. Calculations based on Microsoft FY2017 earnings, "Note 13—Income Taxes," https://www.microsoft.com/en-us/Investor/earnings/FY-2017-Q4/IRFinancialStatements Popups?tag=us-gaap:IncomeTaxDisclosureTextBlock&title=Provision%20for%20 income%20taxes; and Alphabet Inc. (Google's parent company), Form 10-K, https://abc .xyz/investor/pdf/20171231_alphabet_10K.pdf.

33. Johnson & Johnson, "Annual Report," 2015, 2017, available at https://www.jnj .com/about-jnj/annual-reports.

34. Tom Bergin, "Special Report: How Starbucks Avoids UK Taxes," *Reuters,* October 15, 2012.

35. Matthew C. Klein, "What the Foreign Direct Investment Data Tell Us about Corporate Tax Avoidance," *Financial Times,* November 23, 2017; Matthew C. Klein, "How Tax Avoidance Distorts U.S. Trade and Investment," *Barron's,* May 25, 2018.

36. Eurostat, "NUTS3 GDP per Capita (Euros per Inhabitant) for Southwestern Ireland," https://appsso.eurostat.ec.europa.eu/nui/show.do?dataset=reg_area3&lang=en; Charlie Taylor, "Apple's Secretive Cork Facility Opens Up—To an Extent," *Irish Times,* January 11, 2018.

37. Kari Jahnsen and Kyle Pomerleau, "Corporate Income Tax Rates around the World, 2017," *Tax Foundation,* Fiscal Fact No. 559, September 7, 2017; Robert W. Wood, "How Google Saved $3.6 Billion Taxes from Paper 'Dutch Sandwich,'" *Forbes,* December 22, 2016.

38. Based on calculations from BEA data on direct investment and multinational enterprises, https://www.bea.gov/iTable/index_MNC.cfm; see also Matthew C. Klein, "What the Foreign Direct Investment Data Tell Us about Corporate Tax Avoidance," *Financial Times,* November 23, 2017; and Gabriel Zucman, *The Hidden Wealth of Nations* (Chicago: University of Chicago Press, 2015).

39. Apple 2017 10-K, https://www.sec.gov/Archives/edgar/data/320193/000032019 317000070/a10-k20179302017.htm#sCE31BDFF50DA58B8962157DE8467840C; Microsoft, https://www.microsoft.com/investor/reports/ar17/index.html.

40. Treasury Department, "International Capital Flows" data, https://www.trea sury.gov/resource-center/data-chart-center/tic/Pages/ticsec2.aspx; balance sheets from annual reports, https://www.sec.gov/Archives/edgar/data/320193/000119312512444068 /d411355d10k.htm#tx411355_2; Microsoft Corporation, "2012 Annual Report: Balance Sheets," https://www.microsoft.com/investor/reports/ar12/financial-review/balance-sheets /index.html; Brad W. Setser, "Ireland Exports Its Leprechaun," Council on Foreign Relations (blog), May 11, 2018, https://www.cfr.org/blog/ireland-exports-its-leprechaun; Matthew C. Klein, "How Much Do Tax Havens Cost the Rest of Us?," *Barron's,* June 19, 2018; BEA, "International Data: Direct Investment & MNEs," https://apps.bea.gov/iTable /index_MNC.cfm.

TWO   The Growth of Global Finance

1. BIS, "Annual Report," 2017, https://www.bis.org/statistics/ar2017stats.htm.

2. P. L. Cottrell and Lucy Newton, "Banking Liberalization in England and Wales, 1826–1844," in *The State, the Financial System, and Economic Modernization,* ed. Richard Sylla, Richard Tilly, and Gabriel Tortella (Cambridge: Cambridge University Press, 1999), 76–84.

3. Burke Adrian Parsons, *British Trade Cycles and American Bank Credit: Some Aspects of Economic Fluctuations in the United States, 1815–1840* (New York: Arno Press, 1977), 109–14, 324–31.

4. Friedrich Engels, *Socialism: Utopian and Scientific,* in *Marx and Engels,* ed. Lewis F. Feuer (New York: Anchor Books, 1959), 100.

5. H. M. Hyndman, *Commercial Crises of the Nineteenth Century* (1892; reprint ed., London: George Allen and Unwin, 1932), 29; Parsons, *British Trade Cycles,* 118.

6. David Hackett Fischer, *The Great Wave: Price Revolutions and the Rhythms of History* (Oxford: Oxford University Press, 1996), 158.

7. Hackett, *Great Wave,* 26–27.

8. J. Fred Rippy, "Latin America and the British Investment 'Boom' of the 1820s," *Journal of Modern History* 19, no. 2 (June 1947): 122–29.

9. Frank Griffith Dawson, *The First Latin American Debt Crisis: The City of London and the 1822–25 Bubble* (New Haven, Conn.: Yale University Press, 1990), gives statistical tables on pp. 246–49. The list of loans and investments here and below comes from two other sources besides Dawson. These are Rippy, "Latin America and the British Investment 'Boom'"; and Carlos Marichal, *A Century of Debt Crises in Latin America, from Independence to the Great Depression, 1820–1930* (Princeton, N.J.: Princeton University Press, 1989), 12–41.

10. Parsons, *British Trade Cycles,* 209.

11. Parsons, *British Trade Cycles,* 118.

12. Walter Bagehot, *Lombard Street: A Description of the Money Market* (1873; reprint ed., London: John Wiley and Sons, 1999), 39.

13. Hyndman, *Commercial Crises,* 42–43; Cottrell and Newton, "Banking Liberalization in England and Wales," 96–97.

14. There are no good records on the number of banks; these are estimates from Paul Studenski and Herman Krooss, *Financial History of the United States: Fiscal, Monetary, Banking and Tariff, including Financial Administration and State and Local Finance* (New York: McGraw-Hill, 1952), 107.

15. Douglass C. North, "The United States Balance of Payments, 1790–1860," in Conference on Research in Income and Wealth, *Trends in the American Economy in the Nineteenth Century* (NBER, 1960), https://newworldeconomics.com/wp-content/uploads /2017/01/US-Balance-of-Payments-1790-1860.pdf.

16. Bray Hammond, *Banks and Politics in America from the Revolution to the Civil War* (1957; reprint ed., Princeton, N.J.: Princeton University Press, 1985), 455–58; Doug-

lass C. North, *The Economic Growth of the United States, 1790–1860* (New York: W. W. Norton, 1966), 199–203; Parsons, *British Trade Cycles,* 118.

17. Bagehot, *Lombard Street,* 179.

18. Studenski and Krooss, *Financial History of the United States,* 118. For an account of the reasons for the state defaults, see Richard Sylla and John J. Wallis, "The Anatomy of Sovereign Debt Crises: Lessons from the American State Defaults of the 1840s," *Japan and the World Economy* 10, no. 3 (July 1998): 290.

19. Christian Suter, *Debt Cycles in the World Economy: Foreign Loans, Financial Crises, and Debt Settlements, 1820–1990* (Boulder, Colo.: Westview, 1992), 69.

20. Niall Ferguson, *The House of Rothschild: Money's Prophets, 1798–1848* (New York: Penguin, 1999), 374.

21. Bray Hammond, *Sovereignty and an Empty Purse: Banks and Politics in the Civil War* (Princeton, N.J.: Princeton University Press, 1970); John Niven, *Salmon P. Chase: A Biography* (Oxford: Oxford University Press, 1995).

22. Reprinted in Bagehot, *Lombard Street,* 140.

23. Marichal, *Century of Debt Crises,* 97.

24. Charles Kindleberger, *A Financial History of Western Europe* (Oxford: Oxford University Press, 1993), 270; H. M. Hyndman, *Commercial Crises of the Nineteenth Century* (1892; reprint ed., London: George Allen and Unwin, 1932), 99–127.

25. Barry Eichengreen, "The Baring Crisis in a Mexican Mirror," *International Political Science Review* 20, no. 3 (July 1999): 252–54.

26. Eichengreen, "Baring Crisis," 257–58; Niall Ferguson, *The House of Rothschild: The World's Bankers, 1849–1999* (New York: Viking, 1999), 340.

27. "Business Conditions; How High the Rate?," *New York Times,* July 26, 1981.

28. Hyun Song Shin, "Global Banking Glut and Loan Risk Premium," *IMF Economic Review* 60, no. 2 (2012): 155–92; Robert McCauley, "The 2008 Crisis: Transpacific or Transatlantic?," *BIS Quarterly Review,* December 2018; BIS, "Consolidated Banking Statistics," https://stats.bis.org/statx/srs/tseries/CBS_PUB/Q.S.5A.4R.U.C.A.A.TO1.R.US ?t=b4&c=US&m=S&p=2018&i=1.9; FRB, "Assets and Liabilities of Commercial Banks in the United States—H8," https://www.federalreserve.gov/datadownload/Download .aspx?rel=H8&series=b61c440afd7c4e471552632b71488023&filetype=csv&label=include &layout=seriescolumn&from=01/01/2005&to=12/31/2018.

THREE Saving, Investment, and Imbalances

1. Robert C. Allen, "Engels' Pause: Technical Change, Capital Accumulation, and Inequality in the British Industrial Revolution," *Explorations in Economic History* 46, no. 4 (October 2009): 418–35; Robert C. Allen, "The High Wage Economy and the Industrial Revolution: A Restatement," University of Oxford, Discussion Papers in Economic and Social History No. 115, June 2013; Elise Brezis, "Foreign Capital Flows in the Century of Britain's Industrial Revolution: New Estimates, Controlled Conjectures," *Economic History Review,* n.s., 48, no. 1 (February 1995): 46–67.

2. Alan L. Olmstead and Paul W. Rhode, "Cotton, Slavery, and the New History of Capitalism," *Explorations in Economic History* 67 (January 2018): 1–17.

3. Robert E. Lipsey, "U.S. Foreign Trade and the Balance of Payments, 1800–1913," NBER Working Paper No. 4710, April 1994; Robert E. Gallman, "Gross National Product in the United States, 1834–1909," in *Output, Employment, and Productivity in the United States after 1800,* ed. Dorothy S. Brady (New York: National Bureau of Economic Research, 1966); U.S. Census, table 4, "Population: 1790 to 1990," https://www.census.gov/population/censusdata/table-4.pdf.

4. E. Peshine Smith, *A Manual of Political Economy* (New York: George P. Putnam, 1853); Michael Hudson, "E. Peshine Smith: A Study in Protectionist Growth Theory and American Sectionalism" (Ph.D. diss., New York University, 1968).

5. Kenichi Ohno, *The Economic Development of Japan: The Path Japan Traveled as a Developing Country,* trans. Azko Hayashida (Tokyo: GRIPS Development Forum, 2006).

6. Stephen Kotkin, *Stalin: Paradoxes of Power, 1878–1928* (New York: Penguin, 2014); Stephen Kotkin, *Stalin: Waiting for Hitler, 1929–1941* (New York: Penguin, 2017); "Notes from the Meeting between Comrade Stalin and Economists concerning Questions in Political Economy, January 29, 1941," Wilson Center Digital Archives, https://digitalarchive.wilsoncenter.org/document/110984.

7. GGDC, Maddison Project Database 2018, https://www.rug.nl/ggdc/historicaldevelopment/maddison/releases/maddison-project-database-2018.

8. OECD, "Labor Force Statistics," https://stats.oecd.org/.

9. FRB, "Industrial Production and Capacity Utilization—G.17," https://www.federalreserve.gov/releases/g17/.

10. Peter Chen, Loukas Karabarbounis, and Brent Neiman, "The Global Rise of Corporate Saving," Federal Reserve Bank of Minneapolis Working Paper 736, March 2017.

11. Based on calculations from BEA, "National Income and Product Accounts," tables 1.5.4, 1.5.5, 2.1, https://apps.bea.gov/iTable/index.cfm; Matthew C. Klein, "Least Productive Sectors Only Thing Keeping Inflation Going," *FT Alphaville,* September 12, 2016, https://ftalphaville.ft.com/2016/09/12/2174415/least-productive-sectors-only-thing-keeping-inflation-going/.

12. John M. Robertson, *The Fallacy of Saving: A Study in Economics* (London: Swan Sonnenschein, 1892).

13. Michael Kumhof, Romain Rancière, and Pablo Winant, "Inequality, Leverage, and Crises," *American Economic Review* 105, no. 3 (2015): 1217–45.

14. Marriner S. Eccles, *Beckoning Frontiers: Public and Personal Recollections,* ed. Sidney Hyman (New York: Alfred A. Knopf, 1951). See also Robert J. Barro, "Double-Counting of Investment," Working Paper, April 2019, which argues that national income is overstated because investment is valuable only if it enables consumption.

15. IMF, "World Economic Outlook Database," October 2018, https://www.imf.org/external/pubs/ft/weo/2018/02/weodata/weorept.aspx?pr.x=53&pr.y=7&sy=1980&ey=2018&scsm=1&ssd=1&sort=country&ds=.&br=1&c=001&s=NID_NGDP%2CNGSD_NGDP&grp=1&a=1.

16. IMF, "World Economic Outlook Database," October 2018, https://www.imf
.org/external/pubs/ft/weo/2018/02/weodata/weorept.aspx?pr.x=55&pr.y=9&sy=1980
&ey=2018&scsm=1&ssd=1&sort=country&ds=.&br=1&c=924%2C184%2C134%2C174
%2C111&s=NID_NGDP%2CNGSD_NGDP&grp=0&a=.

17. IMF, *Balance of Payments and International Investment Position Manual*, 6th
ed., November 2013, https://www.imf.org/external/pubs/ft/bop/2007/pdf/bpm6.pdf.

18. Korea International Trade Association, "Balance of Trade," http://kita.org/kStat
/overview_BalanceOfTrade.do; Martin Sandbu, *Europe's Orphan: The Future of the Euro
and the Politics of Debt* (Princeton, N.J.: Princeton University Press, 2015).

19. Franziska Hünnekes, Moritz Schularick, and Christoph Trebesch, "Export-
weltmeister: The Low Returns on Germany's Capital Exports," Center for Economic Policy Research Discussion Paper 13863, July 2019; author's calculations based on balance of
payments and international investment position data from the Deutsche Bundesbank,
https://www.bundesbank.de/en/statistics/external-sector.

20. BIS, "Effective Exchange Rate Indices," https://www.bis.org/statistics/eer.htm;
Central Bank of the Republic of Turkey, "Weighted Average Interest Rates for Banks'
Loans," https://www.tcmb.gov.tr/wps/wcm/connect/EN/TCMB+EN/Main+Menu/Statis
tics/Interest+Rate+Statistics/Weighted+Average+Interest+Rates+For+Banks+Loans/.

21. Matthew C. Klein, "If Spain Didn't Need Capital Controls, Why Would Anyone?," *FT Alphaville*, July 15, 2016, https://ftalphaville.ft.com/2016/07/15/2168347/if-spain
-didnt-need-capital-controls-why-would-anyone/; Bank of Spain, "Spanish Securities
Markets," https://www.bde.es/webbde/en/estadis/infoest/temas/sb_tiimerval.html; Bank
of Spain, "Consumer Price Index (CPI) and Harmonised Index of Consumer Prices
(HICP)," https://www.bde.es/webbde/en/estadis/infoest/temas/sb_ipc.html; Bank of
Spain, "Economic Indicators," https://www.bde.es/webbde/en/estadis/infoest/indeco
.html; Bank of Spain, "Interest Rates and Exchange Rates," https://www.bde.es/webbde
/en/estadis/infoest/tipos/tipos.html; BIS, "Effective Exchange Rates," https://www.bis
.org/statistics/eer.htm; BIS, "Residential Property Prices: Detailed Series (Nominal),"
https://www.bis.org/statistics/pp_detailed.htm.

22. Geoffrey Wawro, *The Franco-Prussian War: The German Conquest of France
in 1870–1871* (Cambridge: Cambridge University Press, 2003).

23. Charles P. Kindleberger, *Manias, Panics, and Crashes: A History of Financial
Crises*, 5th ed. (New York: John Wiley and Sons, 2005).

24. Arthur E. Monroe, "The French Indemnity of 1871 and Its Effects," *Review of
Economics and Statistics* 1, no. 4 (October 1919): 269–81; Asaf Zussman, "The Rise of
German Protectionism in the 1870s: A Macroeconomic Perspective," Working Paper,
July 2002.

25. Australian Government, Department of Foreign Affairs and Trade, "China
Fact Sheet," http://dfat.gov.au/trade/resources/Documents/chin.pdf, and "United States
Fact Sheet," http://dfat.gov.au/trade/resources/Documents/usa.pdf.

26. Nick Timiraos, "Trump Adviser Peter Navarro: Trade Deficits Endanger U.S.
National Security," *Wall Street Journal*, March 6, 2017; Peter Navarro, "Why the White
House Worries about Trade Deficits," *Wall Street Journal*, March 5, 2017.

27. BEA, "International Transactions Accounts," table 1.3, https://www.bea.gov/iTable /index_ita.cfm; Navarro, "Why the White House Worries."

28. OECD, "Trade in Value Added: Origin of Value Added in Gross Imports," https://stats.oecd.org/Index.aspx?datasetcode=TIVA_2018_C1; IMF, World Economic Outlook Database," April 2019, https://www.imf.org/external/pubs/ft/weo/2019/01/weo data/index.aspx.

FOUR From Tiananmen to the Belt and Road

1. Consulate-General of the People's Republic of China in San Francisco, "Premier Wen Jiabao's Press Conference," March 17, 2007, http://www.chinaconsulatesf.org /eng/xw/t304313.htm.

2. Based on data from National Bureau of Statistics of China, "Annual Data," http://data.stats.gov.cn/english/easyquery.htm?cn=C01; China, State Administration of Foreign Exchange, "Balance of Payments," https://www.safe.gov.cn/en/BalanceofPay ments/index.html; and BIS, "Credit to the Non-Financial Sector," https://www.bis.org /statistics/totcredit.htm.

3. An Baije, "Reform Drive Will Smash Fences of Vested Interests, Li Pledges," *China Daily,* March 13, 2014.

4. United Nations Population Division, "World Population Prospects 2019," https:// population.un.org/wpp/Download/Standard/Population/.

5. GGDC, Maddison Project Database 2018, https://www.rug.nl/ggdc/historical development/maddison/releases/maddison-project-database-2018; IMF, "World Economic Outlook Database," April 2019, https://www.imf.org/external/pubs/ft/weo/2019 /01/weodata/index.aspx.

6. Barry Naughton, *The Chinese Economy: Transitions and Growth* (Cambridge, Mass.: MIT University Press, 2007); Barry Naughton, "China: Economic Transformation before and after 1989," paper prepared for the conference "1989: Twenty Years After," UC Irvine, November 6–7, 2009.

7. Alexander Gerschenkron, *Economic Backwardness in Historical Perspective* (Cambridge, Mass.: Harvard University Press, 1962).

8. FRED Economic Data, "China/U.S. Foreign Exchange Rate," FRB, https://fred .stlouisfed.org/series/DEXCHUS; National Bureau of Statistics of China, "Annual Data"; IMF, "World Economic Outlook Database," April 2019, https://www.imf.org/external /pubs/ft/weo/2019/01/weodata/weorept.aspx?pr.x=47&pr.y=3&sy=1997&ey=2018 &scsm=1&ssd=1&sort=country&ds=.&br=1&c=924&s=BCA_NGDPD&grp=0&a=.

9. China, State Administration of Foreign Exchange, "The Time-Series Data of Balance of Payments of China," https://www.safe.gov.cn/en/BalanceofPayments/index .html; BIS, "Effective Exchange Rate Indices," https://www.bis.org/statistics/eer.htm.

10. National Bureau of Statistics of China, "Annual Data."

11. Michael Pettis, *Avoiding the Fall: China's Economic Restructuring* (Washington, D.C.: Carnegie Endowment for International Peace, 2013).

12. Qin Hui, "Dilemmas of Twenty-First Century Globalization: Explanations

and Solutions, with a Critique of Thomas Piketty's Twenty-First Century Capitalism," trans. David Ownby, orig. publ. in Chinese in 2015, https://www.readingthechinadream .com/qin-hui-dilemmas.html; Yuan Yang, "Foxconn Stops Illegal Overtime by School-Age Interns," *Financial Times*, November 22, 2017; Javier C. Hernández, "China's Leaders Confront an Unlikely Foe: Ardent Young Communists," *New York Times*, September 28, 2018; Rossalyn A. Warren, "You Buy a Purse at Walmart. There's a Note Inside from a 'Chinese Prisoner.' Now What?," *Vox* October 10, 2018, https://www.vox.com/the-goods /2018/10/10/17953106/walmart-prison-note-china-factory; Emily Feng, "Forced Labour Being Used in China's 'Re-Education' Camps," *Financial Times*, December 15, 2018.

13. IMF, Fiscal Affairs Department, "People's Republic of China: Tax Policy and Employment Creation," March 28, 2018, https://www.imf.org/en/Publications/CR/Issues /2018/03/28/Peoples-Republic-of-China-Tax-Policy-and-Employment-Creation-45765; Philippe Wingender, "Intergovernmental Fiscal Reform in China," IMF Working Papers, April 13, 2018; Sonali Jain-Chandra et al., "Inequality in China—Trends, Drivers and Policy Remedies," IMF Working Papers, June 5, 2018; National Bureau of Statistics of China, "Annual Data."

14. GGDC, Maddison Project Database 2018; Qu Hongbin and Sun Junwei, "China Inside Out: What Over-Investment?," HSBC Global Research, February 14, 2012, https://www.research.hsbc.com/midas/Res/RDV?p=pdf&key=1xZsmfl7Yi&n=320939 .PDF.

15. Wei Fan and Michelle J. White, "Personal Bankruptcy and the Level of Entre-preneurial Activity," *Journal of Law and Economics* 46, no. 2 (October 2003): 543–67; John Armour and Douglas Cumming, "Bankruptcy and Entrepreneurship," *American Law and Economics Review* 10, no. 2 (Fall 2008): 303–50; Christian Bjørnskov, "Social Trust and Economic Growth," Working Paper, January 2017.

16. Harry X. Wu and David T. Liang, "China's Productivity Performance Revisited from the Perspective of ICTs," *VoxEU*, December 9, 2017, https://voxeu.org/article/china -s-productivity-performance-revisited; and Harry X. Wu, "China's Forty Years of Pro-ductivity Performance: Towards a Theory-Methodology-Measurement-Coherent Anal-ysis," unpublished paper, December 6, 2018.

17. People's Bank of China, "Aggregate Financing to the Real Economy (Stock)," http://www.pbc.gov.cn/diaochatongjisi/resource/cms/2018/12/2018121716010887709. htm; National Bureau of Statistics of China, "Investment Actually Completed in Fixed Assets, Accumulated Growth Rate," http://data.stats.gov.cn/english/easyquery.htm?cn =A01.

18. Gabriel Wildau and Yizhen Jia, "China's Subway Building Binge Is Back on Track," *Financial Times*, December 18, 2018.

19. China, State Administration of Foreign Exchange, "The Time Series of the Balance of Payments of China"; National Bureau of Statistics of China, "Annual Data"; Brad W. Setser, "President Xi, Still the Deglobalizer in Chief . . . ," CFR (blog), June 25, 2019, https://www.cfr.org/blog/president-xi-still-deglobalizer-chief.

20. Mark Wu, "The 'China, Inc.' Challenge to Global Trade Governance," *Harvard International Law Journal* 57, no. 2 (Spring 2016): 261–324; Curtis J. Milhaupt and Wen-

ton Zheng, "Beyond Ownership: State Capitalism and the Chinese Firm," *Georgetown Law Journal* 103 (2015): 668; "The Communist Party's Influence Is Expanding—in China and Beyond," *Bloomberg,* March 11, 2018, https://www.bloomberg.com/news/articles /2018-03-11/it-s-all-xi-all-the-time-in-china-as-party-influence-expands; Matthew C. Klein, "The People's Republic of Protectionism," *Barron's,* May 4, 2018; Brad W. Setser, "China Should Import More," CFR (blog), November 7, 2018, https://www.cfr.org/blog/china -should-import-more.

21. China, State Administration of Foreign Exchange, "The Time-Series Data of Balance of Payments of China"; Anna Wong, "China's Current Account: External Rebalancing or Capital Flight?," International Finance Discussion Papers 1208 (2017); Peter Lorentzen and Xi Lu, "Personal Ties, Meritocracy, and China's Anti-Corruption Campaign," Working Paper, November 21, 2018; Matthew Higgins, Thomas Klitgaard, and Anna Wong, "Does a Data Quirk Inflate China's Travel Services Deficit?," *Liberty Street Economics,* August 7, 2019, https://libertystreeteconomics.newyorkfed.org/2019/08/does -a-data-quirk-inflate-chinas-travel-services-deficit.html.

22. Laurie Chen, Zhou Xin, and Raphael Blet, "HNA Group Chairman Wang Jian Dies in 15-Metre Fall onto Rocks while Posing for a Photo in France," *South China Morning Post,* July 4, 2018.

23. Matt Ferchen and Anarkalee Perera, "Why Unsustainable Chinese Infrastructure Deals Are a Two-Way Street," Carnegie-Tsinghua Center for Global Policy, July 23, 2019, https://carnegietsinghua.org/2019/07/24/why-unsustainable-chinese-infrastructure -deals-are-two-way-street-pub-79548.

24. Brad W. Setser, "The Continuing Chinese Drag on the Global Economy," July 18, 2019, CFR (blog), https://www.cfr.org/blog/continuing-chinese-drag-global-economy; People's Bank of China, "Aggregate Financing to the Real Economy (Stock)"; Matthew C. Klein, "China's Household Debt Problem," *FT Alphaville,* March 6, 2018, https://ftalpha ville.ft.com/2018/03/06/2199125/chinas-household-debt-problem/.

25. Wei Chen et al., "A Forensic Examination of China's National Accounts," *Brookings Papers on Economic Activity,* March 2019; Matthew C. Klein, "China's Slowdown Is Worse Than You Thought," *Barron's,* March 15, 2019.

26. Xinhua, "Third Plenary Session of 18th CPC Central Committee," http://www .xinhuanet.com/english/special/cpcplenum2013/topnews.htm.

27. BEA, "National Income and Product Accounts," table 1.1.3, https://apps.bea .gov/iTable/index_nipa.cfm; Matthew C. Klein, "Did Japan Actually Lose Any Decades?," *FT Alphaville,* December 4, 2014, https://ftalphaville.ft.com/2014/12/04/2059371/did -japan-actually-lose-any-decades/.

FIVE The Fall of the Wall and the *Schwarze Null*

1. Henry Kamm, "Solidarity Takes Its Elected Place in the Parliament," *New York Times,* July 5, 1989; Lawrence Weschler, "A Grand Experiment," *New Yorker,* November 13, 1989; John Borrell, "Poland Living with Shock Therapy," *Time,* June 11, 1990.

2. Walter Mayr, "Hungary's Peaceful Revolution: Cutting the Fence and Changing

History," *Der Spiegel,* May 29, 2009; Joseph Rothschild and Nancy M. Wingfield, *Return to Diversity: A Political History of East Central Europe since World War II,* 3rd ed. (New York: Oxford University Press, 2000); Adam Roberts, "Civil Resistance in the East European and Soviet Revolutions," Albert Einstein Institution Monograph Series No. 4, 1991.

3. Mark Kramer, ed. and trans., "Soviet Deliberations during the Polish Crisis, 1980–1981," Cold War International History Project, Special Working Paper No. 1, April 1999; "Spot Oil Price," *Wall Street Journal,* via FRED Economic Data, https://fred.st louisfed.org/series/OILPRICE; U.S. Department of Agriculture, Economic Research Service, "Wheat Data," https://www.ers.usda.gov/data-products/wheat-data/; Dan Morgan and Bradley Graham, "Money Is Often Bottom Line in East-West Ties," *Washington Post,* May 11, 1982.

4. "No. 1383: Protocol of the Proceedings of the Berlin Conference," August 1, 1945, in *Foreign Relations of the United States: Diplomatic Papers, The Conference of Berlin (The Potsdam Conference), 1945,* ed. Richardson Dougall, vol. 2 (Washington, D.C.: U.S. Government Printing Office, 1960).

5. "Helmut Kohl's Ten-Point Plan for German Unity," November 28, 1989, German History in Documents and Images, http://germanhistorydocs.ghi-dc.org/pdf/eng /Chapter1_Doc10English.pdf.

6. Serge Schmemann, "Upheaval in the East; East Germans Form 'Grand Coalition,'" *New York Times,* April 10, 1990; "De Maziere Accused of Ties to East's Secret Police," AP, December 9, 1990.

7. Peter Bofinger, "The German Monetary Unification (Gmu): Converting Marks to D-Marks," Federal Reserve Bank of St. Louis, *Review,* July–August 1990, 17–36.

8. George A. Akerlof et al., "East Germany in from the Cold: The Economic Aftermath of Currency Union," Brookings Papers on Economic Activity, 1991, No. 1; Destatis, "Population, Persons in Employment, Unemployed Persons, Economically Active Population, Economically Inactive Population: Länder, Years," https://www-genesis .destatis.de/genesis/online/link/tabelleErgebnis/12211-0005&language=en.

9. Rupert Wiederwald, "Treuhand Took the Heat for Privatization of East German Economy," *Deutsche Welle,* September 20, 2010; Wendy Carlin and Colin Mayer, "The Treuhandanstalt: Privatization by State and Market," in *Transition in Eastern Europe,* vol. 2, ed. Olivier Blanchard, Kenneth Froot, and Jeffrey Sachs (Chicago: University of Chicago Press, 1994), 189–207.

10. Katrin Bennhold, "One Legacy of Merkel? Angry East German Men Fueling the Far Right," *New York Times,* November 5, 2018; Alberto Abadie, Alexis Diamond, and Jens Hainmueller, "Comparative Politics and the Synthetic Control Method," *American Journal of Political Science* 59, no. 2 (2015): 495–510.

11. Karl Brenke, "Eastern Germany Still Playing Economic Catch-Up," *DIW Economic Bulletin* 4, no. 11 (2014); Alexander Eickelpasch, "Manufacturing in East Germany since Reunification," DIW Berlin, November 25, 2015, https://www.diw.de/documents /vortragsdokumente/220/diw_01.c.525594.de/v_2015_eickelpasch_manufacturing _kistep.pdf.

12. Destatis, "Gross Domestic Product, Quarterly Data," https://www.destatis.de

/EN/FactsFigures/NationalEconomyEnvironment/NationalAccounts/DomesticProduct
/Tables/GDPQuarterly1970_xls.html; FRED Economic Data, "Consumer Price Index,
All Items Non-Food and Non-Energy for Germany," https://fred.stlouisfed.org/series
/CPGRLE01DEM659N; Deutsche Bundesbank, "Discount and Lombard Rates of the
Bundesbank," https://www.bundesbank.de/Redaktion/EN/Downloads/Statistics/Money
_Capital_Markets/Interest_Rates_Yields/S510TTDISCOUNT.pdf?__blob=publication
File; Deutsche Bundesbank, "Public Finances in Germany," https://www.bundesbank
.de/Navigation/EN/Statistics/Time_series_databases/Public_Finances_in_Germany
/public_finances_in_germany_list_node.html?listId=www_v27_web012_11a; Deutsche
Bundesbank, "National Accounts," https://www.bundesbank.de/Navigation/EN/Statistics
/Macroeconomic_accounting_systems/National_Accounts/Tables/table.html; "Treaty on
European Union" (1992), https://eur-lex.europa.eu/legal-content/EN/TXT/?uri=celex
:11992M/TXT.

13. European Commission, "Europeans and Their Languages," Special Eurobarom-
eter 243, February 2006; EU decision to launch accession process from minutes of European Council meeting in Luxembourg, December 12–13, 1997, http://www.consilium
.europa.eu/media/21114/luxembourg-european-council.pdf; Eurostat, "Labour Cost Levels by NACE Rev. 2 Activity," https://appsso.eurostat.ec.europa.eu/nui/show.do?dataset
=lc_lci_lev&lang=en.

14. IMF, European Department, "German-Central European Supply Chain-Cluster
Report: Staff Report, First Background Note, Second Background Note, Third Background Note," Country Report No. 13/263, August 20, 2013; Verband der Automobilin-
dustrie, "Automobile Production," https://www.vda.de/en/services/facts-and-figures
/annual-figures/automobile-production.html; International Organization of Motor Vehicle Manufacturers, "1999 Production Statistics," http://www.oica.net/category/produc
tion-statistics/1999-statistics/; European Automobile Manufacturers Association, "EU
Production, 2017," https://www.acea.be/statistics/tag/category/eu-production; OECD,
"Trade in Value Added," https://stats.oecd.org/index.aspx?queryid=75537; Augustin
Carstens, "Global Market Structures and the High Price of Protectionism," speech at the
Federal Reserve Bank of Kansas City's 42nd Economic Policy Symposium, Jackson Hole,
Wyo., August 25, 2018.

15. Christian Odendahl, "The Hartz Myth: A Closer Look at Germany's Labor
Market Reforms," Centre for European Reform, July 2017; Harald Blau et al., "Labor
Market Studies: Germany," ifo Institute for Economic Research, May 1997; FRED Economic Data, "Harmonized Unemployment Rate: All Persons for Germany" https://fred
.stlouisfed.org/series/LRHUTTTTDEM156S; Eurostat, "Part-Time Employment as a Percentage of the Total Employment, by Sex and Age," https://appsso.eurostat.ec.europa.eu
/nui/show.do?dataset=lfsq_eppga&lang=en; Eurostat, "Temporary Employees as a Percentage of the Total Number of Employees, by Sex and Age," https://appsso.eurostat.ec
.europa.eu/nui/show.do?dataset=lfsq_etpga&lang=en; Destatis, "Persons in Paid Employment: Germany, Years, Extent of Employment, Sex," https://www-genesis.destatis
.de/genesis/online/link/tabelleErgebnis/12211-0011&language=en; Christian Dustmann
et al., "From Sick Man of Europe to Economic Superstar: Germany's Resurgent Econ-

omy," *Journal of Economic Perspectives* 28, no. 1 (2014): 167–88; Wolfgang Dauth, Sebastian Findeisen, and Jens Südekum, "Sectoral Employment Trends in Germany: The Effect of Globalisation on Their Micro Anatomy," *VoxEU,* January 26, 2017, https://voxeu.org /article/globalisation-and-sectoral-employment-trends-germany; Deutsche Bundesbank, "National Accounts Statistics," https://www.bundesbank.de/Navigation/EN/Statistics /Macroeconomic_accounting_systems/National_Accounts/Tables/table_zeitreihenliste .html?id=24928.

16. "Berlin Speech by Federal President Roman Herzog at the Reopening of the Hotel Adlon on April 26, 1997," German History in Documents and Images, http://german historydocs.ghi-dc.org/pdf/eng/Ch12Doc04.pdf.

17. Germany, Federal Returning Officer, "Election to the 14th German Bundestag on 27 September 1998," https://www.bundeswahlleiter.de/en/bundestagswahlen/1998 .html.

18. Deutsche Bundesbank, "National Accounts," https://www.bundesbank.de /Navigation/EN/Statistics/Macroeconomic_accounting_systems/National_Accounts /Tables/table.html.

19. Neal E. Boudette, "New Scandal Emerges to Roil a Rehabilitating Neuer Markt," *Wall Street Journal,* April 11, 2002; "After Greed, Fear: No End to the Troubles of the Neuer Markt," *Economist,* May 23, 2002; "Germany's Neuer Markt to Close," *BBC,* September 26, 2002, http://news.bbc.co.uk/2/hi/business/2283068.stm; Hans-Peter Burghof and Adrian Hunger, "Access to Stock Markets for Small and Medium Sized Growth Firms: The Temporary Success and Ultimate Failure of Germany's Neuer Markt," Working Paper, October 2003.

20. Deutsche Bundesbank, "Liabilities Consolidated," https://www.bundesbank .de/Navigation/EN/Statistics/Time_series_databases/Macroeconomic_accounting_sys tems/macroeconomic_accounting_systems_list_node.html?listId=www_v39_nuverb.

21. Deutsche Bundesbank, "National Accounts."

22. Deutsche Bundesbank, "Expected Real Interest Rates Germany of German Government Bonds with 10 Years Maturity," https://www.bundesbank.de/Navigation/EN /Statistics/Time_series_databases/Money_and_capital_markets/money_and_capital _markets_list_node.html?listId=www_skms_realzinsen; Edmund L. Andrews, "Hard Money for a Softer Europe; Leftist Politics Complicates the Job of the Euro's Banker," *New York Times,* November 5, 1998; ECB, "Introductory Statement Willem F. Duisenberg, President of the European Central Bank, Christian Noyer, Vice-President of the European Central Bank, Frankfurt am Main, 11 April 2001," https://www.ecb.europa.eu /press/pressconf/2001/html/is010411.en.html.

23. IMF, "World Economic Outlook Database: General Government Structural Balance," https://www.imf.org/external/pubs/ft/weo/2018/01/weodata/weorept.aspx?pr .x=79&pr.y=12&sy=1991&ey=2018&scsm=1&ssd=1&sort=country&ds=.&br=1&c =134&s=GGSB_NPGDP%2CGGXONLB_NGDP&grp=0&a=.

24. Stephan Danninger and Fred Joutz, "What Explains Germany's Rebounding Export Market Share?," IMF Working Paper No. 07/24, February 2007; Eurostat, "Intra- and Extra-EU Trade by Member State and by Product Group," https://appsso.eurostat

.ec.europa.eu/nui/show.do?dataset=ext_lt_intratrd&lang=en; Destatis, "Sector Accounts—Annual Results 1991 Onwards," https://www.destatis.de/EN/Themes/Economy/National -Accounts-Domestic-Product/_node.html.

25. Peter Haan and Viktor Steiner, "Distributional and Fiscal Effects of the German Tax Reform 2000: A Behavioral Microsimulation Analysis," Discussion Papers of DIW Berlin 419, 2004; Stefan Homburg, "German Tax Reform 2000: Description and Appraisal," *FinanzArchiv/Public Finance Analysis* 57, no. 4 (2000): 504–13; Michael Keen, "The German Tax Reform of 2000," *International Tax and Public Finance* 9 (2002): 603–21; Destatis, "Labour Market: Unemployed," https://www.destatis.de/EN/FactsFigures /NationalEconomyEnvironment/LabourMarket/Unemployment/Tables_/lrarb003.html.

26. "A Plan to Put Germans Back into Jobs," *Economist,* August 22, 2002; Mark Landler, "The Heart of the Hartz Commission," *New York Times,* November 26, 2004; Lena Jacobi and Jochen Kluve, "Before and after the Hartz Reforms: The Performance of Active Labour Market Policy in Germany," IZA Discussion Paper No. 2100, October 2006.

27. Robert Rohrschneider and Michael R. Wolf, "The Federal Election of 2002," *German Politics and Society* 21, no. 1 (2003): 1–14; Peter James, "The 2002 German Federal Election: The 'Fotofinish,'" *Representation* 39, no. 2 (2003): 129–36; Germany, Federal Returning Officer, "Election to the 15th German Bundestag on 22 September 2002," https://www.bundeswahlleiter.de/en/bundestagswahlen/2002.html.

28. Gerhard Schröder, "Courage for Peace and Courage for Change," speech to the Bundestag, March 14, 2003, http://gerhard-schroeder.de/en/2003/03/14/speech -agenda-2010/.

29. John Hooper, "Schröder Faces Day of Reckoning," *Guardian,* May 29, 2003; Georg Bönisch et al., "The Unsettled People," *Der Spiegel,* August 16, 2004.

30. Daryl Lindsey, "Bundestag Clears Way for New Elections," *Der Spiegel,* July 1, 2005; Uwe Hessler, "SPD Presents Election Manifesto," *Deutsche Welle,* July 5, 2005; Kyle James, "Social Justice or Economic Folly?," *Deutsche Welle,* August 2, 2005; Dietmar Hawranek, Padma Rao, and Sven Röbel, "With Prostitutes and Shady Executives, There's No Love Left in This Bug," *Der Spiegel,* August 29, 2005.

31. Germany, Federal Returning Officer, "Party Seats to the 16th German Bundestag 2005," https://www.bundeswahlleiter.de/en/bundestagswahlen/2005.html; NSD, European Election Database, http://www.nsd.uib.no/european_election_database/about /about_data.html. (Some of) the data applied in the analysis in this publication are based on material from the European Election Database. The data are collected from original sources, prepared and made available by the NSD, which is not responsible for the analyses and interpretation of the data presented here.

32. Odendahl, "Hartz Myth."

33. Eurostat, "People at Risk of Poverty or Social Exclusion by Most Frequent Activity Status (Population Aged 18 and Over)," https://appsso.eurostat.ec.europa.eu/nui /show.do?dataset=ilc_pepso2&lang=en; Eurostat, "Employment and Activity by Sex and Age—Quarterly Data," https://appsso.eurostat.ec.europa.eu/nui/show.do?dataset=lfsi _emp_q&lang=en ; Destatis, "Persons in Paid Employment: Germany, Years, Extent of

Employment, Sex," https://www-genesis.destatis.de/genesis/online/link/tabelleErgebnis/12211-0011&language=en.

34. Marcel Fratzscher, *The Germany Illusion: Between Economic Euphoria and Despair* (Oxford: Oxford University Press, 2018); Schröder, "Courage for Peace and Courage for Change."

35. Deutsche Bundesbank, "National Accounts"; Bundesregierung, "Government Report on Wellbeing in Germany," 2016, available at https://www.gut-leben-in-deutschland.de/static/LB/about.

36. Destatis, "Sector Accounts," https://www.destatis.de/EN/Themes/Economy/National-Accounts-Domestic-Product/_node.html; Deutsche Bundesbank, "National Income," https://www.bundesbank.de/Navigation/EN/Statistics/Macroeconomic_accounting_systems/National_Accounts/Tables/table_zeitreihenliste.html?id=24920; "Investment Activity in Germany under the Influence of Technological Change and Competition among Production Locations," *Bundesbank Monthly Report* 59, no. 1 (January 2007): 17–31.

37. ECB, "Household Finance and Consumption Survey Wave 2 Statistical Tables," https://www.ecb.europa.eu/home/pdf/research/hfcn/HFCS_Statistical_Tables_Wave2.pdf?58cf15114aab934bcd06995c4e91505b; "Household Wealth and Finances in Germany: Results of the 2014 Survey," *Bundesbank Monthly Report*, March 2016; Paul De Grauwe and Yuemi Ji, "Are Germans Really Poorer Than Spaniards, Italians and Greeks?," *VoxEU*, April 16, 2013, https://voxeu.org/article/are-germans-really-poorer-spaniards-italians-and-greeks.

38. Special issue, "Inheritance Tax and Wealth Tax in Germany," *DIW Economic Bulletin* 6, January 27, 2016; James Shotter, "Germany Changes Inheritance Tax to Protect Family Business," *Financial Times*, September 22, 2016; Matthew C. Klein, "Marcel Fratzscher on the Dark Side of the German Economy—Now with Transcript!!," *FT Alphaville*, March 28, 2018, https://ftalphaville.ft.com/2018/03/29/2199403/marcel-fratzscher-on-the-dark-side-of-the-german-economy-now-with-transcript/; Cathrin Schaer, "Germany's Convoluted Property Tax Could Be Illegal," *Handelsblatt*, January 16, 2018; Alena Bachleitner, "Abolishing the Wealth Tax—A Case Study of Germany" (M.Sc. thesis, University of Vienna, 2017); Dan Andrews and Aida Caldera Sánchez, "The Evolution of Homeownership Rates in Selected OECD Countries: Demographic and Public Policy Influences," *OECD Journal: Economic Studies* 2011, no. 1 (2011): 8; Christian Dustmann, Bernd Fitzenberger, and Markus Zimmerman, "Housing Expenditures and Income Inequality: Shifts in Housing Costs Exacerbated the Rise in Income Inequality," *VoxEU*, October 22, 2018, https://voxeu.org/article/housing-expenditures-and-income-inequality.

39. Odendahl, "Hartz Myth"; Destatis, "Collective Bargaining Coverage," https://www.destatis.de/EN/FactsFigures/NationalEconomyEnvironment/EarningsLabourCosts/AgreedEarnings/Tables_CollectiveBargainingCoverage/CollectiveBargainingCoverage.html; Christian Dustmann et al., "From Sick Man of Europe to Economic Superstar: Germany's Resurgent Economy," *Journal of Economic Perspectives* 28, no. 1 (Winter 2014): 167–88; Charlotte Bartels, "Top Incomes in Germany, 1871–2013," World Income Database Working Paper Series, December 2017.

40. "Private Consumption in Germany since Reunification," *Bundesbank Monthly Report* 59, no. 9 (September 2007): 41–55.

41. Eurostat, "Intra and Extra-EU Trade by Member State and by Product Group," https://appsso.eurostat.ec.europa.eu/nui/show.do?dataset=ext_lt_intratrd&lang=en; OECD, "Trade in Value Added 2018," https://stats.oecd.org/Index.aspx?datasetcode =TIVA_2018_C1; IMF, European Department, "Germany: Selected Issues," Country Report No. 19/214, July 10, 2019.

42. Deutsche Bundesbank, "External Sector Statistics (Monthly)," https://www .bundesbank.de/en/statistics/external-sector.

43. Deutsche Bundesbank, "Lending to Foreign Nonbanks, Total," https://www .bundesbank.de/Navigation/EN/Statistics/Time_series_databases/Banks_and_other _financial_institutions/banks_and_other_financial_institutions_list_node.html?list Id=www_s100_mb3031_08_01; Deutsche Bundesbank, "Lending to Foreign Banks (MFIs), Total," https://www.bundesbank.de/Navigation/EN/Statistics/Time_series_data bases/Banks_and_other_financial_institutions/banks_and_other_financial_institutions _list_node.html?listId=www_s100_bh16_3_01; Matej Senkarcin, "German Landesbanks in the Post-Guarantee Reality," (Ph.D. diss., Wharton School, University of Pennsylvania, 2015).

44. BIS, "Locational Banking Statistics," table A7, https://stats.bis.org/statx/srs /table/a7?c=DE&p=20181; BIS, "Consolidated Banking Statistics," table B3, https://stats .bis.org/statx/srs/table/B3?c=&m=S&p=20181&i=10.1; BIS, "Consolidated Banking Statistics," table B4, https://stats.bis.org/statx/srs/table/b4.

45. Bank of Spain, "Monetary Financial Institutions," https://www.bde.es/webbde /en/estadis/infoest/bolest6.html; Bank of Spain, "Balance of Payments and International Investment Position," https://www.bde.es/webbde/en/estadis/infoest/temas/sb_extbppii .html; Bank of Spain, "Gross External Debt by Institutional Sector, Financial Instrument, and Term," https://www.bde.es/webbde/en/estadis/infoest/temas/sb_extdeu.html.

46. Eurostat, "GDP and Main Components." https://appsso.eurostat.ec.europa.eu /nui/show.do?dataset=namq_10_gdp&lang=en.

47. Eurostat, "International Investment Position—Quarterly and Annual Data," https://appsso.eurostat.ec.europa.eu/nui/show.do?dataset=bop_iip6_q&lang=en; Eurostat, "Balance of Payments by Country," https://appsso.eurostat.ec.europa.eu/nui/show .do?dataset=bop_c6_q&lang=en; Eurostat, "GDP and Main Components."

48. Tobias Buck, "Spanish Ghost Airport Costing €1bn Attracts Offer of Just €10,000," *Financial Times,* July 17, 2015; Philip Reid, "Out of Bounds: The Death of an Irish Golf Course," *Irish Times,* February 1, 2017.

49. Philippe Martin and Thomas Philippon, "Inspecting the Mechanism: Leverage and the Great Recession in the Eurozone," *American Economic Review* 107, no. 7 (2017): 1904–37.

50. Deutsche Bundesbank, "Lending to Foreign Nonbanks, Total"; Deutsche Bundesbank, "Lending to Foreign Banks (MFIs), Total"; Deutsche Bundesbank, "Balance of Payments," https://www.bundesbank.de/en/statistics/external-sector/balance-of -payments.

51. Konstantin von Hammerstein and René Pfister, "Merkel's Dispassionate Approach to the Euro Crisis," *Der Spiegel,* December 12, 2012.

52. Wolfgang Streeck, "Endgame? The Fiscal Crisis of the German State," Max Planck Institute for the Study of Societies, MPIfG Discussion Paper 07/7.

53. Federal Ministry of Finance, Economics Department, "Reforming the Constitutional Budget Rules in Germany," September 2009, http://www.kas.de/wf/doc/kas _21127-1522-4-30.pdf?101116013053; Federal Ministry of Finance, "Germany's Federal Debt Brake," March 2015, https://www.bundesfinanzministerium.de/Content/EN/Stan dardartikel/Topics/Fiscal_policy/Articles/2015-12-09-german-federal-debt-brake.pdf ?__blob=publicationFile&v=6; IMF, "World Economic Outlook Database: General Government Structural Balance," April 2018 vintage, https://www.imf.org/external/pubs/ft /weo/2018/01/weodata/weorept.aspx?pr.x=44&pr.y=8&sy=1991&ey=2018&scsm=1&ssd =1&sort=country&ds=.&br=1&c=134&s=GGSB_NPGDP&grp=0&a=#cs1.

54. Eurostat, "Quarterly Nonfinancial Accounts for General Government," https:// appsso.eurostat.ec.europa.eu/nui/show.do?dataset=gov_10q_ggnfa&lang=en.

55. Fratzscher, *Germany Illusion,* chaps. 5, 6.

56. Stephan Brand and Johannes Steinbrecher, "Municipal Investment: Growing Needs, Limited Capacities," KfW Research, KfW Municipal Panel 2018—Executive Summay, June 2018; Gabriel Borrud, "A Long, Strange Trip for German Truckers near Duisburg," *Deutsche Welle,* July 3, 2015; Guy Chazan, "Cracks Appear in Germany's Cash-Starved Infrastructure," *Financial Times,* August 3, 2017.

57. OECD, "Broadband and Telecom Statistics," http://www.oecd.org/sti/broad band/broadband-statistics/.

58. Germany, Federal Ministry of Finance, "2014 Federal Budget: No New Borrowing Was Required," Press Release, January 13, 2015, https://www.bundesfinanzminis terium.de/Content/EN/Pressemitteilungen/2015/2015-01-13-2014-federal-budget.html; Eurostat, "Quarterly Nonfinancial Accounts for General Government"; Germany, Federal Ministry of Finance, "Schuldenbremse 2015: Struktureller Überschuss—das zweite Jahr in Folge," September 22, 2016, https://www.bundesfinanzministerium.de/Content/DE /Monatsberichte/2016/09/Inhalte/Kapitel-3-Analysen/3-3-Schuldenbremse-2015.html.

59. Deutsche Bundesbank, "Daily Term Structure of Interest Rates in the Debt Securities Market—Estimated Values," https://www.bundesbank.de/en/statistics/money -and-capital-markets/interest-rates-and-yields/term-structure-of-interest-rates.

60. Ben Knight, "Schäuble Clings to 'Black Zero' Fetish in German Budget," *Deutsche Welle,* July 6, 2016; Cat Rutter Pooley, "Schäuble Sent Off with a 'Black Zero,'" *Financial Times,* October 24, 2017.

61. European Commission, "Communication from the Commission to the European Parliament, the European Council, the Council, the European Central Bank, the Economic and Social Committee, and the Committee of the Regions: Reinforcing Economic Policy Coordination," May 12, 2010, http://ec.europa.eu/economy_finance/articles /euro/documents/2010-05-12-com(2010)250_final.pdf; Treaty on Stability, Coordination, and Governance in the Economic and Monetary Union, March 2, 2012, https://www .consilium.europa.eu/media/20399/st00tscg26_en12.pdf.

62. Eurostat, "Government Deficit/Surplus, Debt, and Associated Data," https://appsso.eurostat.ec.europa.eu/nui/show.do?dataset=gov_10dd_edpt1&lang=en; Matthew C. Klein, "The Euro Area's Fiscal Position Makes No Sense," *FT Alphaville*, March 14, 2018, https://ftalphaville.ft.com/2018/03/14/2199197/the-euro-areas-fiscal-position-makes-no-sense/.

63. Matthew C. Klein, "What the U.S. Should Demand from Europe," *Barron's*, July 27, 2018.

64. Eurostat, "GDP and Main Components."

65. European Commission, "VAT Rates Applied in the Member States of the European Union: Situation at 1st January 2018," https://ec.europa.eu/taxation_customs/sites/taxation/files/resources/documents/taxation/vat/how_vat_works/rates/vat_rates_en.pdf; Zsolt Darvas, "EU Income Inequality Decline: Views from an Income Shares Perspective," *Bruegel*, July 5, 2018, http://bruegel.org/2018/07/eu-income-inequality-decline-views-from-an-income-shares-perspective/.

66. Matthew C. Klein, "European Leaders Seem Determined to Remake the 'Global Savings Glut' on a Massive Scale," *FT Alphaville*, November 8, 2017, https://ftalphaville.ft.com/2017/11/08/2195596/european-leaders-seem-to-determined-to-remake-the-global-savings-glut-on-a-massive-scale/.

SIX The American Exception

1. Based on BEA, "International Transaction Accounts," tables 1.1, 9.1, https://apps.bea.gov/iTable/index_ita.cfm; Tamim Bayoumi, Joseph Gagnon, and Christian Saborowski, "Official Financial Flows, Capital Mobility, and Global Imbalances," Peterson Institute for International Economics Working Paper No. 14-8, October 23, 2014; and Brad W. Setser, "Mapping Capital Flows into the U.S. over the Last Thirty Years," CFR (blog), February 16, 2018, https://www.cfr.org/blog/mapping-capital-flows-us-over-last-thirty-years.

2. Thomas Piketty, Emmanuel Saez, and Gabriel Zucman, "Distributional National Accounts: Methods and Estimates for the United States," *Quarterly Journal of Economics* 133, no. 2 (May 2018): 553–609; Emmanuel Saez and Gabriel Zucman, "Wealth Inequality in the United States since 1913: Evidence from Capitalized Income Tax Data," *Quarterly Journal of Economics* 131, no. 2 (May 2016): 519–78; Tax Policy Center, "Historical Capital Gains and Taxes," https://www.taxpolicycenter.org/statistics/historical-capital-gains-and-taxes; Matthew C. Klein, "How Should a 'Workers' Party' Cut Taxes?," *FT Alphaville*, May 5, 2017, https://ftalphaville.ft.com/2017/05/04/2188305/how-should-a-workers-party-cut-taxes/; Peter B. Edelman, "Poverty and Welfare: Does Compassionate Conservatism Have a Heart?," 2001 Edward C. Sobota Memorial Lecture, Albany Law School, Albany, N.Y.

3. FRB, "Industrial Production and Capacity Utilization—G.17," https://www.federalreserve.gov/releases/g17/; Robert Shiller, stock market data used in *Irrational Exuberance*, http://www.econ.yale.edu/~shiller/data.htm.

4. Based on BEA, "National Income and Product Accounts," tables 1.1.5, 1.14, 5.1, 5.2.6, https://apps.bea.gov/iTable/index_nipa.cfm.

5. Robert Skidelsky, "Winning Back Europe's Heart; Rogue Dollar," *New York Times*, February 20, 2005; George P. Shultz and Martin Feldstein, "Everything You Need to Know about Trade Economics, in 70 Words," *Washington Post*, May 5, 2017; Jason Furman, "Worry about the Trade Deficit—a Bit," *Wall Street Journal*, May 1, 2018; Joseph E. Stiglitz, "The US Is at Risk of Losing a Trade War with China," *Project Syndicate*, July 30, 2018, https://www.project-syndicate.org/commentary/trump-loses-trade-war-with-china-by-joseph-e-stiglitz-2018-07.

6. Joseph W. Gruber and Steven B. Kamin, "The Corporate Saving Glut in the Aftermath of the Global Financial Crisis," International Finance Discussion Papers 1150, June 2015; Matthew C. Klein, "Aging, Real Rates, and Labour Bargaining Power: The Case of Japan," *FT Alphaville*, December 8, 2015, https://ftalphaville.ft.com/2015/12/08/2147125/aging-real-rates-and-labour-bargaining-power-the-case-of-japan/.

7. Based on BEA, "National Income and Product Accounts," tables 1.1.5, 5.1, 5.2.6, https://www.bea.gov/iTable/index_nipa.cfm.

8. Perry Mehrling, "A Money View of Credit and Debt," paper prepared for the INET/CIGI "False Dichotomies" conference, Waterloo, Ont., November 18, 2012, https://www.cigionline.org/sites/default/files/inet2012mehrling_amoneyviewofcreditanddebt.pdf.

9. Gary Gorton, *Misunderstanding Financial Crises: Why We Don't See Them Coming* (Oxford: Oxford University Press, 2012).

10. Michael D. Bordo and Robert N. McCauley, "Triffin: Dilemma or Myth?," BIS Working Papers No. 684, December 2017; P. H. Lindert, *Key Currencies and Gold, 1900–1913* (Princeton, N.J.: Princeton University Press, Department of Economics, 1969).

11. Liaquat Ahamed, *Lords of Finance: The Bankers Who Broke the World* (New York: Penguin, 2009); Adam Tooze, *The Deluge: The Great War, America, and the Remaking of the Global Order, 1916–1931* (New York: Penguin, 2014); Douglas A. Irwin, "The French Gold Sink and the Great Deflation of 1929–1932," Cato Papers on Public Policy, vol. 2, 2012; Barry Eichengreen and Douglas A. Irwin, "The Slide to Protectionism in the Great Depression: Who Succumbed and Why?," *Journal of Economic History* 70, no. 4 (December 2010): 871–97; Robert L. Hetzel, "German Monetary History in the First Half of the Twentieth Century," *FRB Richmond Economic Quarterly* 88, no. 1 (Winter 2002): 1–35; Adam Tooze, *The Wages of Destruction: The Making and Breaking of the Nazi Economy* (London: Allen Lane, 2006); Stephen Kotkin, *Stalin: Waiting for Hitler, 1929–1941* (New York: Penguin, 2017); "Foreign Trade in German Economy," *Editorial Research Reports, 1939*, vol. 1 (Washington, D.C.: CQ Press, 1939).

12. Benn Steil, *The Battle of Bretton Woods: John Maynard Keynes, Harry Dexter White, and the Making of a New World Order* (Princeton, N.J.: Princeton University Press, 2013); Barry Eichengreen, *Exorbitant Privilege: The Rise and Fall of the Dollar* (Oxford: Oxford University Press, 2011); Nicholas Crafts, "Walking Wounded: The British Economy in the Aftermath of World War I," *VoxEU*, August 27, 2014, https://voxeu.org/article/walking-wounded-british-economy-aftermath-world-war-i.

13. Sylvia Nasar, "Robert Triffin, an Economist Who Backed Monetary Stability," *New York Times*, February 27, 1993.

14. Testimony of Robert Triffin, U.S. Congress, Joint Economic Committee, *Employment, Growth, and Price Levels: Hearings before the Joint Economic Committee*, 86th Cong., 1st sess., October 28, 1959, 2905–14; BEA, "National Income and Product Accounts," tables 1.1.5, 4.1, https://www.bea.gov/iTable/index_nipa.cfm.

15. Federal Reserve System, Board of Governors, *Banking and Monetary Statistics, 1941–1970* (Washington, D.C.: FRS, 1976), tables 14.1, 14.2, available at https://fraser.st louisfed.org/files/docs/publications/bms/1941-1970/BMS41-70_complete.pdf.

16. Bordo and McCauley, "Triffin: Dilemma or Myth?"

17. Robert Triffin, "Gold and the Dollar Crisis: Yesterday and Tomorrow," Essays in International Finance No. 132, Princeton University, Department of Economics, December 1978.

18. Gold Fixing Price in London Bullion Market, FRED Economic Data, https://fred.stlouisfed.org/series/GOLDAMGBD228NLBM; Robert L. Hetzel, "German Monetary History in the Second Half of the Twentieth Century: From the Deutsche Mark to the Euro," *FRB Richmond Economic Quarterly* 88, no. 2 (Spring 2002): 29–64; Michael Bordo, Eric Monnet, and Alain Naef, "The Gold Pool (1961–1968) and the Fall of the Bretton Woods System: Lessons for Central Bank Cooperation," NBER Working Paper No. 24016, November 2017.

19. Bureau of Labor Statistics, Consumer Price Index, all items, https://www.bls.gov/cpi/.

20. Bordo and McCauley, "Triffin: Dilemma or Myth?"; Ashoka Mody, *Eurotragedy: A Drama in Nine Acts* (Oxford: Oxford University Press, 2018).

21. Michael P. Dooley, David Folkerts-Landau, and Peter Garber, "An Essay on the Revived Bretton Woods System," NBER Working Paper No. 9971, September 2003; Gita Gopinath, "The International Price System," NBER Working Paper No. 21646, November 2015.

22. George Soros, "General Theory of Reflexivity," *Financial Times,* October 26, 2009; George Soros, "Financial Markets," *Financial Times,* October 27, 2009.

23. Central Bank of the Republic of China (Taiwan), "Monthly Releases: Foreign Exchange Reserves," https://www.cbc.gov.tw/ct.asp?xItem=1866&ctNode=511&mp=2; IMF, "IMF Country Information," https://www.imf.org/en/Countries.

24. Timothy Lane, "The Asian Financial Crisis: What Have We Learned?," *Finance and Development* (IMF) 36, no. 3 (September 1999): 44–47.

25. Michael Pettis, *The Volatility Machine: Emerging Economies and the Threat of Financial Collapse* (Oxford: Oxford University Press, 2001), esp. chaps. 4–6.

26. Seth Mydans, "Indonesia Agrees to I.M.F.'s Tough Medicine," *New York Times,* January 16, 1998.

27. Timothy Lane et al., "IMF-Supported Programs in Indonesia, Korea, and Thailand: A Preliminary Assessment," IMF Occasional Paper No. 178, 1999; IMF Staff, "Recovery from the Asian Crisis and the Role of the IMF," June 2000, https://www.imf.org/external/np/exr/ib/2000/062300.htm; IMF, "World Economic Outlook Database," October 2018, https://www.imf.org/external/pubs/ft/weo/2018/02/weodata/weoselgr.aspx.

28. Based on IMF, "Composition of Foreign Exchange Reserves" database; and Setser, "Mapping Capital Flows."

29. See, e.g., C. Fred Bergsten and Joseph E. Gagnon, *Currency Conflict and Trade Policy: A New Strategy for the United States* (Washington, D.C.: Peterson Institute for International Economics, 2017).

30. China, State Administration of Foreign Exchange, "The Time-Series Data of China's Foreign Exchange Reserves," https://www.safe.gov.cn/en/2018/0408/1426.html.

31. IMF, "World Economic Outlook Database," October 2018; FRED Economic Data, "Crude Oil Prices: Brent–Europe," https://fred.stlouisfed.org/series/DCOILBRENTEU.

32. Based on U.S. Treasury Inflation-Protected Securities, which incorporate inflation expectations, https://fred.stlouisfed.org/series/DTP30A28; and inflation-adjusted Broad Dollar Index, FRB, H.10 release, https://www.federalreserve.gov/releases/h10/summary/indexbc_m.htm.

33. FRED Economic Data, "Federal Debt Held by the Public," https://fred.stlouisfed.org/series/FYGFDPUN; FRED Economic Data, "Federal Debt Held by Foreign and International Investors," https://fred.stlouisfed.org/series/FDHBFIN; Treasury Department Fiscal Service, Monthly Bulletin; FRB, "Financial Accounts of the United States," https://www.federalreserve.gov/releases/z1/current/default.htm; FRB, "Mortgage Debt Outstanding," https://www.federalreserve.gov/data/mortoutstand/current.htm; SIFMA statistics, "US Mortgage-Related Issuance and Outstanding," https://www.sifma.org/resources/research/us-mortgage-related-issuance-and-outstanding/; SIFMA statistics, "US ABS Issuance and Outstanding," https://www.sifma.org/resources/research/us-abs-issuance-and-outstanding/.

34. Atif Mian and Amir Sufi, *House of Debt: How They (and You) Caused the Great Recession and How We Can Prevent It from Happening Again* (Chicago: University of Chicago Press, 2014); John Geanakoplos, "What's Missing from Macroeconomics: Endogenous Leverage and Default," Cowles Foundation Paper No. 1332, 2011; Alan Greenspan and James Kennedy, "Estimates of Home Mortgage Originations, Repayments, and Debt on One-to-Four-Family Residences," FEDS Working Paper No. 2005-41; Alan Greenspan and James Kennedy, "Sources and Uses of Equity Extracted from Homes," FEDS Working Paper No. 2007-20; updated estimates of mortgage equity withdrawal provided by James Kennedy via Bill McBride, "Equity Extraction Data," March 24, 2009, https://www.calculatedriskblog.com/2009/03/equity-extraction-data.html; "Mortgage Equity Withdrawal Positive," December 13, 2016, CalculatedRISK (blog), https://www.calculatedriskblog.com/2016/12/mortgage-equity-withdrawal-positive-in.html; FRB, "Financial Accounts of the United States, table B.101," https://www.federalreserve.gov/apps/fof/DisplayTable.aspx?t=b.101.

35. Based on BEA, "National Income and Product Accounts," tables 1.4.3, 5.2.3U, 7.1, https://apps.bea.gov/iTable/index_nipa.cfm; FRB, "Industrial Production and Capacity Utilization—G17," https://www.federalreserve.gov/releases/g17/download.htm; OECD, "Trade in Value Added" database, https://stats.oecd.org/index.aspx?queryid=75537; and David Autor et al., "Foreign Competition and Domestic Innovation: Evidence from US Patents," *American Economic Review: Insights* (forthcoming).

36. Bureau of Labor Statistics, Establishment Survey, https://fred.stlouisfed.org /series/MANEMP and https://fred.stlouisfed.org/series/USPRIV, and Household Survey, https://fred.stlouisfed.org/series/LNS12300060.

37. Kerwin Kofi Charles, Erik Hurst, and Matthew J. Notowidigdo, "Housing Booms, Manufacturing Decline, and Labor Market Outcomes," Working Paper, July 2017; Michael Spence and Sandile Hlatshwayo, "The Evolving Structure of the American Economy and the Employment Challenge," Council on Foreign Relations Working Paper, March 2011.

38. David Autor, David Dorn, and Gordon Hanson, "The China Shock: Learning from Labor-Market Adjustment to Large Changes in Trade," *Annual Review of Economics* 8 (2016): 205–40; David Autor, David Dorn, and Gordon Hanson, "When Work Disappears: Manufacturing Decline and the Falling Marriage Market Value of Young Men," *American Economic Review: Insights* 1, no. 2 (September 2019): 161–78; Justin R. Pierce and Peter K. Schott, "Trade Liberalization and Mortality: Evidence from U.S. Counties," FEDS Working Paper No. 2016-094, November 2016; Leo Feler and Mine Z. Senses, "Trade Shocks and the Provision of Local Public Goods," IZA Discussion Paper No. 10231, 2015.

39. FRB, "Summary Measures of the Foreign Exchange Value of the Dollar," https://www.federalreserve.gov/releases/h10/summary/default.htm.

40. Jean-Noël Barrot et al., "Import Competition and Household Debt," Federal Reserve Bank of New York Staff Reports No. 821, August 2017.

41. Based on BEA, "National Income and Product Accounts," tables 1.1.5, 1.5.3, 4.1, 4.2.3, 4.2.5, 5.2.3U, 7.1, https://apps.bea.gov/iTable/index_nipa.cfm; Bureau of Labor Statistics, Household Survey; FRB, "Industrial Production and Capacity Utilization—G.17."

42. Setser, "Mapping Capital Flows"; China, State Administration of Foreign Exchange, "The Time-Series Data of Balance of Payments of China," https://www.safe.gov .cn/en/2018/0928/1457.html; China, State Administration of Foreign Exchange, "The Time-Series Data of China's Foreign Exchange Reserves."

43. Benoît Cœuré, "The Persistence and Signalling Power of Central Bank Asset Purchase Programmes," speech presented at the 2018 U.S. Monetary Policy Forum, New York, February 23, 2018, ECB; BEA, "National Income and Product Accounts," table 4.2.3, https://apps.bea.gov/iTable/index_nipa.cfm; BEA, "International Transaction Accounts," table 1.3, https://apps.bea.gov/iTable/index_ita.cfm; ECB, "Statistical Data Warehouse," http://sdw.ecb.europa.eu/quickview.do?SERIES_KEY=338.BP6.Q.N.I8.W1.S1.S1 .T.A.FA.P.F3.T.EUR._T.M.N and http://sdw.ecb.europa.eu/quickview.do?SERIES_KEY =338.BP6.Q.N.I8.US.S1.S1.T.A.FA.P.F3.T.EUR._T.M.N.

44. Adam Tooze, *The Deluge: The Great War, America and the Remaking of the Global Order, 1916–1931* (New York: Penguin, 2014); Nicholas Crafts, "Walking Wounded: The British Economy in the Aftermath of World War I," *VoxEU*, August 27, 2014, https:// voxeu.org/article/walking-wounded-british-economy-aftermath-world-war-i; Barry Eichengreen, "The British Economy between the Wars," in *The Cambridge History of Modern Britain*, ed. Roderick Floud and Paul Johnson (Cambridge: Cambridge University Press, 2004), 314–43.

Conclusion

1. Bernie Sanders, "Sanders: Party Platform Still Needs Work," *Philadelphia Inquirer,* July 3, 2016; "Hillary Clinton Says She Does Not Support Trans-Pacific Partnership," *PBS News Hour,* October 7, 2015, https://www.pbs.org/newshour/politics/hillary-clinton-says-she-does-not-support-trans-pacific-partnership; Larry Summers, "A Setback to American Leadership on Trade," *Financial Times,* June 14, 2015.

2. "Presidential Memorandum Regarding Withdrawal of the United States from the Trans-Pacific Partnership Negotiations and Agreement," January 23, 2017, https://www.whitehouse.gov/presidential-actions/presidential-memorandum-regarding-with drawal-united-states-trans-pacific-partnership-negotiations-agreement/; Chad P. Brown and Melina Kolb, "Trump's Trade War Timeline: An Up-to-Date Guide," Peterson Institute for International Economics, https://www.piie.com/blogs/trade-investment-policy-watch/trump-trade-war-china-date-guide; BEA, "National Income and Product Accounts," table 3.2, https://apps.bea.gov/iTable/index_nipa.cfm; Jeff Stein, "Democrats Struggle to Present a United Front on Trump's Trade War," *Washington Post,* August 7, 2019.

3. New Zealand Immigration, "Buying or Building a House in New Zealand," https://www.newzealandnow.govt.nz/living-in-nz/housing/buying-building; Jamie Smyth, "Australia Targets Foreign Homebuyers with Property Tax Rise," *Financial Times,* May 31, 2017; Paul Vieira, Rachel Pannett, and Dominique Fong, "Western Cities Want to Slow Flood of Chinese Home Buying. Nothing Works," *Wall Street Journal,* June 6, 2018; U.S. Congress, S.2357 (116th), "Competitive Dollar for Jobs and Prosperity Act," https://www.baldwin.senate.gov/imo/media/doc/Competitive%20Dollar%20for%20Jobs%20 and%20Prosperity%20Act%20FINAL.pdf.

4. Mary Childs, "Former Fed Chairman Blasts McKinsey and Hedge Fund Billionaires," *Barron's,* December 12, 2018.

5. FRB, "Credit Liquidity Programs and the Balance Sheet: Central Bank Liquidity Swaps," https://www.federalreserve.gov/monetarypolicy/bst_liquidityswaps.htm.

6. Matthew C. Klein, "Why Is the Netherlands Doing So Badly?," *FT Alphaville,* June 16, 2016, https://ftalphaville.ft.com/2016/06/16/2166258/why-is-the-netherlands-doing-so-badly/.

Index

Figures and notes are indicated by f and n following the page number.